Thinking About Insanity, Religion, and Terrorism

Answers to Frequently Asked Questions
With Case Examples

Edited by
Ellsworth Lapham Fersch

iUniverse, Inc.
New York   Bloomington

Thinking About Insanity, Religion, and Terrorism
Answers to Frequently Asked Questions with Case Examples

iUniverse books may be ordered through booksellers or by contacting:

iUniverse
1663 Liberty Drive
Bloomington, IN 47403
www.iuniverse.com
1-800-Authors (1-800-288-4677)

ISBN: 978-1-4502-2866-4 (sc)
ISBN: 978-1-4502-2867-1 (ebook)

Printed in the United States of America

iUniverse rev. date: 5/18/2010

Contents

About the Book

This volume grew out of my Harvard seminar on *The Insanity Defense*. The seminar reconsidered and updated earlier attention to mental disorder in relation to the law and also expanded its focus to examine at greater length the roles of religion and terrorism in conceptualizing and implementing the insanity defense. The contributors reviewed the earlier book, *Thinking About the Insanity Defense*, as well as current research and comment on the broader topics of this volume. All participants discussed these topics and cases and research and collaboratively wrote these materials. Profiles of all appear in *About the Contributors*.

This book follows the format of former seminar volumes by posing and answering basic and additional frequently asked questions. Because the answer to each question is self-contained and because readers may choose to explore the book in various ways, some materials are repeated where necessary to answer each question. For simplicity, the masculine pronoun has been used throughout when both males and females may be involved. On some occasions, a plural accompanies a singular to make the same point.

Embedded within the questions and answers are a number of case examples which illustrate the general points about the topics. Although this volume includes an extensive bibliography, it does not refer specifically to the listings within the text itself. To facilitate reading, specific references were removed. The effort of the contributors while preparing this volume was to summarize what others discovered, learned, thought, and presented, and then, finally, to offer some of their own reflections. As with a *New Yorker* piece on psychopathy or a *New York Times Magazine* piece on neurolaw, this volume is intended for the general reader and not for the researcher or for the scholar.

The aim of this volume is to assist that reader in thinking about the insanity defense in its relation to mental disorder, religion, and terrorism by presenting a number of competing materials. The book includes as many alternatives as possible in order to address the widely varying approaches to this controversial interaction between legal and psychological approaches to human behavior. At the same time, the bibliography provides a complete list of references for those who may wish to examine further some aspect of the overall topic. All who have been involved with this volume urge those who read it to explore at length many of the contributions of those authors and others, and to continue the important work of following the controversies surrounding the use in law and in psychology of the insanity defense. It is the hope of everyone who contributed to *Thinking About Insanity, Religion, and Terrorism* that the book will encourage all readers to pursue cases and concepts in the exciting world where psychology, neuroscience, genetics, law, religion, terror, and public policy interact.

About the Contributors

Josh Abram concentrates in Psychology at Harvard University and pursues a secondary field in Economics. He has worked in several social psychology laboratories as a research assistant. He has conducted research under Professor Daniel Schacter on the relationship between sleep and memory and under Professor Joshua Greene on how people make moral decisions.

Aditi Balakrishna concentrates in Neurobiology with a secondary field in Psychology at Harvard University. She serves as the Associate Managing Editor for *The Harvard Crimson*, where she reported on the Dean of the College. She also served as Managing Editor for Content for *The Harvard Undergraduate Research Journal*.

Ellsworth Lapham Fersch has taught at Harvard University during the three decades since receiving his J.D. in law and his Ph.D. in clinical psychology there. He has been a visiting faculty member at a number of colleges and universities. A licensed clinical psychologist and member of the Massachusetts bar, he served as the long-time director of The Massachusetts Court Clinic, and has practiced clinical and forensic psychology and written about psychoforensic topics. As General Editor of this volume, he guided its preparation in his seminar on *The Insanity Defense*, contributed material, and wrote the Introduction.

Rachel Flynn studies Comparative Religion at Harvard University with secondary fieldwork in the Dramatic Arts. An active member of the Harvard-Radcliffe Dramatic Club, she has directed, designed and acted in over thirty productions on campus. She completed her religion coursework with a thesis on the construction of social meaning through religious ritual, utilizing the letters and sermons of Martin Luther and the works of theorists Rene Girard and Catherine Bell. She is the 2009 recipient of the Radcliffe Doris Cohen Levi Prize for Musical Theater.

Justin Hall concentrates in Psychology and has received a citation in Spanish at Harvard University. He has worked as a research assistant in Professor Wendy Mendes' Psychophysiology Laboratory studying emotion, health, and stress. He has also been involved in weekly community service with the Big Brother Big Sister Boston program and plays junior varsity basketball for Harvard.

Eesir Kaur studies Psychology at Harvard University with a focus on social and cognitive neuroscience. She has coached the Boston Urban Debate League for three years and is actively involved with the Crimson Summer Academy.

Patrick Lahue concentrates in Psychology at Harvard University where he has worked in psychology laboratories at both the Business School and the Kennedy School. He has spent much of his time at Harvard singing with his co-ed a cappella group, the Harvard Opportunes, and participating in a variety of English teaching programs in Asia.

Alex Lipton concentrates in Psychology with a secondary field in Economics at Harvard University, where he has worked as a research assistant in Professor Steven Pinker's Social Psychology Laboratory. For two years he composed the annual show for The Hasty Pudding Theatricals and conducted it and other productions as well. He also serves as a Peer Advising Fellow.

Kevin Mee concentrates in Economics with a secondary field in Psychology and a foreign language citation in German at Harvard University. He is the chair of the Harvard College Events Board and also serves as a coordinator for the Mission Hill After School Program and is a Peer Advising Fellow.

Tara Moross is an English and American Literature concentrator at Harvard University. She is primarily interested in dramatic literature and wrote a thesis on the works of Tom Stoppard, focusing on *Arcadia* and *The Invention of Love*. She is also involved in several theatrical organizations including the Harvard-Radcliffe Dramatic Club and The Hyperion Shakespeare Company.

Renée Pastel concentrates in Visual and Environmental Studies in the Film Studies track, with a secondary field in Psychology and a citation in French at Harvard University. She participates in the Harvard-Radcliffe Dramatic Club in various roles including actor, director, and dramaturg, and in *Cinematic*, Harvard's film journal, as Theory Editor. Her senior thesis involved the editing and manipulation of memory in terms of impact on personal identity as portrayed in film. She has also served as research assistant to Visual and Environmental Studies faculty members David Rodowick and Dominique Bluher.

Joseph Peter Resnek studies Government at Harvard, where he competes on the Mock Trial Team. He also participates in the Model Congress. His principal interest is in contemporary American political theory.

Danielle Schnur concentrates in Sociology with a secondary field in Psychology at Harvard University, focusing on gang violence and juvenile delinquency. She is the director of Franklin After School Enrichment and South Boston Outreach Summer, and serves as an adviser to first year students through the Peer Advising Fellows program.

Eric Schultz concentrates in Psychology with a secondary field in Economics at Harvard University. A former Harvard football player, he played linebacker during all his four years with the Crimson. He is also a member of Veritas Financial Group, a student organization focused on providing financial education for undergraduates through Harvard Business School.

Barry Shafrin is a Psychology concentrator with a secondary field in Dramatic Arts at Harvard University where he has spent most of his time performing. An active member of the Harvard-Radcliffe Dramatic Club, he has worked on two dozen shows as an actor, director, producer, and dramaturg. Additionally, he has traveled the world with his a capella group, the Harvard Krokodiloes, performed in drag with the Hasty Pudding Theatricals, and taught local middle schoolers with Citystep.

Tracy Spetka concentrates in Psychology with a secondary field in Human Evolutionary Biology and a foreign language citation in Spanish at Harvard University. She is the treasurer of Kappa Kappa Gamma sorority and the Yardfest Coordinator for the Harvard College Events Board. She has participated as a tutor for English as a Second Language adults and works in Professor Christine Hooker's Social Neuroscience and Psychopathology Laboratory.

Roberta Steele concentrates in Economics with a secondary field in Government at Harvard University. During her time at Harvard, she served on the Executive Board of the Harvard Undergraduate Women in Business, as well as the Executive Board of her sorority, Kappa Alpha Theta. During her senior spring, she chaired the Senior Gift Campaign for Kirkland House.

Jennifer Sullivan concentrates in Psychology at Harvard University. She has spent three years working in Professor Elizabeth Spelke's Laboratory for Developmental Studies, focusing primarily on implicit social bias in toddlers and its relationship to reciprocity. She has also spent time as a child rights advocate in Geneva, Switzerland, and is an active member of the Harvard-Radcliffe Dramatic Club and a member of Harvard Ladies' Improvisational Troupe.

Camden Vilkin studies Government at Harvard University, with a particular interest in law and public policy. She has served as President of the Harvard College Law Society and as a research assistant to Senator Jeanne Shaheen and the Institute of Politics. She has written a book entitled *Profiles in Service: Young Americans Ask What They Can Do for Their Country.*

Clement Wright concentrates in English with a secondary field in Psychology at Harvard University. He has worked in Professor Marc Hauser's Cognitive Evolution Laboratory, studying economic decision making in common marmosets, and has completed a book of original poetry for his English thesis.

Introduction

Five years after the publication of *Thinking About the Insanity Defense*, the insanity defense remains as controversial and current as it was then, and as much in the public view. With the publicity over the November 2009, Fort Hood massacre of military personnel by a major in the service and with an increasing focus on those termed American jihadists, that scrutiny will continue and undoubtedly intensify. And given such continuing interest, this volume answers the need to review briefly the essentials of the insanity defense and then to go beyond the earlier volume by including materials on terrorism, by expanding the focus on religion, by addressing the impact of neuroscience on the legal foundations of free will and criminal responsibility, by reassessing the role that psychopathy may play in the defense, by examining brainwashing, and by considering what each of the insanity defense standards offers or does not offer to the law.

The insanity defense spurred a storm of controversy when John Hinckley, Jr., who attempted to assassinate President Reagan, was found not guilty by reason of insanity. And half a decade ago, the controversy received extensive coverage when a mother was convicted of murder in the drowning deaths of her children in one trial and then found not guilty by reason of insanity in a retrial. Now, a quarter century after the assassination attempt, more widespread controversy has emerged in efforts to understand the motivation of the Fort Hood killer and to determine how legally to proceed. In fact, the insanity defense, though rarely invoked, is, when entered in high profile cases, the most prominent and controversial interaction between the mental health and the legal systems.

The insanity defense remains one of the most talked about and controversial interactions between a deterministic psychological approach to human behavior and a free will based legal approach. An excellent example of the way in which our legal system has emphasized psychology rather than religion or sociology or economics or biology, the insanity defense has raised questions which lie at the root of our political views of society, our moral and religious notions of good and evil, our medical and psychological conclusions about healing and sickness, our philosophical ideas about free will and determinism, and our linguistic concerns about language and semantics.

As is generally known, the criminal law attempts to hold people accountable for their actions. The insanity defense, on the contrary, attempts to excuse some individuals from responsibility for their actions on the theory that their legal insanity prevented them from choosing the lawful act, knowing what they were doing, or understanding that their action was wrong. Two incompatible, contradictory theories about what motivates human beings meet in the insanity defense. One is the modern determinist theory of causation which underlies psychology, neuroscience, and related disciplines. The other is the continuing free will theory of morality which underlies the criminal law.

As stated in the earlier volume, however individual cases are resolved, the controversy remains because two great theories about human nature and human action are involved, the criminal justice theory that individuals of their own free will choose to act as they do and ought to be punished for wrongful acts, and the psychological and modern scientific theory that individuals' actions are determined by their personality, genetics, culture, environment, and other factors largely beyond their rationality and self-control and ought rather to be understood and helped. When terrorism is added to the volatile mix, the controversy captures even more public interest and concern.

Much has happened since that earlier book was published in 2005. At the time of its publication, there was controversy over the conviction of Andrea Yates. She had then been recently convicted of murder for killing her five children by methodically drowning them in the bathtub. Her insanity defense had failed. Insanity, as that book detailed and this volume summarizes, is a legal, not a psychological concept, and the law provides tests or standards to determine whether the facts of a case fit that legal defense. The general public as well as those who represented Yates and those they engaged to testify for the prosecution or the defense pointed to varying explanations for her motivation to kill. Among the most prominent explanations for her behavior were those derived from psychology and psychiatry in the form of an increasing mental illness for which she had been hospitalized and received some, though often inadequate, treatment; from medicine because of inadequate and contradictory prescriptions for her condition; from biology in that postpartum depression led to psychosis; from religion, as she had received religious instruction from a radical preacher whose teachings she had followed; from simple opportunity, afforded by the hour-long time she had daily between her husband's leaving for work and her mother-in-law's arrival to help and to supervise her; from suicidology, as her previous suicidal ideation and gestures had now turned outward to homicide; and from the media, especially as one psychiatrist testified that Yates had copied a television drama in which a mother drowned her children and then escaped punishment through a successful insanity plea. After listening to the many explanations and to expert testimony about them, the jury concluded that Yates was not insane, but was guilty of murder.

Yates was sentenced to prison but sent to the mental health unit of the state correctional system. While she was legally guilty, the state recognized her serious mental problems. The Texas appellate court, however, overturned her conviction that year. It concluded that the testimony of the psychiatrist about the television drama, for which he had been a consultant, but which had not aired, was false. Yates's motivation could not have derived from the acts and the successful insanity plea in that television drama.

In a later, second trial of Andrea Yates after the earlier book was published, everything was the same inside the courtroom except for a different jury and the testimony of that psychiatrist which did not then include anything about that television drama. But outside the courtroom, starting with the horrific events in the case and continuing through all the pretrial, trial, and post-trial coverage leading up to the earlier trial, mistrial, and then the retrial, the intense and widespread comments about it caused many to reconsider the entire case including the jury's verdict. Some considered Yates' husband or her preacher or her clinicians or any number of others to have been central to her debilitated condition and to her extreme acts, and that led some to consider the jury's verdict mistaken.

As the materials in this volume indicate, the jury in her second trial found Andrea Yates not guilty by reason of insanity. Though not guilty, she remained in a secure mental hospital setting. So, aside from the labeling of her as either guilty or not guilty by reason of insanity, the practical consequence of the two trials remained much the same for Andrea Yates. And the intermingling of psychological, religious, cultural, environmental, and related factors in her case remain relevant to this volume, though the factor of terrorism does not. Because Andrea Yates did not seek to spread fear to other mothers or to those suffering from postpartum depression or psychosis, or to society in general, no one considered her acts to be those of a terrorist. Undoubtedly fear and terror seized her children as they struggled while she drowned them one by one, but her motive did not appear to derive from terrorism. In that respect she is similar to many others who have killed while motivated by rage or jealousy or any other human emotion. Some have had mental disorders as well and have pleaded not guilty by reason of insanity. Despite those disorders, most of those who enter such a plea have been found criminally responsible.

Now, as this book is published, equally notorious cases are capturing the public attention and raising new controversies, about the definition of a terrorist and about whether those considered terrorists are mentally ill enough to have an insanity plea available to them. The earlier volume dismissed that suggestion in a brief answer, but the cases of the Fort Hood killer and others as well have brought it up in a newly significant way raising all of the issues that this volume on insanity, religion, and terrorism considers. Throughout the 2010s and well beyond, these new cases and others will resonate whenever the insanity plea is considered.

In briefly summarizing a most relevant case involving insanity, religion, and terrorism, these facts seemed important to the subject of this book. Nidal Hasan, then 39 years old, an Army major, a military psychiatrist, the son of Muslim parents who emigrated from Palestine to Virginia, was unmarried and characterized as a loner. His military service involved treating military personnel who were suffering psychological disorders from their tours of duty in Iraq and Afghanistan. He wrote and spoke favorably about jihadists, corresponded with an influential Islamist terrorist, contacted prosecutors to inform them of acts his military patients had committed which he considered illegal. He had business cards printed with SoA (SWT) on them, the one referring to Soldier of Allah and the other meaning Subhanahu Wu Ta'ala or Glory to God. He used a first name on his official email of Abduwall, meaning Slave of God, rather than his actual first name. It was said that he shouted Allahu Akbar, meaning Glory to God, as he opened fire in a military installation building in Texas killing thirteen and wounding thirty-two. He was charged with thirteen counts of premeditated murder and thirty-two counts of attempted murder. These and other emerging facts made clear that discussion of the case would involve all three elements in the title of this book, insanity, religion, and terrorism. In this instance, insanity referred both to the mental disorders presumably used to advance the legal defense and to the insanity defense itself. Religion referred to Hasan's Islamic faith and possible Islamist approach. And terrorism raised the question of whether his acts were terrorist or simply criminal. A more detailed presentation of the case later in the book explains the variety of responses made to a discussion of his motivation. Suffice it to say here that Hasan's defense lawyer indicated that he would consider an insanity defense.

While the earlier volume filled a special need as it answered almost one hundred of the most frequently asked questions about the defense, this volume fills an additional need. It answers in a concise and easily available format nearly three hundred of the most frequently asked questions about the insanity defense and its relation to religion and to terrorism as well as to mental disorder. Beyond the expansion of discussion to include more about terrorism and religion and mental disorder, this volume revisits and expands upon an earlier topic of brainwashing and its related deprogramming or reeducation or deradicalization, as well as on the emerging influence of neuroscience and law on the continuing controversy about free will and responsibility. Finally, this volume summarizes the various arguments favoring each of the possible insanity defense standards. And, like the earlier volume, this book encourages further exploration of the subject through a comprehensive bibliography as it focuses, in the editor's view, on the importance of thinking about the insanity defense, religion, and terrorism.

Chapter 1.   Insanity Defense Basics

Some of this chapter has been adapted from *Thinking About the Insanity Defense* (2005).

What is the insanity defense?

The insanity defense is one of a number of defenses available to individuals who have committed an act which the law has declared criminal. An individual who commits such an act may be found not criminally responsible for the act with a successful plea of insanity. The individual is, in other words, determined to be not guilty by reason of insanity. Because insanity is a legal and not a psychological term, the defense is often misunderstood by the public at large and by juries who must grapple with it. A more clearly understood defense which, when successful, may excuse an individual from criminal responsibility is self-defense. When that plea is successful, the individual is simply found not guilty, though the phrase by reason of self-defense would be an appropriate way to understand the finding. Because of the connotations of insanity and of mental illness and because of the history of attempts to deal with those mentally disordered individuals who come to the attention of the police and the courts, the insanity defense has been the center of controversy within the legal and mental health professions and with the public at large.

What is mens rea?

Mens rea means guilty mind. In other words, one has mens rea when he commits an act intending to do something wrong. That is one of the two elements making the behavior a crime. This idea follows the provision that people should only be punished when they have acted in a way that makes them morally blameworthy.

What is actus reus?

Actus reus refers to the wrongful act which is an element of a criminal statute.

What is an affirmative defense?

An affirmative defense is one in which the defendant provides evidence that removes civil or criminal responsibility, regardless of whether the defendant has been proven to have actually committed the acts. Self-defense is a prominent example of an affirmative defense. In most jurisdictions insanity is an example of an affirmative defense.

How is the insanity defense related to diminished capacity?

The diminished capacity defense, as does the insanity defense, examines the mental state of the defendant at the time of the antisocial act which has been charged as a crime. It is similar to the insanity defense in that it involves evidence related to mental illness, but differs in that it does not require the defendant to be unaware of the difference between right and wrong. It differs in that a successful insanity defense means the defendant has been found not guilty while a successful diminished capacity defense means that the defendant has been found guilty, but of a lesser offense. The legal doctrine concerning diminished capacity applies to defendants who lack the necessary mens rea, or guilty mind, to commit a more serious crime with the knowing purpose and intent required for it. While both the insanity defense and the diminished capacity defense focus on the cognitive question of whether the defendant knew his or her behavior was wrong, and on the motivational question of whether they were able to control that behavior, they differ in the role that mental disease or defect played in the antisocial act. Diminished capacity negates the mens rea required for the more serious crime, but does not prove insanity. A successful diminished capacity defense results in a conviction for a lesser offense, but not in acquittal. The rationale for the diminished capacity defense is that the crime for which the offender is convicted should accord with his mental state.

What are the primary tests of insanity?

The primary tests of insanity are the M'Naghten rule and American Law Institute rule. Each state and the federal government can use any one it chooses, or it can choose none, or it can add irresistible impulse as a test, or it can choose the somewhat related test of guilty but mentally ill or guilty but insane.

What is the M'Naghten test?

The M'Naghten rule provided one of the earliest definitions of insanity and was derived from English case law in 1843. The House of Lords issued the M'Naghten ruling, which called for stricter standards for defining insanity. Under the M'Naghten rule, the defense must clearly prove that the defendant was suffering from such a defect of reason from disease of the mind that he either did not understand the nature and quality of the act he committed, did not in other words know what he was doing, or did not know that it was wrong.

For over a century this narrow definition of insanity was adopted and used in both English and American courts of law. Today, about one-third of the states use some variation of the M'Naghten rule. Modifications to the standards of insanity were eventually made in numerous states due to the criticisms that accompanied the M'Naghten rule. Those mental health professionals who opposed the M'Naghten rule argued that it was too restrictive in its focus on the cognitive distinction between right and wrong. They thought that the focus of a suitable test ought to be on affective or emotional factors as well, and that volitional ability to control one's acts ought also to be a consideration.

What is Clark v. Arizona?

Eric Clark shot and killed a police officer when he was stopped while driving. His lawyers argued that he was seriously mentally ill, that he suffered from paranoid schizophrenia, and that he thought he was shooting an alien not a police officer which he knew to be against the law. Lawyers argued that Clark did not have the requisite criminal intent to commit a crime and that he was insane at the time of the killing. Arizona used a version of the M'Naghten test of insanity and Clark had the burden of proof on that. His lawyers also argued that he could not have formed the criminal intent necessary for the crime because of his serious mental illness. On this second argument, the state had to prove his intent beyond a reasonable doubt. But Arizona law, while it permitted Clark to plead insanity and use expert witnesses under the M'Naghten standard, where he had the burden of proof, it did not permit the lawyers to use expert witnesses to show he could not form the criminal intent required by the crime. Arizona, when it enacted a guilty except insane verdict eliminated the first prong of the M'Naghten test. That prong excused the individual if he did not know the nature and quality of the act he was performing. It retained only the second prong, that the individual did not know it was wrong. Clark, who knew it was wrong to kill a police officer, was convicted and sentenced to prison for twenty-five years to life. His lawyers appealed.

The U. S. Supreme Court ruled in a five to four decision that the state of Arizona's limitation of expert witnesses to testimony about Clark's mental state for the insanity defense but not to the mens rea requirement in the law was constitutional. The Supreme Court declared that Arizona could prevent expert evidence about Clark's mental state to rebut the prosecution's contention that Clark had formed the criminal intent to commit the crime of murder. The defense was attempting to show that the mental illness meant, if not insanity, then diminished capacity and therefore diminished responsibility. Arizona presumed sanity and criminal responsibility and Clark could not use evidence concerning insanity to rebut that presumption. Critics and the dissenters argued that the decision did not meet the basic test of fairness or due process of law.

What is the American Law Institute test?

The American Law Institute rule, promulgated by the Model Penal Code in 1962, found favor in the *Brawner* case in 1972. It tried to combine the cognitive component of the M'Naghten test with the focus on mental disease or defect in the *Durham* test. It was broader than the M'Naghten test, but narrower than the *Durham* test. In other words, when followed, it appeared to permit more defendants to be found not guilty by reason of insanity than did the M'Naghten test and fewer than did the *Durham* test.

The American Law Institute test stated that a defendant was not criminally responsible if, at the time of his act, he lacked, as a result of mental disease or defect, either substantial capacity to appreciate the wrongfulness of his conduct or to conform his conduct to the requirements of the law. The part of the test about appreciation contained the cognitive or knowledge component of the test. The part of the test about conforming contained the volitional component of the test. The part of the test about mental disease or defect contained the psychological component of the test. And the part of the test about substantial capacity defined the degree of impairment necessary.

What is the guilty but mentally ill verdict?

Since 1976, approximately twenty-five percent of the states have passed reforms incorporating guilty but mentally ill as a possible verdict in trials involving the insanity defense. The uses and consequences of a guilty but mentally ill verdict have varied from state to state. Typically, guilty but mentally ill has been added to the possible verdicts of not guilty, guilty as charged, guilty of a lesser offense because of diminished capacity, and not guilty by reason of insanity. Occasionally it has replaced not guilty by reason of insanity. Under this verdict, an offender found guilty but mentally ill would be sentenced to the same amount of time as a simple guilty verdict would require, but would begin serving his term in a mental institution instead of jail. The mentally ill offender would receive appropriate treatment before being transferred to prison in order to serve the remainder of his sentence.

The guilty but mentally ill verdict arose out of an attempt to avoid certain criticisms associated with the not guilty by reason of insanity verdict. Jurors and the public had trouble grappling with the issue that a defendant could be found not guilty by reason of insanity but still have committed the crime, meaning the act itself, in essence making him guilty. They had difficulty distinguishing the issue of factual guilt, that is having committed the act, from the issue of legal guilt, which could result in a finding of not guilty by reason of insanity. The guilty but mentally ill option was proposed as a compromise between factual guilt on the one hand and legal guilt on the other.

Critics of the option have argued that it does not make conceptual sense because mental illness of the degree that would be specified in the verdict should lead to a finding of not guilty by reason of insanity. They have said that the option simply gives jurors an easy way out of making a difficult decision by allowing them to agree to both possibilities, mental illness and guilt. They have also argued that adding a phrase to a guilty verdict in order to direct the corrections department where to place the convicted mentally ill offender makes as much sense as adding a phrase that a defendant is guilty but physically ill as a way of suggesting to the corrections system where that defendant should initially be placed. Critics also have stated that the guilty but mentally ill option confuses jurors even more than regular insanity instructions because jurors are then faced with making the distinction between regular mental illness and mental illness that results in insanity. Finally such groups as the American Psychiatric Association have contended that the guilty but mentally ill option eliminates the jury's legal function of making decisions regarding responsibility for criminal acts.

Proponents of guilty but mentally ill verdicts have denied the contentions of the critics. They have suggested that its addition would lessen the number of not guilty by reason of insanity verdicts, which they have supported, and would allow for better treatment of offenders suffering from mental illness, which they have said everyone, proponents and critics alike, have favored. Studies have produced mixed conclusions as to whether or not the inclusion of a guilty but mentally ill verdict has actually decreased the number of defendants acquitted due to insanity. In addition, overcrowding in mental hospitals has eliminated the option of hospitalization from many defendants found guilty but mentally ill with the majority going directly to prison without treatment or after very brief periods of treatment.

What is the guilty but insane verdict?

Seemingly a variant of the guilty but mentally ill verdict, guilty but insane uses the legal term, insane, rather than the mental health term, mentally ill. Because a finding of insanity means that a person is not guilty, the terminology of this verdict seems logically impossible making it more objectionable to those who take seriously the meanings of the words themselves. But those who want to incorporate the concept of insanity while allowing for a verdict of guilty might prefer this formulation.

What happens in states where there is no insanity test?

In the minority of states that have abolished the insanity defense, evidence of the defendant's mental state may be presented to the court as a mitigating factor. In these states, the issue of *mens rea*, or requisite guilty mind, is assessed. The defense may attempt to negate *mens rea*, by showing that the defendant did not know the nature or quality of his illegal act, and therefore the crime was not committed with the necessary guilty mind needed for a specific conviction. If the defense is able to negate mens rea, charges in the case can be reduced. The defendant would still be found guilty of a lesser charge and sentenced to prison, rather than being sent to a mental hospital for treatment.

What is the Texas insanity standard?

Texas law sets forth the M'Naghten rule and irresistible impulse as insanity defense tests. It does not include a bifurcated trial; the verdict is known as Not guilty by reason of insanity, NGBI; treatment is mandatory for violent acts; and release authorization from treatment can only be by direction of the court. The burden of proof of insanity rests with the defense.

What is the Federal insanity standard?

The M'Naghten rule is the Federal insanity defense test. It does not include a bifurcated trial, the verdict is known as Not guilty by reason of insanity, NGBI, and treatment is mandatory. Authorization for release from treatment can only be by direction of the court.

How many guilty persons were executed last year in Texas and in the Federal system?

In 2009, Texas led all states in the number of executions, with twenty-four. There were no Federal executions that year.

When is a person guilty of treason?

According to the United States *Constitution*, a person is guilty of treason only when levying war against the United States, or adhering to the enemies of the United States, giving them aid or comfort. The punishment is death.

Why did **Mental Health America** *support the not guilty by reason of insanity plea, oppose laws incorporating*

guilty by insane, and declare its preference for the American Law Institute Model Penal Code Standards?

The organization said it sought the maximum diversion from the criminal justice system of all persons accused of crimes where mental health treatment is a reasonable alternative to criminal sanctions.

What is competence to stand trial?

Competence to stand trial requires the defendant's cognitive and affective ability to aid meaningfully in his court case. It is a completely separate inquiry from the question of insanity, which refers to the defendant's mental state at the time of the act which brought him to court. The question of competence arises at all stages of the proceedings, from arrest, to preparation of the case, to sentencing, even to execution when that is the sentence. In order to be found competent to stand trial, the defendant must demonstrate that he understands the charges and the proceedings, can communicate knowingly with their attorney, and can make legally rational decisions. The premise behind competence to stand trial is that people should not be placed on trial if they do not understand their own and others' roles at the trial, or the purpose of the proceedings. Whether the standard is a difficult one to meet or is much more readily met is arguable. As an argument that the standard is incredibly low, the prosecutor in the Ralph Tortorici case, for example, said that the standard is so low that a defendant's ability to distinguish a judge from a grapefruit meets the standard.

What is the relation between competence to stand trial and the insanity defense?

The relation between competence to stand trial and the insanity defense may or may not be a close one. Where insanity is raised as a defense, the question of competence to stand trial often accompanies it, and where the question of competence to stand trial arises, the issue of insanity at the time of the offense often accompanies it. If a defendant is found incompetent to stand trial, the trial halts

9

until the defendant is restored to competency. In some instances, the defendant is never found competent. In some less serious cases, the charges might be dismissed; in more serious cases, hospitalization of the defendant as incompetent may serve much the same purpose as would hospitalization as not guilty by reason of insanity. In fact, it has often been suggested that in states which have abolished the insanity defense, such alternative institutionalization of mentally ill defendants has taken the place of insanity acquittals.

Is insanity a psychological concept?

No. Insanity is a legal concept, not a psychological diagnosis. In fact, there are no psychological criteria to determine insanity. Insanity is a purely legal concept used to determine the degree to which a defendant is responsible for his actions.

Is insanity the same as mental illness?

No. Insanity is a legal concept, while mental illness is a psychiatric and psychological concept. Consequently, a person could be minimally or even seriously mentally ill but not found to be insane, and thus could be held partially or even fully criminally responsible for his acts. A manslaughter verdict, in place of a murder conviction, and a verdict of guilty but mentally ill are examples of these discrepancies. Additionally, it is possible for a person who is not mentally ill to be deemed insane by a jury. For example, if a person ingests a drug involuntarily and this severely impairs his judgment and actions he may be found to be insane despite no history of mental illness.

What is mental illness?

There is no universally accepted federal or state definition of mental illness. In fact, researchers examining clinical literature have discovered two major classification systems. The first system, called by some broad-based, has used the American Psychiatric Association's *Diagnostic and Statistical Manual of Mental Disorders*. That manual features a multiaxial classification system and states that mental disorders are characterized by a behavioral or psychological syndrome associated with disability or suffering. Those who evaluate and testify as experts in court and other settings rely almost exclusively on the *Diagnostic and Statistical Manual of Mental Disorders*, and often differentiate between serious and less serious mental illnesses. The second system classifies mental illnesses as brain disorders and organizes them by their biochemical markers, their heritability, and their lesions. This biologically-based view of mental illness is considerably less used in legal settings.

What did the American Psychiatric Association recommend in its statement almost three decades ago about the insanity defense?

It stated in 1982 that a person who is not morally blameworthy should not be punished but that persons with antisocial personality disorder should, for heuristic reasons, be accountable for their behavior; that the defense should not be abolished; that guilty but mentally ill should not be used; that the cognitive test should be strict; and that the volitional test should be eliminated as confusing to jurors,

What position did the American Psychiatric Association take more recently about the insanity defense?

In 2007, the Association strongly reiterated its support for the insanity defense. It stated that the law would be unfair to punish someone who had substantial impairment of mental function who acted in what would otherwise be a criminal manner. It said that serious mental disorder can substantially prevent someone from reasoning and behaving lawfully. The Association said it did not favor any one of the legal standards for the insanity defense, but wanted whatever standard was used to be broad. The Association wanted full consideration of the way in which serious mental disorders diminished or eliminated individual legal guilt, responsibility, culpability.

What types of mental illnesses does the American Psychiatric Association consider for an insanity defense?

Officially, the American Psychiatric Association has endorsed defining someone as legally insane if because of mental disease or mental defect he was not able to understand the wrongfulness of his conduct at the time of the offense. Consequently, the American Psychiatric Association stated that only severely abnormal mental conditions, like schizophrenia, fit properly within the insanity defense. And they excluded disorders resulting from the voluntary ingestion of alcohol or other psychoactive substances. Further, the Association did not support the irresistible impulse test for insanity.

Is insanity the same as psychosis?

No, it is important to differentiate psychosis from insanity. Psychosis is a psychiatric concept and insanity is a legal concept. Psychosis is essentially defined as a state of mind during which one's perception of reality is distorted. Psychosis is sometimes accompanied by hallucinations, personality changes, disorganized thinking, and delusional beliefs. As with mental illness, someone who was found legally insane may have been experiencing psychosis; however psychosis does not mandate legal insanity and being found insane does not necessarily mean that psychosis was present.

What is the relation between psychopathology and psychosis?

Psychopathology is basically a synonym for mental disease. It indicates the presence of disturbed, abnormal, or pathological conditions either mentally or behaviorally. As a result, psychosis is a form of psychopathology.

How do the various diagnoses in the official **Diagnostic and Statistical Manual of Mental Disorders** *fit with the insanity defense?*

Many of the diagnoses in the *Diagnostic and Statistical Manual of Mental Disorders* could theoretically be used as the basis for an insanity defense. This fact underscores one of the major issues with the insanity defense: How serious a mental disorder must be to persuade the legal system that an individual with that mental disorder should be excused from criminal responsibility, where, in other words, the line should be drawn between mental disorders which may qualify as legitimate causes of insanity, and those which either merely seek to reduce an individual's culpability or which do not impact the degree of culpability at all.

As an initial dividing line, those disorders which are the most serious, schizophrenia and bipolar disorder, are generally thought to be good candidates for a plea of insanity. Most legal and mental health experts agree that either schizophrenia with its potential for hallucinations and delusions and consequent loss of touch with reality, or manic-depressive illness, renamed bipolar disorder, with its potential for psychotic features, may potentially fit the requirements for a plea of insanity. Similarly, multiple personality disorder, renamed dissociative identity disorder, is, according to those who agree that it exists and is independent of therapist-induced origins, serious enough to be a good candidate as well. Less generally acceptable for pleas of insanity are such disorders as attention deficit hyperactivity disorder, obsessive compulsive disorder, post-traumatic stress disorder, and Asperger disorder, the latter one rejected by a Massachusetts jury which found a youth, fifteen at the time he killed another youth, guilty of murder rather than not guilty by reason of insanity. After the conviction and sentencing, an unscientific newspaper poll reported that only nine percent of the fifteen hundred respondents thought he should have been found not guilty by reason of insanity. The rest agreed with the verdict and life sentence with no chance for parole, but were split on where he should be held, with more favoring state prison than a mental hospital. Least acceptable for pleas of insanity, in fact rejected by the American Psychiatric Association, are the disorders of antisocial personality disorder, characterizing individuals formerly labeled as psychopaths or sociopaths, and of conduct disorder, for those younger than the eighteen required for antisocial personality disorder. Individuals, in other words, whose behavior is characterized by repeated criminality cannot argue that their criminality ought to be excused because it is itself a mental disorder. Finally, although substance use, abuse, or dependence and related disorders are often associated with crime, they are rarely used as the basis for the insanity defense. Nearly all of the people who have committed a crime while under the influence of a substance ingested the substance voluntarily. Those who ingested a substance unknowingly or against their will would not require an insanity defense.

What is malingering?

Malingering is pretending to have a mental disorder for a certain purpose, such as to avoid legal sanctions or to gain monetary advantage. Malingering can also occur when one actually has a mental disorder but exaggerates the severity of the condition.

Why have psychological explanations for behavior dominated in the legal system as opposed to economic or racial or cultural or other explanations?

As a field of study, psychology has attempted to understand human behavior. As the field has evolved and as the public's faith in psychological science has grown, society has become increasingly willing to explain most behavior in psychological terms. The criminal justice system has especially opened up to the field. Psychology and psychological experts are now used to evaluate many aspects of the criminal process. In fact, there has been a reciprocal escalation. The legal system has asked psychology and psychologists to do more. Psychology and psychologists have claimed they can do more and have been willing participants within the legal system. The legal system has then asked more and the science of psychology and its practitioners have complied. This psychoforensic escalation has by far outstripped other sciences or explanations or fields. Wherever one turns in the criminal justice system, psychoforensic professionals participate. Thus criminal profilers analyze crime scenes to develop a psychological description of the suspect. Forensic psychologists and psychiatrists evaluate a defendant's competency to stand trial, and evaluate defendants and testify regarding the insanity defense. Psychoforensic specialists participate in sentencing and correctional and institutional release issues and in myriad other issues as well, and that is only within the criminal justice system. These specialists also participate in the civil justice system in such probate matters as awarding custody of children or determining the need for guardianship, to name but a few examples.

Because the criminal justice system often requires judges and juries to look inside the mind of a criminal, such as when assessing criminal intent, it is natural that psychology, the study of the mind, would gain importance in the courts. As such risk factors for criminal behavior as low socioeconomic status, ethnic or racial minority status, and housing conditions have emerged, psychology has often been used to explain these factors as well. The reciprocal escalation between the legal and mental health systems has reduced the impact of new theories.

How can the legal assumption of free will and full criminal responsibility be compatible with the psychological assumption of determinism and lessened or no criminal responsibility?

Much time has been spent debating the insanity defense in terms of criminal responsibility. The question has been raised whether someone with a severe mental illness, in a legal condition of insanity, should be held less responsible for their actions than someone else or not held responsible at all. This question and the law itself presume that most of us are responsible for our actions. The law is based on free will, an assumption of one's freedom and capacity to choose to act or not to act. Determinism, on the other hand, is a scientific theory that presumes that every action is explainable by analyzing the state of the universe before the action and integrating all natural and scientific laws. Consequently, in a deterministic view, every action is in essence a reaction. This set of reactions, according to deterministic theory, is understandable and ought to excuse individuals from what would otherwise flow from their freely willed choice.

The law has largely maintained the theory of free will in the face of much of society's deterministic thrust. The insanity defense has been used to carve out a reserved space for the deterministic theory within a system oriented toward free will. In fact those who argue for the insanity defense see it as a way of maintaining the morality of a system which otherwise would force everyone to accept responsibility for what many consider to be acts beyond their control. The insanity defense proponents see it as allowing the criminal justice system to operate largely on a theory of free will. And they recognize that determinism could not exclusively work in our legal system because then no one would be guilty. The therapeutic state, with its focus on treatment, would dominate. The insanity defense appears to allow determinism and free will to coexist. Many philosophers, psychologists, and lawyers, however, suggest that the insanity defense wraps in scientific garb what is essentially a philosophical argument about the nature of action and of free will. It creates for some and appears to create for others a bridge between the extremes of determinism and free will.

Are terrorists mentally ill?

When an atrocious crime is committed, society has a tendency to question immediately the mental health of the perpetrator. The public asks itself what person in his right mind could do such a thing and often labels both the act and the person as crazy. That initial reaction becomes even more pronounced when the crime concerned was a result of terrorism and especially when it included self-destruction of the perpetrator as well. The forces that led groups and individuals to commit mass murder of innocent citizens, especially as suicide bombers willing to donate their lives in order to kill others, were beyond the comprehension of most citizens. Compounding the difficult to understand nature of terrorism was the fact that many terrorist acts are committed in the name of religion. As these terrorist acts have spread around the world, more have called them evil, and previous efforts to deal with them solely through the criminal law have given way to efforts to understand and deal with them in a more military fashion.

However they might be viewed, it is not the nature of these acts of terrorism that qualifies a defendant as insane, but rather, his state of mind at the time of the act. There must be a serious mental disease or defect to qualify as the insanity that prevented responsibility for the crime. The horrendous quality of a terrorist attack, even the suicidality, may well indicate underlying mental illness, but it is the illness and not the act itself that would possibly render the terrorist insane. While some argue that indoctrination into the belief system that turns one into a suicide bomber is a form of brainwashing which ought to excuse the perpetrator, others argue that such a belief system is better understood as evil rather than as a symptom of mental illness.

Why have some considered terrorists sane, altruistic, heroic?

Terrorists have been characterized as focused, motivated, disciplined. They have been motivated by religious, political, and/or nationalist ideology. They view themselves and are seen by supporters as heroic. Some, often leaders, are middle-class, educated individuals. While they may be antisocial in the diagnostic sense, they exhibit no major mental illness. As has often been said, depending on one's own orientation and perspective and values, one man's terrorist is another man's patriot, and vice versa.

Should an insanity defense be available to terrorists?

In the courts many argue that a terrorist defendant is no different from any other defendant, and, therefore, both must have all of the same defenses available, including the insanity defense, and both must be subjected to the same standard of insanity. Regardless of how reprehensible the terrorist act was, the nature of the crime does not either qualify the defendant as insane or disqualify him. Instead, the defendant must prove that he was sufficiently mentally ill as to not be responsible for the crime, whether that crime was terror related or not. Others argue that a terrorist defendant is different and society must fashion different ways of dealing with terrorists.

What might happen to some individuals found not guilty by reason of insanity?

Depending on the state, there are two routes that an individual acquitted for insanity might take. In some states, the individual may be automatically committed to a mental institution. After treatment, the judge would later decide whether it was safe enough to release the individual to his community. One study showed that the average period of confinement in a mental institution for defendants found not guilty by reason of insanity in New York was three years, and was increasing. The period of confinement was also shown to lengthen with the degree of seriousness of the crime.

In other states, the individual may be released to his community after a brief hospital stay, while continuing to receive monitoring by mental health professionals and outpatient care. This option is termed conditional release and is the mental health equivalent to parole. Under the conditional release system, a four-state study showed that sixty percent of five-hundred twenty-nine insanity defendants were conditionally released within five years of being institutionalized. The median length of confinement for released violent offenders was approximately three and a half years, and one and a third years for minor offenders.

A common belief of the public is that individuals found not guilty by reason of insanity are quickly released, as in the case of Lorena Bobbitt, who was released only after several weeks in a mental institution. At times, however, insanity defendants have been confined more frequently, and for longer periods of time, than non-insanity defendants who have committed similar crimes. For example, Michael Jones was acquitted under a plea of not guilty by reason of insanity for shoplifting but was institutionalized for decades longer than the maximum possible prison sentence for the offense. One explanation for this phenomenon is that under the commitment system, the standards by which the judge decides whether the individual should be released are civil and may be stricter than those for a prison inmate. Though an individual can remain committed to a mental institution only so long as he or she is considered mentally ill and dangerous, the circumstances which brought an individual to the attention of the police in a misdemeanor case may replay themselves sufficiently to insure longer term commitment to a mental hospital.

What shifts have taken place in the placement of individuals found not guilty by reason of insanity?

Before mental health laws were revised, individuals found not guilty by reason of insanity were often given what amounted to life sentences in hospitals specially designated for the criminally insane. Because of this result, only the most serious charges saw a plea of not guilty by reason of insanity. While the finding of insanity might satisfy the moral view of its advocates, the conditions in the special hospitals were often as bad as or worse than those in prisons to which guilty individuals were sent. With the revision of civil commitment laws and with the conceptualizing of the insanity acquittee as the equivalent of a civil committee, changes took place in the placement of individuals found not guilty by reason of insanity and in their potential length of confinement.

Two primary options replaced lengthy inevitable commitments. One remained automatic commitment to a mental institution after an evaluation following a verdict of not guilty by reason of insanity, with periodic reviews as to whether the committed individual remained dangerous by reason of mental illness. The other involved conditional release of the individual into society with requirements for continuing care for the mental illness. While there were few complaints from the public over the harsh earlier consequences for insanity acquittees, many more complaints surfaced with these changes in the system.

One objection has been that criminals have faked mental illness while pleading not guilty by reason of insanity to avoid serving their sentence in prison. Then, once they have been committed to a mental institution, they have feigned recovery, and have been released. Although this complaint may be valid, the public has overestimated the actual number of instances where this strategy has been successful.

Another source of complaint have been studies that show that recidivism rates of those committed to mental institutions through the insanity plea are similar to those of average criminals placed in prison. For instance, a study showed that half of all insanity defendants committed to the Oklahoma state forensic hospital in a five-year period were hospitalized or arrested again within two years of being released from mental facilities. Studies comparing the status of insanity acquittees who were legally discharged and those who escaped also show conflicting results about whether hospitalization benefited the individuals themselves.

One of the suggested reforms has been to have those acquitted by reason of insanity remain in institutions until they showed no symptoms of mental illness. A criticism of it has been that while it may indeed increase the safety of society, it would jeopardize the rights of the wider institutionalized population because of a few violent individuals. Another suggested reform has been to give those found not guilty by reason of insanity a combination of prison and hospital time. As is clear, this type of sentence has been associated with the verdict of guilty but mentally ill, and has placed the defendant first in a mental hospital, and then in a prison to serve the remainder of his sentence.

Should a person found not guilty by reason of insanity be automatically committed to a mental hospital?

Presumably, the individual is found not guilty by reason of insanity because he was insane at the time of his offense. Thus, the expected reaction would be that these individuals belong in mental hospitals, at least initially, especially if the individual is a danger to himself or herself. After all, it seems inhumane to confine the mentally ill in a hostile prison environment that is not equipped to tend to their needs adequately. Yet there may be some lapse between the offense and the verdict and the individual may have recovered in that time. Based on this possibility, some argue that automatic commitment is not warranted. While it seems clear that most insanity defendants should first be treated in a mental hospital, their status should be regularly reviewed in order to prevent either premature release or excess confinement. Current practice seems to show that laws require indeed monitoring by judges and mental health professionals.

Why would someone found not guilty by reason of insanity be evaluated as if he were simply a civilly committed individual?

Both the defendant who is found not guilty by reason of mental illness of a violent act and the individual who is found to be dangerous by reason of mental illness share two factors: Each has been judged to be mentally ill and each has been found to be dangerous. As a consequence, both should be evaluated for commitment to a mental hospital in a similar fashion. Yet, the fact that the defendant in the criminal proceeding has actually committed a dangerous act ought, some argue, to make his bid for freedom less easily accepted. But for his mental illness he would be guilty as charged and however serious the offense was, the fact of his having done it means that he is different from the individual who has not faced a criminal proceeding but who is deprived of freedom nonetheless. Many critics of the insanity defense have feared that individuals who are found not guilty by reason of insanity will be quickly treated and then released back into society, as civilly committed individuals often are. Short hospital stays have become the norm for philosophical, psychological, and economic reasons. The fact that insanity defendants are indeterminately committed ought, these critics have said, to mean that they will not be so readily released. Advocates of the system, however, say that many studies have shown that because of their civil commitment status, most individuals who are acquitted by reason of insanity spend equal or longer periods of time in mental institutions than defendants found guilty of similar crimes and sent to prison.

For civil commitment generally, proof must be given through clear and convincing evidence that a person is both mentally ill and dangerous. After a trial and a verdict of not guilty by reason of insanity, both of these prerequisites appear to have been met for the defendant. Therefore, advocates of the present system have said, the trial has proven that the person committed a criminal act and thus may pose a threat to society or themselves, and in addition, a jury has deemed the person mentally ill. Consequently, they conclude, an insanity acquittal in itself meets the standards of civil commitment.

If the best predictor of future behavior is past behavior, why would not a person found not guilty of a very serious act due to insanity be committed for a long time as a precaution?

In the case of a person found not guilty by reason of insanity, many states follow a procedure of automatically committing that person to a mental institution. That person can then only be released when a judge is convinced that he can be released safely. Therefore, the procedure places a focus on the evaluation and progress of a defendant who has become a patient. A person's future progress cannot be determined at the time of his commitment, and as a result, it would be impossible to sentence a person to a certain length of commitment, because this would assume that the judge could predetermine the minimum length of time the patient would need to get better.

Furthermore, the insanity defense operates on the assumption that people were not aware of their actions at the time of their crime, or that mental illness prevented them from understanding that their actions were wrong. This assumes that their past behavior was influenced by a mental illness. When a defendant who is found not guilty by reason of insanity is committed to a mental institution, the purpose is to treat them for their mental illness. If patients are not released until they are satisfactorily treated for that illness, then their behavior would no longer be under the influence of that illness. As a consequence, after release, their future behavior should not actually resemble past criminal behavior because the cause of that behavior, the mental illness, has ideally been eliminated or mitigated.

Under this system of treatment, it cannot then be assumed that past behavior would be a predictor of future behavior, and the notion that there should be minimum lengths of commitment falls within punitive ideals, not rehabilitative ideals, which are fundamental to procedures of commitment and treatment of those found not guilty by reason of insanity.

As critics note, the system is not flawless, however, and in order to protect against the possibility of releasing back into society a person who is not fully treated and dangerous, some states have instituted a procedure known as conditional release. In this procedure, people found not guilty by reason of insanity are placed in confinement until a judge or mental health professional deems their illness adequately treated. Mental health professionals continue to monitor the released patients for a period of time in order to ensure their safety to the community and to themselves.

Should a person who was sane at the time of the crime and sentenced to death but who becomes insane be executed while insane?

A variety of arguments have been offered regarding this question. Most of them revolve around the reasoning behind capital punishment. Many proponents of capital punishment claim that it is an effort both at deterrence for others and at just desserts for the criminal. A sentence of death, they argue, sets a precedent for similar crimes, which theoretically should prevent their repeated occurrence while at the same time meting out suitable punishment in the case. With such a perspective, the answer to the question is an obvious one. The convict's metal state should have little to no bearing on the decision to execute. The state is setting an example by executing the criminal.

On the other hand, opponents argue that the purpose of capital punishment is to seek retribution from an individual who has violated a societal code. If the individual is mentality incapacitated to the extent that he or she does not understand the punishment, it is scarcely a punishment at all. In such a case, they argue, capital punishment does not meet its designed end and ought not to be imposed until the individual has regained his sanity.

Should a lawyer be able to prevent forcing a psychotic client to take medication in order to

preserve, for the jury, the state of mind in which that person committed acts for which he is charged?

Whatever their position on this question, most respondents would agree that the justice system has an interest in proceeding with a case, in having a defendant able to assist his attorney, and in having an attorney vigorously representing his client. All would agree that a lawyer has the responsibility of acting in his client's best interest. If a defendant's lawyer believes that the defendant will be better served by avoiding a conviction than being treated for psychosis, then some would argue that it is the lawyer's right to make that decision. They argue that if a judge believes that such behavior would not be in the defendant's best interests, the judge should not simply make the client take medication. Instead, the judge should find that the lawyer is not acting in the client's best interest and dismiss the lawyer from the case entirely.

Others would argue, however, that a defendant must be deemed mentally fit to stand trial, for the defendant must be able to assist his lawyer fully in the case. Thus, the defendant must know what is in his or her own best interest, and if the defendant is psychotic how is he to know this. This argument would hold that instead of forcing the client to not take medication, the lawyer should file for a reexamination of his client on the grounds that he does not deem the client to be competent enough to understand what is in his best interest. Finally, some would argue for a middle ground that would force the defendant to take enough medicine to become less psychotic at which time he could then make the rational decision as to whether to continue taking medication and remaining free from psychosis or stopping the medication and becoming psychotic again.

Chapter 2. Further Questions about the Insanity Defense and Mental Illness

What is the relation among insanity, mental illness, and mental disorder?

Mental disorder and mental illness seem to be used interchangeably in psychological and psychiatric literature. The American Psychiatric Association's official list is found in what the organization terms the *Diagnostic and Statistical Manual of Mental Disorders*, but governmental units often imply the term mental illness by naming, as does Massachusetts for example, their bureaucracy the Department of Mental Health. Logically, the department should be called the Department of Mental Illness or the Department of Mental Disorder. Some states more curiously call theirs the Department of Mental Hygiene. It is interesting that the three terms, especially the first two, seem in the public mind to mean the same thing. Yet they have such different contextual power, the former as a legal term and the latter as a psychological term. Some have argued that law, especially through the courts' working to determine a person's mental stability based on psychological standards and measures, should also adhere to psychological terminology. For the law to have its own language only complicates the issue and creates a larger area of confusion for the public. Further, while not guilty by reason of insanity is the standard formulation, some states which have adopted a guilty but or guilty except verdict, call it guilty but insane, which is a logical impossibility, while others call it guilty but mentally ill. Psychologists and psychiatrists have adopted the term mental illness in part to destigmatize patients, painting them as suffering from something akin to a physical illness, rather than as aberrant members of society. The legal world, on the other hand, may not have the same goals or even the same need to be politically correct, inasmuch as it is dealing with criminals, and preserving their feelings often is not high on the list of priorities. The legal world may not see this same need to be politically correct, as it is dealing with criminals and preserving their feelings often is not high on the list of priorities.

In what historical perspective does American use of the insanity defense fit?

Defenses dealing with the insanity of the perpetrator date back to criminal proceedings in ancient Greece and Rome. The modern American insanity defense had its beginnings in court proceedings in 19th century England. Though the United Kingdom's Criminal Lunatics Act of 1800 did not clearly distinguish how insane individuals should be treated differently from their sane counterparts, the insanity plea itself was codified in English law with the M'Naghten Rules of 1843. The United States, as well as most jurisdictions where human rights are advocated, include some form of the insanity defense.

Does committing an evil crime imply an offender is insane?

Evil crimes and crimes of insanity can often be one and the same. An evil depraved act, however, does not imply the offender was legally insane. Many individuals who commit severely heinous crimes are referred to as crazy by the public. Yet several of these individuals, as Yates, have been found not guilty by reason of insanity. Nonetheless, the public perception persists that an individual who committed a horrific, evil act must be insane because a normal person would never commit such an act. The depravity of an individual's act, however, does not imply that the individual is legally insane. Although the offender may have a severe mental illness and be perceived by the public as crazy, the offender can only be found legally insane based on each state's requirements for the insanity defense. Many states require offenders to know the acts they committed were wrong. And many psychopathic individuals who commit heinous crimes realized what they were doing was wrong but chose to perform the acts anyway. Dahmer, convicted of killing at least fifteen victims and desecrating their bodies through acts of cannibalism and necrophilia, was seen as evil and crazy in the public's eye, but was not found legally insane. This meant that while crimes and offenders may be considered evil, in the sense that they were depraved and horrible, there were no acts of insanity and the offenders were therefore legally guilty of the crimes.

Should the intensity of the crime be relevant to the use of the insanity defense and the subsequent disposition?

There should be a point at which, if the seriousness of an act committed is bad enough, the law would mandate a specified amount of time in jail or in a mental institution. If a person were to be found not guilty by reason of insanity, but their crime was on the level of what Yates did to her children, he should have to spend the majority of his life without complete freedom. Also, some have argued that if the crime committed is at that level of seriousness then the insanity defense should probably not be relevant at all. With someone like Yates or Hinckley or others, even if they were mentally rehabilitated, the possibility of relapse or of repeat criminality ought to permit removal of the individual from society for an extremely long time. If the balance of freedom is between someone who has not been convicted and someone who has been, the already-convicted should be kept in confinement to protect the innocent but potentially harmable.

What test is used to determine whether or not experts may testify in court?

Experts occupied extremely important roles in court cases. Since they rendered opinions central to court cases, and since they were the most credible witnesses in any trial, their opinions were monitored closely in trials. As a consequence, judges determined when and how experts testified to their opinions in court. Before 1993, the standard determining the admissibility of expert scientific testimony was derived from the Federal Circuit Court case of *Frye v. United States*. It provided that expert opinion based on a scientific technique was admissible only where the technique was generally accepted as reliable in the relevant scientific community. It was replaced by the standard derived from the U S Supreme Court case of *Daubert v. Merrell Dow Pharmaceuticals*. The *Daubert* standard required that the evidence was relevant and reliable, that it was derived from the scientific method, that it could be empirically tested, and that it was generally accepted by the scientific community. The *Daubert* standard was somewhat more rigorous than the Frye standard.

✦What is fMRI?

The letters mean functional Magnetic Resonance Imaging. This form of neuroimaging measures the change in blood flow related to neural activity in the brain. It has become an essential element of neuroscientific studies. While it appears to be scientifically explanatory in a number of situations, as in memory and truth-telling, interpretations also raise important issues in its use, including the dangers of assuming correlation and causation are the same. It is a technique increasingly used in research, and by extension, in legal and other contexts beyond the psychological and neuroscientific. Its use runs the same danger of reciprocal escalation that more traditional psychological research has. As researchers claim more ability to understand, diagnose, and predict, and as courts and law ask for more explanations, diagnoses, and predictions, the demands of each may outrun the ability of the other to provide thoroughly tested answers, and yet each may be tempted or encouraged to produce answers beyond that capacity, or even as likely the media may encourage and report that escalation as if all of it were proven.

How are general questions of morality, as in the hypothetical Trolley Problem, connected to the insanity defense?

Many have asked whether recent studies performed by neuroscientists and psychologists on morality, ethics, and the brain have begun to have any impact on the insanity defense. In particular, studies have examined the ways in which people make moral decisions in hypothetical situations like the *Trolley Problem*. The *Trolley Problem*, a popular moral dilemma, posed a series of hypothetical problems for the subject, usually beginning with a bystander near a switch watching a train hurtle down the track. The track is currently leading to five workmen, while the track to which the train could be switched has one workman. The question is whether the bystander should switch the track and kill the single workman to save the five. This problem was examined in several iterations by a Harvard neuroscientist. As research increased on whether moral decisions are visible in the brain, as with fMRI, for example, has there been a commensurate increase in attempts to use brain science evidence in courts to support the insanity defense following the precedent set by the judge in the Hinckley case.

What legal alternatives are there to the standard insanity defense trial?

One alternative to the standard insanity defense trial was the bifurcated trial system. Each trial was separated into two different segments. The first segment simply determined guilt or innocence in the sense of committing the acts and did not discuss any of the intricacies of sanity, mental disorders, or psychiatric or psychological ideas. The second part of the trial discussed the issue of sanity only. Proponents of the bifurcated system argued that splitting trials into two segments made it easier for the jury to faithfully digest complicated expert testimony. They also observed that it eliminated the need to introduce such complicated evidence if the person wished to argue that he or she did not actually commit the crime in the first place. State supreme courts have consistently held that this practice was unconstitutional, yet the practice still remained in several states, including Colorado, Wisconsin, and California. This bifurcated system presented an alternative which could have possibly made it easier for the lay jury to better understand the very complicated issues at work in any insanity defense trial.

Should an individual be immediately committed to a mental institution following an acquittal on the basis of insanity?

The type and duration of medical treatment the individual received in the interim between his crime and trial should be of primary concern. From a psychopharmacological perspective, commitment to an asylum, where conditions have sometimes been reported as equal to if not worse than those of prisons, may be wholly unnecessary if the psychotic individual has undergone successful neuroleptic treatment during this period. While monitoring by health and legal representatives may be in order, a successful application of the insanity defense should not be necessarily followed by a minimum institutional sentencing, but dealt with on a case-by-case basis, where the status of ongoing medical treatment should be strongly considered.

Given how seldom it is used, how and why has the insanity defense occupied such a prominent position in the interaction between psychology and the law?

A misunderstanding of the function of the insanity defense on the part of the American public has resulted in a distorted sense of the frequency with which it is employed. This is further exacerbated by popular media's fascination with the insanity defense, and the effect this fascination has had on the public. This fascination has been bolstered by fictional dramatizations of the insanity defense, as well as in newspapers, blogs, and such. The realms of film and written fiction have influenced a broader sense of the insanity defense in the national psyche. The dramatization of cases concerning the insanity defense has had an equivalent effect on public opinion to the broader non-fictional exposure of these trials in traditional print media?

What is antisocial personality disorder?

The official *Manual* describes antisocial personality disorder as a persistent disregard for the rights of others which begins by age fifteen and continues into adulthood, though it cannot be diagnosed before age eighteen. It says other terms for the disorder are psychopathy and sociopathy. While individuals with antisocial personality disorder do appear to have an aversion to complying with societal norms, their behavior involves more aggression towards society than withdrawal from society. They not only exhibit disregard for the rights of others, they violate them for their own benefit. Their lawless behavior is usually persistent. They may react with indifference when caught, often blaming their victim and offering no compensation. Antisocial personality disorder is a condition in which an individual completely ignores the rights of others. To receive this diagnosis, an individual first has to show at least three of the following behaviors: repeated acts that result in arrest such as theft or assault, regularly lying or conning, inability to plan ahead, high levels of physical aggressiveness, engaging in activities that endanger others, inability to hold onto a job, and lack of remorse for causing harm to others. Additionally, the individual must have a history of conduct problems in childhood or adolescence, preferably with a diagnosis of conduct disorder. Finally, the diagnosis of antisocial personality disorder can only be given to adults. Due to the emphasis on aggression and criminal behavior, the disorder is often underdiagnosed in females. Although the term is often used interchangeably with psychopathy, there are differences between this disorder and psychopathy.

Though antisocial personality disorder is often comorbid with a number of other disorders, it cannot be diagnosed if the symptoms only occur during a schizophrenic or manic episode. Although many psychopaths have all the markers of antisocial personality disorder,

Ellsworth Lapham Fersch

most of those diagnosed with antisocial personality disorder are not psychopaths because psychopathy is considered a smaller, stringently defined subpopulation of antisocial personality disorder. While most psychopaths satisfy the criteria for antisocial personality disorder, most of those diagnosed with antisocial personality disorder are not psychopaths.

Why does the court treat antisocial personality disorder differently from other psychological disorders?

The American Psychiatric Association and the courts have not considered a diagnosis of antisocial personality disorder grounds for insanity. Antisocial personality disorder is loosely defined as a lack of moral conscience, and a large portion of current inmates have been or could be diagnosed as having antisocial personality disorder. Since the criminal behavior is itself an indicator of antisocial personality disorder, acquittal on grounds of insanity should not be an option. Further, many consider the disorder to have no effective treatment or considerably more problematic than individuals found insane due to schizophrenia or bipolar disorder who might possibly be rehabilitated through psychopharmacology or clinical treatment.

What is psychopathy?

Psychopathy does not appear as a diagnostic category in the current official *Diagnostic and Statistical Manual of Mental Disorders-IV*. Nonetheless, the MacArthur Foundation Neuroscience and the Law Project listed psychopathy as one of its three primary subjects of study. While *DSM-5* is in its initial stages of preparation, it is not scheduled for release until May 2013. So, until then, the current status of psychopathy as a mental disorder and its relation to the insanity defense remains as it is presented in *DSM-IV*. Confusion about the term has continued.

That confusion started with the very terms psychopath and psychopathy. While they have occurred in the popular literature, and have been deeply embedded in the public imagination, they appeared only indirectly in the official scientific literature. The index to the authorized list of psychological and psychiatric illnesses, as defined by the American Psychiatric Association in its current *Diagnostic and Statistical Manual of Mental Disorders-IV*, did not contain the word psychopath at all. The *Manual* did say in its general discussion of antisocial personality disorder that the pattern of disregard for, or violation of, the rights of others has also been called psychopathy, sociopathy, or dyssocial personality disorder. In so doing, the *Manual* equated the four terms. But the *Manual* only authorized the use of antisocial personality disorder for diagnostic, treatment, insurance, legal, and other purposes.

The preeminent investigator of psychopathy, Robert Hare, argued that research on psychopathy showed that it was more complex and nuanced than antisocial personality disorder. It included, he determined, two explicit factors, the first of which was only implicitly presented in the *Manual*'s discursive essay material. As opposed to the *Manual*'s seven limited diagnostic criteria, Hare operationalized twenty in his *Psychopathy Checklist-Revised*, the *PCL-R*. He described the first factor as an emotional one. It referred to the selfish, callous, and remorseless use of others. With information obtained from files and from semi-structured hour-and-a-half to two-hour interviews, it included eight items: glibness and superficial charm, a grandiose sense of self-worth, pathological lying, manipulativeness, a lack of empathy, and of remorse, shallow affect, and a failure to accept personal responsibility. He described the second factor as a behavioral one. It referred to a chronic, unstable lifestyle. With information gathered from files and other ancillary sources it included ten items: proneness to boredom, with accompanying need for stimulation, parasitic lifestyle, poor behavioral control, early behavioral problems, including juvenile delinquency, and failure to succeed with lesser forms of sanction, lack of realistic long-term goals, impulsivity, and irresponsibility. Two items, promiscuous sexual behavior and many short-term marital relationships, though they were used, did not load on either factor. And he concluded that while reliable diagnoses of psychopathic personality disorder could be made based solely on extensive file and ancillary material, interviews alone did not lead to reliable diagnoses.

The consequences of the label psychopath have extended far beyond a limited diagnostic purpose. Use of the results of the diagnostic labeling occurred in the legal as well as in the mental health system. Because many practical decisions, involving diagnosis, treatment, sentencing, classification, confinement, even death, required the drawing of lines separating the degrees of psychopathy, the PCL-R scoring system accommodated that effort. Scoring each factor as 0, 1, or 2, an individual's total could range from 0 to 40. Lines then were generally drawn at scores of 30 or more for psychopaths, 21-29 for possible or partial psychopaths, and 20 or less for non-psychopaths. Research showed that the overall difference among these groups was highly significant.

Why was psychopathy not included as a *diagnosis in the* Diagnostic and Statistical Manual of Mental Disorders-IV?

The American Psychiatric Association made the decision that behaviors are more easily and reliably quantifiable than affective and interpersonal traits. Because a diagnosis of psychopathy requires evaluation of affective and interpersonal factors as well as of antisocial behaviors, the Association chose to include only antisocial personality disorder which can be diagnosed solely on the basis of the antisocial behaviors.

Will psychopathy be included as a *diagnosis in the* Diagnostic and Statistical Manual of Mental Disorders-5?

Psychopathy has not been considered as a stand-alone diagnosis in the *Manual's* revision. Rather, it has been put forth as one of the five prototypes for personality disorders, termed the antisocial/ psychopathic type. The traits associated with it would include six forms of antagonism, namely callousness, aggression, manipulativeness, hostility, deceitfulness, and narcissism. And they would include three forms of disinhibition, namely irresponsibility, recklessness, and impulsivity. The revised *Manual* would rate the individual's match to the type on a five point scale from very good match to no match at all and the traits associated with it on a four-point scale from not descriptive to extremely descriptive. Unlike *DSM-IV*, this personality disorder would encompass both behavior and personality.

How might DSM-5 *differ from* DSM-IV?

Work and study groups of the American Psychiatric Association have been considering revisions to the *Diagnostic and Statistical Manual of Mental Disorders-IV*, in preparation for making *DSM-5* official in May 2013. A number of changes, especially relevant to the insanity defense, have been proposed for the fifth edition. One of those introduces dimensional, rather than dichotomous, assessments. A second introduces quantitative tools in the form of rating scales to measure the severity of psychiatric disorders. A third consolidates the eleven personality disorders in the fourth edition into one general diagnostic category in the fifth consisting of five personality disorder types, antisocial/psychopathic type being the one most relevant to the insanity defense. In a fourth, no mention of which was made in *DSM-IV*, *DSM-5* would provide seven suicidal risk factor groups, only one of which might link terrorists to mental illness, namely a current, meaning this week, preoccupation with or plans for suicide. And finally, in a sixth, *DSM-5* would emphasize gender and cultural sensitivity, specifically considering how gender, race, and ethnicity might affect diagnoses of mental illness. Given that some of the general material in this book and some of its cases focus on the interplay between insanity and religion, and further than that, on the interplay among those two and terrorism, it is noteworthy that religion has not been included in the American Psychiatric Association's reworking of its *Manual*. Either those in the work and study groups have concluded that cultural sensitivity does not include religion or they have been wary of approaching the topic of religion from what they consider a scientific point of view. Yet, as some of the materials in this book make clear, religion, whether viewed as standard, extreme, or idiosyncratic, has figured prominently in cases widely-covered in the media and thus exerting important influence on the public at large.

What characteristics of post-traumatic stress disorder make it suitable or not for an insanity defense?

Post-traumatic stress disorder was officially introduced in the third edition of the *Diagnostic and Statistical Manual of Mental Disorders.* Post-traumatic stress disorder occurs after a person has been exposed to a traumatic stimulus, either once, as in a car accident, or repeatedly, as in recurring physical, sexual, or emotional abuse. The most common symptoms of post-traumatic stress syndrome include reexperiencing of the traumatic event, avoidance of stimuli associated with the trauma, extreme fear and anxiety or numbness when exposed to stimuli associated to the trauma, and the presence of hypervigilance or hyperarousal symptoms.

Post-traumatic stress disorder has had an interesting relationship with the insanity defense. Though it has occasionally been thought of in cases involving temporary insanity, as for example when an abused woman is said to have snapped and killed her abusive husband, the more common use has been when the crime was one of inaction. For example, as in the case of Hedda Nussbaum, when a woman has been severely abused by her partner, she may have suffered from post-traumatic stress syndrome. As a result, it could be argued, when he beat their children she might have been unable to respond because of her own trauma. In cases such as that, post-traumatic stress syndrome could be the basis for an insanity defense as one could argue that the defendant was not responsible for the abuse of her children since she was unable to intercede on their behalf because of post-traumatic stress syndrome.

What is the relation among psychopathology, psychopathy, and psychosis?

These words are often confused. Psychopathology simply combines pathology or sickness with psycho or mind, and therefore refers to mental illness or mental disorder. Psychopathy, as addressed in another question, is a mental disorder characterized by lack of conscience and emotional disconnect from others. Psychosis refers to any mental disorder which involves a serious distortion of or separation from reality. Schizophrenia and bipolar disorders often involve psychoses such as hallucinations or delusions.

Is insanity the same as mental illness?

Much of the public has thought that insanity and mental illness were essentially synonymous, but that does not appear to be the case. Many suggest there needs to be a reformation in the way in which insanity is viewed and defined. Only in cases where judgment is impaired, whether through substance abuse, brainwashing, or other means, should one allowed to be able to claim insanity. Talking about insanity without a discussion of mental illness is not a useful debate about the insanity defense.

What factors determine a defendant's competency to stand trial?

Courts usually agree with one or more of the forensic evaluators' decisions concerning the competency of a criminal to stand trial. A study of clinicians showed that from zero to sixty-two percent of the defendants they evaluated were incompetent to stand trial. However, twelve percent of the variability could be attributed to the evaluators. The other significant variables that influenced an evaluator's decision were characteristics of the defendants referred for evaluation such as their degree of impairment and the setting under which the evaluation was performed. Characteristics of the system also had an effect on the competency evaluation, including availability and quality of psychiatric facilities, compensation, and evaluator characteristics such as training and professional discipline.

Should the M'Naghten rule be revised to redefine wrong to include wrongs outside of the legality?

Although some crimes were committed by the insane who could not comprehend their actions, the majority did know that the act they were committing was technically illegal, but could not control their compulsion to commit the act anyways. Many argue that a person who was extremely paranoid and believed that the whole world would blow up if he did not kill one person should not be considered less insane than someone who either did not know the total extent of the law or whose mental illness made him believe his act was legal.

What were common misconceptions between the verdicts not guilty by reason of insanity and guilty but mentally ill?

Many previously thought that guilty but mentally ill was an acceptable and even a superior verdict to not guilty by reason of insanity because the fact that the defendant was insane does not necessarily mean that he was not guilty if he did in fact commit the crime. But many are concerned because they believe that guilty but mentally ill is merely a verdict intended to please everyone, not deliver justice. This verdict allowed juries to take the easy way out without leaving the jury room with a guilty conscience. The remark that the overcrowding of hospitals has resulted in many convicted but mentally ill patients being transferred straight to jail without much treatment further discredits the case for the guilty but mentally ill verdict.

What has been advocated as a three-step process to make mens rea *and* actus reus *clearer to jurors, to incorporate society's values, and to replace an abolished insanity defense?*

The first question in the decision-making process would be whether the defendant intended the act itself. An example would be: Did the defendant intend to kill? The second question in the process would be whether the defendant carried out the act he intended. An example would be: Did the defendant kill the person he intended to kill?

The third question in the decision-making process would be whether there was a moral justification society would agree upon for the act. Clear examples of moral justification would be such well-accepted reasons as self defense. Less clear examples of moral justification would be mercy killings in some circumstances. Examples of no moral justification would include commands by aliens or directly from God or for persecutory purposes. The third question would be answered by asking what society would deem acceptable, not what someone who committed the act would find acceptable, as taking commands from aliens or from God or with some other rationale, because it would be clear that that individual had already found the act acceptable.

Does the insanity defense associate violent criminals with mental illness?

Opponents of the insanity defense noted that the defense created an association between the mentally ill and violent criminals. This led to a public stigmatization of mental illness, which undoubtedly harmed the mentally ill. This concept, however, ignored the benefits that could be gained from properly identifying an individual as insane through the insanity defense. When declared insane, individuals were placed in rehabilitation or treatment centers, where some enjoyed positive outcomes and even reintegrated themselves into society. Without the defense, the mentally ill would instead be relegated to prisons, which would cause the public to perceive a much stronger association between criminal and mentally ill populations.

Why does public opinion about the insanity defense appear to be so negative?

In a 1994 study of reform of the insanity defense in eight states, researchers examined public beliefs about the insanity defense in comparison with a sampling of actual statistics on its use in various counties of those states. Not surprisingly, public beliefs were extremely skewed, viewing the insanity defense as commonly relied upon and easy to use as a legal loophole to escape justice. The authors of the study argued that these beliefs were highly influenced by media coverage of the insanity defense, which lent itself to highly sensationalized coverage, both factual and fictional. The main question remaining for the authors was whether a public that was informed of accurate facts and statistics would hold a less negative view of the insanity defense per se.

Why does the public react to someone's causing terrible harm by saying that the perpetrator must have been crazy?

Most people cannot even conceive of causing such harm themselves and thus feel a need to provide an explanation that distances themselves from the perpetrator and highlights the importance of the strict limitations on the definition of insanity. This in large part is because studies have shown that many people can be relatively easily led into committing horrendous acts. Psychologist Stanley Milgram conducted a series of experiments in 1961 to judge people's propensity to obey an authority figure. He found that sixty-five percent of his study participants were willing to deliver a potentially fatal shock of four hundred and fifty volts to another human being on the instructions of a scientist. Situational factors seemed to have more of an impact in this area than an individual's personality. A horrendous, harmful act did not necessarily have a strong correlation to a person's mental health. Many therefore argue that great care must be taken when employing the insanity defense ensure that it springs from the nature of the perpetrator's moral awareness of his crime rather than from the nature of the crime or the nature of the public perception of the crime and the criminal.

Do jurors' intuitive prototypes of insanity and attitudes toward the insanity defense shape their verdicts more than legal definitions of insanity?

Some researchers argued the answer is yes. A questionnaire-based experiment with a pool of prospective jurors revealed that both the prototypes of insanity and jurors' attitudes strongly predicted trial outcomes. They further observed that the predictive utility of prototypes was far less than that of negative attitudes. Hence, they believed that during the empanelling of an impartial jury, jurors' attitudes should be the focus.

Does prior exposure to mental illness influence the likelihood that jurors will accept the insanity defense?

Lawyers interviewing potential jury members have had to take into account a variety of factors, and one of those factors was the exposure a potential juror had had to mental illness in his past. Researchers investigated what the effect of past exposure was on jury decisions on the insanity defense in mock trial situations. Surveyed prior to the study, participants were asked to deliberate on a variety of closing remarks given for a female defendant charged with shooting and killing a convenience store worker. One of four defense arguments given to all participants was the insanity defense. Results revealed that even participants with a history of mental illness in their past, whether in a family member or themselves, were no more sympathetic to the insanity defense argument than those who had no connection to mental illness in their past. While it might natural to think that this would have been an important factor to consider for both defense and prosecution attorneys when selecting jury members, this research showed that was not necessarily the case. Past experience with mental illness had no direct connection to an increased likelihood to accept the insanity defense in a trial.

What are the differences between an insanity defense and a cultural defense?

People v. Kimura provided an interesting case example that highlighted the intersection of law and culture. A Japanese-American woman attempted parent-child suicide, known as oyako-shinju in the Japanese culture, upon discovering her husband's extramarital affair. Her children were killed in the process, while she survived. While acceptable in Japanese culture, this was clearly a violation of American law. Another salient example surfaced when an American resident of the Hmong tribe killed his wife as a result of her adultery. Again, in the Hmong culture, this was not only acceptable, but also necessary.

Those individuals who adhered to cultural norms or practices that were explicitly illegal in the United States faced the difficult choice of either abandoning their cultural traditions or breaking the law. If the individual chose to break the law, a cultural defense might be used. Employing a cultural defense, however, is not a formal defense in American criminal law. But cultural influences might be introduced. Given that mens rea is an important factor in criminal conviction, cultural circumstances may mitigate the extent of defendant's guilty mind. A prosecutor might choose not to prosecute or to agree to a plea deal if significant cultural factors were at play.

Stark differences have existed between a cultural and insanity defense. These differences often render cultural circumstances inapplicable in an insanity plea. The insanity defense has required the testimony of expert witnesses to evaluate and explain the defendant's mental instability and defendants who have committed crimes due to their cultural beliefs often resist or refuse to employ the insanity defense. These defendants believed that employing insanity during prosecution of an act committed according to religious beliefs degraded that culture. Defendants were also hesitant to employed the insanity defense given that a verdict of not guilty by reason of insanity would commit the offender for an indefinite period of time, as opposed to a conviction of guilty, which had a more determinate and finite sentence.

How accurately can psychologists and psychiatrists determine who is malingering?

It has been said that the two most important aids for evaluators trying to detect malingering were a detailed knowledge of the disease and a detailed knowledge of all circumstances concerning the defendant. But it was possible for the defendant to obtain detailed knowledge of the disease and the common symptoms of the disease, especially with modern technology, and the defendant also knew more about himself than the evaluator could ever possibly know. Therefore, it seemed easy for an intelligent defendant to look up the common symptoms of a disease or obtain information from his lawyer and then fake it in front of an evaluator. This also suggested that more intelligent people will be more able to abuse the insanity defense in this way, which means that smart, guilty people, who were also more dangerous because of their intelligence, would be able to avoid long prison sentences in exchange for shorter time in mental institutions, which could have a negative effect on society.

Should mentally ill defendants who refuse to use an insanity defense still be considered insane?

It is not unusual for defendants, who have a history of mental illness and appear to have committed their criminal acts under some kind of delusion or hallucination, to forbid their lawyers from using the insanity defense on their behalf. Ron and Dan Lafferty, for example, committed two murders in the view that they were acting in a righteous manner and would be given a reward in heaven. They refused to let their lawyers use an insanity plea because they wanted their views to be seen as legitimate and rational. Similarly, Ted Kaczynski, who had sent bombs through the mail in order to draw attention to his belief that technology was a great danger to society, was diagnosed as a paranoid schizophrenic but he refused to use the insanity defense because he was afraid that it would discredit his beliefs. In both cases, thought the defendants appeared mentally unstable, a fact which affected the crimes they committed, they were not treated as such. Some argue that lawyers should declare that their clients are insane even when those clients protest that they are not. This they say is important because a sentence of not guilty by cause of insanity can ensure that these criminals get the psychiatric treatment they need, something that is not guaranteed by a verdict of guilty.

What potential problems occur in insanity defense trials?

There are numerous opportunities for bias in the trial of insanity defense. Everyone from the judge, to the court-appointed psychoforensic expert, to the general public and even the jury could have biased opinions about the insanity defense or about what is just that can alter the proceedings of the trial. The right to a fair trial by jury could be complicated by a judge who was not in favor of the insanity defense from the start. Even the psychoforensic experts hired by the defense or the prosecution could advance their own personal opinions which might not help the case that they were hired to argue. Also jurors have their own preconceived notions of the defendant's innocence or guilt in relation to insanity even if they have already been screened by attorneys to determine their impartiality on the defense. If a juror slipped through the screening, and disapproved of the insanity defense, its acceptance would be as unlikely as that of a jury where a juror had firm beliefs against the death penalty and was serving in a capital punishment case.

What is conditional release and how successful has it been?

Individuals who were found not guilty by reason of insanity can be conditionally released into the community following a period of time in a mental hospital. Once an individual no longer exhibited signs of mental illness and was considered to not be dangerous, he was permitted to be conditionally released. Conditional release implied that in order for these individuals to maintain their freedom, they had to continue to receive mental health services and be monitored. There has been controversy surrounding the decision to conditionally release those who were found not guilty by reason of insanity. There was a fear that, once released, these individuals would inflict further damage on society. Reasons for conditional release included overcrowding of mental hospitals and upholding the rights of patients who were no longer a threat to society. The effect of conditional release depended on several characteristics of the individuals being released. Individuals who spent less time in a mental health institution prior to release, who had previous release failures, who had alcohol and other drug problems, and who were diagnosed as schizophrenic were more likely to have their conditional release revoked. The most successful conditional release programs were found to provide substance abuse treatment, close monitoring of mental health symptoms, and intensive supervision for individuals whose release was revoked in the past.

What factors have been important when deciding to conditionally release those who found not guilty by reason of insanity?

The most important factor is whether the person still suffers from a mental illness and whether the person remains dangerous. The process of deciding whether a patient is fit to be released varies from state to state. Most states do not explicitly state what factors need to be considered in assessing whether a patient can be released. Prior to the 1990s, the mental health status of the patient was most heavily considered when determining whether the patient should be released. Gradually, substance use gained more importance in the decision making process. This was because substance abuse combined with mental illness proved to be a good predictor of relapse. More recently a significant amount of attention has been paid to mental illness and future dangerousness. This was because a detailed assessment of future dangerousness was a very labor intensive process and resources did not exist to assess all patients in this manner. Instead, easier factors to assess had been relied upon. Compliance with psychiatric treatment has played a significant role in deciding to conditionally release someone who was found not guilty by reason of insanity. This is because studies have shown that those who are compliant with their treatment at the mental hospital are more likely to attend required meetings once they are released, which is critical for preventing relapse. Release assessments have become more structured over time as mental health facilities become more sophisticated and have acquired more resources for making such decisions. Release decisions still vary widely from state to state and there has been little effort to establish a uniform process for making the decision.

Should someone who receives a verdict of not guilty by reason of insanity be subject to commitment to a mental health institution for longer than he would have been in prison for his crime?

In a way it seemed unjust to institutionalize a person for longer than he would have to be in prison, but at the same time if the purpose of institutionalization was to help a person overcome mental problems, then the patient should really be hospitalized until he was deemed no longer mentally unstable, for his own safety and to prevent any future harm by him. Only by thinking of the defendant as completely not guilty, and therefore not deserving of any loss of liberty, but rather just mental help in order to justify what might be a short period of treatment or one that takes place over decades.

What are the consequences of malingering?

As psychologists may have but a slightly greater ability than chance to determine whether an individual is malingering or faking a condition of insanity, this inevitably means that those who are actually malingering may often go undetected, while those who should fit the description of insane are deemed sane and sentenced accordingly. Society's problems which follow include overly harsh and therefore unsuccessful punishment for truly mentally ill offenders, the release of dangerous, sane and calculating offenders into society, and distrust in a system unable to properly classify sane and insane offenders, to name a few. The United States saw a surge in the overturning of convictions with the introduction of more sophisticated DNA analysis, exonerating criminals who died during imprisonment while

46

serving life sentences or who had been sentenced to the death. If new technological or biological advancements highlight the implausibility of successful distinguishing of the truly insane from the malingerers, this will shame the criminal justice system in a similar way. Overturning convictions based on changes in such classifications will shed light on gross guesses and inaccuracies, which had tremendous implications in the lives of not only offenders, but also the victims and families and friends of victims of countless crimes.

What is the Juvenile Psychiatric Security Review Board *and what are its consequences?*

Some scholars explained that in Oregon legislators were particularly aware of the role of mental illness in juvenile offenses and established the novel and unique JPSRB to manage juvenile insanity acquittees. With an interest in regarding juvenile offenders with serious mental conditions that pose a substantial danger to others as non-criminals, insanity verdicts were renamed responsible except for insanity. Once a juvenile was placed under the jurisdiction of the JPSRB, the Board controlled treatment, placement, early and conditional release and ensured these juveniles were entirely separated from adults. Many recognized that the state of the juvenile justice system in Oregon would be greatly benefited by the JPSRB, which was among the first of juvenile justice programs to recognize the intersection of crime and mental illness in adolescents. However, parts of the statute establishing the JPSRB seemed unclear and inevitably disputed by lawyers and judges, calling into question the statute's effectiveness and long-term durability.

Can juveniles employ the insanity defense in the same manner as adults?

Juvenile courts are primarily modeled after adult courts. The insanity defense is not a fundamental constitutional right for adults, and therefore the same law holds true for juveniles. Additionally, while juveniles generally can plead insane, they are subject to particular statutory rules and restrictions specific to the state they are facing charges in. For example, some states do not have an insanity defense for juveniles or for adults. Most states do explicitly allow adults to plead insane, but do not specify whether that right is or is not afforded to juveniles. On the other hand, a juvenile's right to employ the insanity defense was embedded in statutory law in Texas and New Jersey, for example. California, Massachusetts, Nebraska and New York affirmed this juvenile right in other state codes. Wisconsin and Louisiana were unique in that state case law classified a juvenile's right to plead insane as a fundamental right. Washington D.C. was the only jurisdiction to explicitly forbid juveniles to use the insanity defense. The general consensus among those states that did allow juveniles to plead insane was to allow more subjectivity in the definition of insanity. Given that juvenile courts were subject to different, often more lenient, regulations than adult courts, it was difficult to determine the impact a juvenile's mental disorder would have on a particular case outcome. However, a juvenile who was mentally ill but not legally insane might have found the material presented by the insanity defense lessened or altered the nature of his final sentencing.

What did the MacArthur Juvenile Adjudicative Competence Study *measure and conclude?*

Conducted in 2003 by the MacArthur Foundation Research Network on Adolescent Development and Juvenile Justice, the study analyzed the effects of young age on competency to stand trial. Prevalent mental illness in youthful offenders coupled with developmental immaturity determined an adolescent's trial competency. The researchers examined nine hundred twenty-seven adolescents, all under the age of eighteen, and four hundred sixty-six young adults between the ages of eighteen and twenty-four. The adolescents were broken down into three more specific age groups: eleven to thirteen-year olds, fourteen to fifteen-year-olds, and sixteen to seventeen-year-olds. Half of all subjects were either serving time in jail or in juvenile detention centers. The other half were the former subjects' counterparts, similar in age, gender, ethnicity and social class, yet not incarcerated. All subjects were administered tests that evaluated their competency to stand trial, ability to make legal decisions and other related knowledge.

The study concluded that adolescents in the youngest age cohort, eleven to thirteen-years-old, were on average three times less likely than young adults to possess the necessary attributes to be deemed competent to stand trial. Similarly, juveniles aged fourteen to fifteen were twice as likely to be impaired as young adults. Those juveniles in the two lowest age cohorts were significantly less likely to make successful legal-related decisions than young adults. Given that juveniles with low intelligence were less likely to possess the necessary abilities and cognition to stand trial and that most juveniles in the criminal justice system were of below average intelligence, risk for incompetency to stand trail was very high.

As a result of these and other important findings of the study, the Network made several policy recommendations. Most generally, the commission called on states and policy makers to consider the low competency rates for juveniles to stand trail when evaluating juvenile justice policies. More specifically, the Network asked states to consider automatic competency evaluations for juveniles before transferring them to adult court.

What has been the history of the death penalty for juveniles in the United States?

The first recorded death penalty occurred in 1642 in Plymouth Colony. The offender, age sixteen at the time of his crimes, confessed to crimes of bestiality including sexual relations with a cow, a mare, two goats, five sheep, two calves and a turkey. He was hanged immediately following the slaughtering of each of the animals he had sexual relations with. The youngest offender to receive the death penalty was ten-year-old James Arcene, a Cherokee Indian convicted of robbery and murder in 1885 in the state of Arkansas.

The *Eighth Amendment* to the *United States Constitution* guarantees protection from cruel and unusual punishment. In 1958, *Trop v. Dulles* declared that a punishment is determined to be cruel or unusual if it is disproportionate to the crime, disproportionality measured by both evolving standards of decency and the judgment of modern society.

The specific issue of juvenile capital punishment first came before the Supreme Court in the 1983 case of *Thompson v. Oklahoma.* Fifteen year old Thompson shot and cut the throat, chest and abdomen of his former brother-in-law with the help of three older men. The victim was then tied to a concrete block and dumped into a river. Thompson and his accomplices all received the death penalty. Given that Thompson was fifteen-years-old at the time of the crime, he appealed on the basis that the sentence was a violation of the *Eighth Amendment.* Based on the standards of decency at the time, a plurality of the Supreme Court agreed and Thompson's sentence was overturned.

In 1989, in *Stanford v. Kentucky,* the United States Supreme Court decided five to four that capital punishment of offenders between the ages of fifteen and eighteen was not cruel and unusual punishment. Thirteen years later in *Atkins v. Virginia,* the Court decided that capital punishment of mentally retarded offenders was cruel and unusual punishment. In the decision, the Court explained that mentally retarded offenders had diminished capacity and therefore diminished culpability for their crimes. In this sense, the punishment of death did not meet the crime. This case raised the issue of whether juveniles, like mentally retarded offenders, also had diminished capacity and diminished culpability.

⚖ *What did* Roper v. Simmons *decide?*

In 2005, the Supreme Court declared capital punishment unconstitutional as cruel and unusual punishment for crimes committed when the offender was under the age of eighteen. *Roper,* decided by a divided court, five to four, effectively overruled *Stanford v. Kentucky,* which permitted capital punishment for crimes committed at the age of sixteen or above. This decision upheld the decision by the Supreme Court of Missouri to overturn the death penalty of a seventeen-year-old.

Roper v. Simmons involved the conviction and sentencing of Christopher Simmons, seventeen at the time of his crime, who had been convicted in the murder of Shirley Cook. Simmons expressed plans to his friends to kill someone and claimed he would be acquitted due to his young age. After abducting Cook from her home, he bound her legs and hands with duct tape and threw her off of a bridge into the Meramec River.

Simmons, after confessing to the murder, was tried as an adult. The prosecution focused on the brutality of the murder, while the defense highlighted Simmons' young age as a mitigating factor. At the close of the trial, he was convicted of first-degree murder. The jury recommended the death sentence. After denying two of Simmons' previous appeals, the United States Supreme Court decided *Atkins v. Virginia*, which prohibited capital punishment of mentally retarded offenders. Simmons argued that the Court's justification for *Atkins*, that the mentally retarded had diminished capacity, should also be applied to juvenile offenders. The Supreme Court of Missouri finally granted his appeal and overturned his conviction in light of *Atkins* and current standards of decency regarding the death penalty. Simmons was instead given life imprisonment without the possibility of parole.

The United States Supreme Court upheld the Supreme Court of Missouri's decision in *Roper v. Simmons*. The Court agreed that capital punishment of an offender between the ages of fifteen and eighteen was a violation of the *Eighth Amendment*. Along with the Court's opinion that evolving standards of decency rendered such punishment unconstitutional, the Court also noted the diminished capacity of offenders in that age range. For this reason, retribution and deterrence, the two social purposes of capital punishment, would be rendered ineffective for juvenile defenders and the mentally retarded alike.

❧*What implications does* Roper v. Simmons *have for the insanity defense?*

In 2005 the United States Supreme Court declared capital punishment unconstitutional for offenders under the age of eighteen. That decision as well as the decision abolishing capital punishment for those of low IQ score may well affect the trajectory of the insanity defense in the United States. In *Roper v. Simmons* and *Atkins v. Virginia,* the Court rested their opinions on arguments that adolescents and the mentally retarded had diminished capacity. Neurological and social immaturity increased impulsivity in such offenders and decreased their culpability. Following this logic, adults with low IQs may be just as impulsive and nonculpable as a mentally retarded or juvenile offender. But so may offenders with a range of mental illnesses. The Court's prior categorizations raise the question of whether, eventually, execution of all mentally ill offenders will be cruel and unusual punishment.

What rehabilitation services have been offered to individuals found not guilty by reason of insanity?

Individuals found not guilty by reason of insanity and then returned to the community may be conditionally released. State governments have focused on policies to keep such patients in conditional release and thus to aid their reintegration into society. Since no set terms of institutionalization accompany a finding of not guilty by reason of insanity, specific hospitalization and rehabilitation regimens are meant to be tailored to the needs of the individual. Studies found a fairly large success rate for not guilty by reason of insanity individuals reintegrated through conditional release programs. The most successful programs included alcohol and drug abuse components and continued psychological and psychopharmacological treatment as well as adequate housing and meaningful activities. They also employed risk assessment models to determine which patients were likely to recommit offenses or to relapse into mental illness, with greater caution taken with highly psychotic or formerly dangerous individuals.

Can the court force a mentally ill defendant such as Russell Weston to take antipsychotic medicine in order to make him competent?

This is an extremely important issue because the court cannot put an incompetent person on trial, and therefore some criminals may evade conviction. In *Riggins v. Nevada,* the Court found that drugs that affect one's demeanor and mental state during a trial impede due process and therefore violate the right to a fair trial. The Court stated that forced medication would be appropriate if there were no less intrusive alternatives and the person was a danger to himself or others, or if the government could not obtain a clear understanding of his guilt or innocence in no other manner. The main contribution to doctrine from *Riggins* was that it demanded heightened scrutiny in these cases.

Another concern of the justices in *Riggins v. Nevada,* was that the drugs affect on one's demeanor could create unconstitutional drug prejudice because known side effects of some psychotic drugs were drowsiness and confusion. Although the Court found this argument persuasive in Riggins' case, it stated that involuntary treatment that creates trial prejudice is constitutional as long as the State can justify the prejudice with an essential state interest. The Court did not define what essential meant in these situations. Justice Kennedy, in the concurring opinion, went further and stated that the State has the burden to show that the medication will not impair the defendant's capacity in the trial in any meaningful way or else it will prevent a perfectly fair trial. Kennedy also stated that forcing medicine to make a defendant competent to stand trial is not an important enough state interest on its own.

Further case addition to the doctrine about forcible medication involved Russell Weston. Weston was found incompetent to stand trial The Bureau of Prisons found that Weston suffered from a mental disorder, was dangerous to himself and others, could not function in the open mental health population, and required medication to treat his illness, prevent danger, and in order to be competent to stand trial. The Bureau's findings came with the approval to administer involuntary antipsychotic drugs. After two reviews with the same findings, the district judge allowed the Bureau of Prisons to force medication on Weston. The court relied on the fact that Weston was a danger to himself and others in order to allow the medication. The judge in the district court ignored the defendant's plea that the drugs would hinder his right to a fair trial and thus Weston filed for an appeal. The Circuit Court reversed the District Court's finding, stating that the court had failed to prove that Weston was a danger to himself and others and that forcing the antipsychotic drugs would impair his chances for a fair trial. The case returned to the District Court where the judge once again found that the medicine could be forced, but this time focused on the fact that the actions were serving a compelling government interest, that there were no less intrusive alternatives, and that the medicine would not prevent Weston from receiving a fair trial. The judge also argued that Weston's health had worsened and he was even more dangerous at this point because he had received no treatment whatsoever.

Once again the decision was appealed, but this time the D.C. Circuit Court affirmed the judge's decision. The Circuit Court did not accept the danger argument, but declared that competency restoration was a compelling government interest because the prevention and punishment of criminals is an important role of the government. Both the District and Circuit Courts declared that such medication could even create a more fair trial for the defendant because he would be able to intelligently speak with his counsel and have the ability to testify if he so chose. Therefore competency restoration was enough to force medication on a pretrial defendant.

Weston also ignited many discussions about the ethics of the case. Weston's attorneys were adamant that he not receive medication, and although they argued that it was to procure a fair trial, many also knew that it was because if found competent to stand trial, he would be eligible for the death penalty. This created a huge commotion in the ethics of the situation because proponents felt that the psychotic suffering the defendant endured while not receiving treatment would ultimately save his life, whereas opponents felt this process was causing unnecessary pain for the individual and that the attorneys should avoid the death penalty by arguments during the trial, not avoiding the trial.

What might happen to individuals such as Lorena Bobbitt and others found not guilty by reason of insanity?

Depending on the state, there are two routes that an individual acquitted for insanity might take. In some states, the individual may be automatically committed to a mental institution. After treatment, the judge would later decide whether it was safe enough to release the individual to his community. One study showed that the average period of confinement in a mental institution for defendants found not guilty by reason of insanity in New York was three years, and was increasing. The period of confinement was also shown to lengthen with the degree of seriousness of the crime.

In other states, the individual may be released to his community after a brief hospital stay, while continuing to receive monitoring by mental health professionals and outpatient care. This option is termed conditional release and is the mental health equivalent to parole. Under the conditional release system, a four-state study showed that sixty percent of five-hundred twenty-nine insanity defendants were conditionally released within five years of being institutionalized. The median length of confinement for released violent offenders was approximately three and a half years, and one and a third years for minor offenders.

A common belief of the public is that individuals found not guilty by reason of insanity are quickly released, as in the case of Lorena Bobbitt, who was released only after several weeks in a mental institution. At times, however, insanity defendants have been confined more frequently, and for longer periods of time, than non-insanity defendants who have committed similar crimes. For example, Michael Jones was acquitted under a plea of not guilty by reason of insanity for shoplifting but was institutionalized for decades longer than the maximum possible prison sentence for the offense. One explanation for this phenomenon is that under the commitment system, the standards by which the judge decides whether the individual should be released are civil and may be stricter than those for a prison inmate. Though an individual can remain committed to a mental institution only so long as he or she is considered mentally ill and dangerous, the circumstances which brought an individual to the attention of the police in a misdemeanor case may replay themselves sufficiently to insure longer term commitment to a mental hospital.

Was Lisa Nowak successful in employing the insanity defense in her assault and kidnapping case?

After assaulting and attempting to kidnap a former romantic rival, Lisa Nowak was charged and employed the insanity defense. The former astronaut attempted to demonstrate her insanity through several claims. She lost fifteen pounds over a very short period of time. She suffered from major depression and from obsessive-compulsive disorder. Her defense attorney also claimed that she experienced a brief psychotic disorder, though the stressors of this disorder were not made entirely clear. Considering whether her mental and physical issues qualify as evidence for the insanity defense her weight loss could hardly be considered since the marked loss could be entirely intentional and a mechanism for falsely demonstrating insanity. And her other mental disorders did not seem to prove that she was unaware of her wrongful criminal action.

Why did Kipland Kinkel plead guilty rather than not guilty by reason of insanity in the killing of his parents and attacks at his school?

In May 1998, at age fifteen, Kipland Kinkel shot and killed his parents. The next morning he entered his high school cafeteria where he shot fifty rounds from a semiautomatic rifle. He killed two students and wounded twenty-five more. Kinkel was charged with four counts of aggravated murder and twenty-six counts of aggravated attempted murder. When police eventually discovered Kinkel's dead parents, the soundtrack to the 1996 film *Romeo and Juliet* was set to continuous play.

Kinkel's case did not involve either religion or what were then considered to be terrorist acts, but given Kinkel's psychological history, it seemed clear that his lawyers would employ the insanity defense. Before trial, however, Kinkel pleaded guilty to murder and attempted murder three days before jury selection was scheduled to begin. This effectively eliminated the possibility of pleading insane and being found not guilty by reason of insanity. When later interviewed about this decision, Kinkel's trial lawyer explained that pleading guilty would offer the possibility of a reduced sentence given the discretion of the judge. As a result of past encounters with the particular judge in the case defense counsel thought the judge would be fair and objective. On the other hand, the lawyer worried that the impassioned press and the fear that an insanity defense might render such a brutal murderer a free citizen would negatively influence a jury.

A hearing determined Kinkel's sentencing. The hearing consisted of six days of testimony relating to Kinkel's crime, his psychological history, his mental health, and the opinions of the victims and victims' families. The defense attempted to prove the extent of Kinkel's mental illness by calling psychologists to the stand. One expert met with Kinkel for thirty-two hours following the crime. He extensively reviewed past records and administered extensive psychological examinations. He diagnosed Kinkel with a psychotic disorder and explained that Kinkel exhibited paranoid symptoms. He argued that these symptoms most likely stemmed from early onset schizophrenia, which ran in Kinkel's family. He also argued that Kinkel suffered from auditory hallucinations at the time of the murders, which most likely caused him to commit the acts. An expert, a psychologist, evaluated Kinkel and also diagnosed him as psychotic with pre-schizophrenic tendencies. Lastly, a pediatric neurologist conducted a neurological exam consisting of a mental status evaluation, a cranial nerve examination, and a motor examination. He found a lesion in the prefrontal lobe of Kinkel's brain. He explained that such abnormalities rendered decision making and emotional control virtually impossible. He explained that such abnormalities are found in pre-schizophrenics and made adolescents more susceptible to psychotic episodes. The prosecution called an expert who had interviewed Kinkel prior to the incident. He explained that while Kinkel was angry and depressed, he was not psychotic. At the close of the hearing, the defense and prosecution made sentencing recommendations to the judge. The prosecution suggested the maximum possible sentence, two hundred and twenty years. The judge cited a change to the Oregon State *Constitution*, which highlighted the importance of societal protection and personal responsibility. He then handed down a sentence of one hundred eleven years with no possibility of parole.

Why in the case of Jeffrey Dahmer, where the criminal acts were so grotesque, would insanity still be so difficult to prove?

The case of Jeffrey Dahmer was fascinating because of the unbelievably bizarre nature of his crimes which included not only killing but cannibalizing and storing body parts in his refrigerator. One of the overall tendencies, when looking at a serial killer such as Dahmer, is to dismiss his actions as insane because of the ghastly nature of them. Society does not want to believe that anyone short of a psychotic lunatic would be capable of committing such heinous acts. This was precisely what Dahmer thought. He believed that the crimes he had committed were so grotesque that no jury would believe he was sane.

Despite his efforts, Dahmer was found guilty on fifteen counts of first degree murder. The standard for insanity in Wisconsin, where Dahmer was tried, was the American Law Institute test with the burden of proof on the defendant. The defense argued that such acts as building an altar of human skulls and necrophilia and cannibalism constituted sufficient evidence that Dahmer was operating in a distorted reality. The prosecution's expert psychiatric witnesses countered by testifying that Dahmer understood right and wrong and that he had the capacity to stop his actions at any point.

Dahmer was not found legally insane for many reasons but there were two explanations that seem most convincing. The first was that bizarre behavior was not in itself enough to constitute insanity. If bizarre behavior alone were legitimized as insane an obvious legal loophole would exist for any crime severely out of the ordinary. An intelligent criminal might then reasonably make his crimes as gruesome and grotesque as possible in order to avoid full responsibility. The second explanation was society's desire to make serial killers responsible for their actions and keep them in prison.

Society likely did not want to find serial killers insane because of the nature of their crimes. Unlike delusional perpetrators such as Yates, Dahmer's acts were not impulsive but well thought out and patterned. This repetitive pattern made it more likely for recurrence in the future, and society has a higher stake in keeping these people in prison. Of course, Yates had thought out her acts and had planned. But then she had no more children to kill, whereas Dahmer had many more potential victims.

Chapter 3.   Insanity, Religion, and Mental Illness

How is religiosity defined?

Religiosity, in its broadest sense, is a comprehensive sociological term used to refer to the numerous aspects of religious activity, dedication, and belief. In its narrowest sense, religiosity deals with how religious a person is instead of how a person is religious. Researchers determined that there were multiple dimensions to religiosity. In 1986, Cornwall and colleagues identified six of these dimensions. The cognitive dimensions were traditional orthodoxy and particularistic orthodoxy; the affective dimensions were spiritual feeling, church commitment, and physical feeling; and the behavioral dimensions were religious behavior and religious participation. Most dimensions of religiosity were highly correlated. Individuals who attend church regularly were also likely to score highly on the belief and spirituality dimensions, though this was not always the case as scores also varied by dimension.

What is the relation between religion and psychotic manifestations?

A great deal of research examined the relationship between religion and psychotic manifestations. Imaging studies found evidence that the inferior parietal cortex plays a substantial role in both schizophrenic misattribution in psychotic patients and common religious experiences in healthy individuals. Researchers found a link between religious delusions and overactivation in the left temporal lobe and underactivation in the left occipital lobe. These findings were obviously controversial, since they pointed to a common cause for both psychotic delusions and religious experiences. However, this neurological link between schizophrenia and religious belief, along with the prevalence and frequency of religious imagery from a cultural standpoint, helped to explain religions presence as a consistent theme in schizophrenic delusions.

Is religious belief antithetical to mental health?

A scholar discussed the early 1990s shift in the attitude of mental health professionals over the malignancy of religious belief in relation to mental health. While early psychologists as well as the creators of the *Diagnostic and Statistical Manual* commonly made malignant references to religiosity and religious belief, a significant body of empirical evidence emerged in the 90s, showing that there was actually an inverse relationship between religion and psychopathology. The capstone of this research was the *Handbook of Religion and Health* which presented an analysis of over twelve hundred studies and four hundred reviews. It showed among other things that eighty percent of the one hundred studies on religion and well-being reported positive correlations and that twenty-eight of thirty-six studies found lower crime and delinquency rates among more religious individuals. The scholar ultimately concluded that in order to best understand the complexity of the human mind, the profound influence religious belief has in relation to the human psyche must be considered.

Are there neural correlates of religious understanding?

Researchers explored whether or not there was a neural correlate to the Christian teaching to submit oneself to God and judge oneself from God's perspective. They used fMRI to contrast Christian and non-Christian subjects performing trait-assignment tasks. The scientists determined that self-referential processing resulted in increased ventromedial prefrontal cortex activity for non-religious participants and the dorsal-medial prefrontal cortex for self-identified Christians. Those two brain regions are generally engaged when representing self-relevance of a stimulus and the evaluation of self-referential stimuli, respectively. The researchers argued that religious belief in Christianity was associated with depressed encoding of self-relatedness but increased encoding of evaluating self-referential stimuli. Thus these individuals were more wired to evaluate the self through God than directly, a clear representation of the religious and cultural expectations of their belief system.

What is the neurological basis for religious experiences like the sensation of being visited by God?

It has been argued that because the brain is the source of all human experience, by stimulating the brain in certain ways one should be able to produce religious experiences such as the sensation of being visited by God. Years of experimentation showed that patterns of weak magnetic fields near the temporal lobes could produce religious experiences in subjects. Subjects used their own cultural belief systems to put a name, such as God, to what has been called the sensed presence of a sentient being. These experiences were not only religious in nature, but also included other paranormal experiences such as visitation by extraterrestrials. Re-analysis of prior experiments proved that these paranormal experiences were not the result of the suggestibility of the subjects.

Are there any similarities in how the brain responds to psychotic and to religious episodes?

Some researchers explored the concurrence of religious episodes and temporal lobe epileptic. They explained that 2.2 percent of temporal lobe epilepsy patients have after-seizure religious experiences. Moreover, 3.9 percent of all epilepsy patients reported some sort of religious symptoms or auras. The paper said that patients with post-seizure psychosis were also likely to experience between-seizure hyper-religiosity, which the authors argued supported a pathological increase in interictal religiosity. They went on to explain that the limbic system, which is affected during temporal lobe epilepsy, was likely involved due to the emotional nature of the experiences. Parts of the neocortex might also play a role, as religious experiences can sometimes result in auditory and visual hallucinations and complex ideation. The paper seemed to suggest a correlation between the occurrence of psychosis and religious experience in temporal lobe epilepsy patients and also identified activation in brain regions during religious experiences that were dysfunctional in several psychotic disorders. Though there was clearly not any causal link between religion and psychosis, the fact that similar brain regions were involved may help explain why some psychotic individuals identify their delusions as having a religious basis.

What is the relationship between religion and psychosis?

Religion is an enduring theme in psychosis across cultures but there is a distinction between cultural conceptions of religion and pathological religion known as religiosity. Religion, defined as a particular system of faith and worship, plays a role in psychosis due to its cultural role, but also due to overactivity in the temporolimbic region of the brain which causes perception to be interpreted spiritually since religion and psychosis share a common pathway in the brain. Prevalence of religious beliefs in pathology has been shown to be as high as fifty-six percent which occurred in schizophrenic patients. While Freud viewed religion as a mechanism to overcome the Oedipal complex,

William James considered personal religious experiences as part of abnormal psychological processes. There can be an unclear boundary between normal religious beliefs and psychosis. Mentally ill patients often cite their unusual perceptions as divine religious experiences.

What is the relation between religion and mental illness in schizophrenia?

Frequently, people with schizophrenia have heard the voices of God or the devil speaking to them in their auditory hallucinations. In many cases, these people had some exposure to religious ideals previously in their lives. Oftentimes, when schizophrenics believed they were acting according to the will of an outside agent, they felt justified to commit a crime. Even if they knew that it was wrong to do so, it seemed to be acceptable because they were coerced by a higher power. This has caused courtroom disputes over whether criminal behavior can be justified if instructions to commit the crime came from an auditory hallucination from God or an auditory hallucination from the devil. Religious beliefs, religious values, and cognitive dissonance were the three significant predictors of attribution of causes and treatments of schizophrenia to religious factors. Also, a significant percentage of followers of Protestant denominations indicated demonic causes of mental illness.

Under the American Law Institute test of insanity, can acting criminally to satisfy a fundamentalist religious belief lead to a verdict of not guilty by reason of insanity?

Committing criminal acts due to religious convictions, however strong they may be, does not inherently qualify one for insanity. Only if mental illness caused a person to believe he was acting on a god's behalf, and he did not understand the wrongfulness of his actions or was unable to conform to the law due to that could a defendant plead insanity. Merely acting upon extremist religious beliefs would not necessarily qualify for the insanity defense.

How did the case of Phineas Gage inform modern brain-imaging practices?

The evolving debate over psychopathology and the role the different parts of the brain play has been an interesting one. fMRI technology has highlighted the significance of the frontal lobe and its correlation to mental disorders such as antisocial personality disorder. An important physical case that underscored the idea of localization of brain functions was that of Phineas Gage. Gage was a railroad construction worker who accidentally had an iron rod driven through his head. He survived the accident, but significant and irreversible damage was done to one, or maybe both, of his fontal lobes. Several reports indicated that his friends no longer thought he was the same person, and that he had poor work habits, was quick to temper, fitful, profane, impatient, and lacked an ability to plan for the future, all characteristics in direct opposition to his personality before the accident.

Have there been successful treatment programs for psychopaths?

One issue with the insanity defense is the question of the extent to which seriously mentally ill offenders can be reformed. Despite a common perception among both clinicians and laypersons that there are problems with treatments, many treatments have empirically been shown to work. Among them are both effective cognitive-behavioral and psychodynamic therapies. Success has often been measured by the extent to which interpersonal relationships have improved.

How much freedom of speech should one have when preaching about religion?

Because religion is a very sensitive and personal topic, it is often hard to draw definite lines determining what is and is not appropriate. But based on cases such as Yates more recently and even such notorious cases such as Schroevers in 1900 in the Netherlands, it is hard to claim that preaching had no effect on the perpetrators. A closer examination of the cases finds a history of bizarre, hateful preaching. Under the First Amendment, there are essentially nine categories of speech that are not protected: obscenity, fighting words, libel or slander, child pornography material, perjury, blackmail, incitement to imminent lawless action, true threats, and solicitations to commit crimes. If these types of speech are not constitutionally protected, then many argue that more stringent laws should be applicable to religious preaching which mirrors intense hate and calls for bizarre or dangerous actions.

Have religious institutions promoted mental health treatment?

Religious beliefs play a part in insanity defense cases. In fact some people have pointed to religious visions as responsible for their crimes. This has led many to believe their religious devotion was a potential cause of mental illness. Yet a 2006 study revealed that, since religious institutions were a strong source of mental health information, religion could actually have had a positive overall effect on the mentally ill. While the religious institution, itself, was not often responsible for the curing of mental illness, it acted as an entry point into the formal treatment system. Often, the study observed, religious organizations detected early signs of mental illness and directed parishioners to mental health services. In fact, roughly twenty-five percent of mentally ill persons turned to their religious institutions first for help with their problems. And while the study did reveal that religion offered less support to the seriously mentally ill, it still suggested that religion did not necessarily have a negative impact on the mentally ill. In fact, it suggested that religious institutions probably helped more than they hurt.

Does the Eighth Amendment require the acceptability of the insanity defense in all states?

The *Eighth Amendment* to the *United States Constitution* prohibits the federal government from imposing cruel and unusual punishments. Given that the *Fourteenth Amendment* extends that to apply to the states, meaning that no state can impose such punishment on any individual, a 1979 Montana law abolishing the insanity defense might seem to be unconstitutional. After all if a person lacks awareness and moral culpability it would seem cruel or unusual to indict, convict, and sentence that individual. Yet in a 1994 case challenging the Montana law the United States Supreme Court denied certiorari to the petitioner. This meant that the Supreme Court allowed individual states to prohibit the use of the insanity defense. Because of the court's silence on the issue, states are allowed to prevent the use of the insanity defense. Only a few states do so.

Can someone who commits a crime to satisfy a fundamentalist religious belief be found not guilty by reason of insanity?

Committing a crime due to religious convictions, however strong they may be, does not inherently qualify one for insanity. Instead, the defendant must show that he conforms to the jurisdiction's insanity defense. If a mental illness caused a defendant to believe he was acting on a god's behalf, and he did not understand the wrongfulness of his actions or was unable to conform to the law due to that defect, then that defendant might be found not guilty be reason of insanity. However, merely acting upon extremist religious beliefs does not necessarily qualifying for the insanity defense.

How do psychiatrists and psychologists distinguish between authentic or legitimate religious beliefs and religious based psychosis?

A balance must be struck between understanding religious belief from a cultural and philosophical standpoint and recognizing religiously themed psychopathology. This is difficult because of the varying feelings about religion and mental health. Freud, for example, believed that all religious ideology was a symptom of unsound psychological processes, but other authorities, such as William James, had a more centered view of religion and psychology. Some have advanced a theory about the basic cognitive difference between a genuine religious experience and a psychotic religious experience. A genuine religious experience might be characterized as an abnormal interpretation of a normal event, whereas a psychotic religious experience might be characterized as an abnormal perceptual experience. In the first instance, the individual associated a higher level of affect, whether profound joy or feelings of harmony or oneness, to a normal event. In the second, the individual perceived a reality that was not there. The person's fundamental perception of the world was altered in a psychotic way. But the distinction might be difficult. The challenge would lie in understanding the difference between religious culture and pathology without jumping to conclusions regarding unfamiliar religious beliefs.

What should be the verdict on faith based killings?

A scholar argued that faith based killings driven by purported messages from God should not be punishable and those who follow them should be exculpated from blame through the insanity defense. Just as God told Abraham to sacrifice his only son Isaac and Abraham willingly complied, one who believes he hears God must listen to his command above all else. Abraham was fortunate enough to have an angel stop him from killing his son, but in cases such as Yates' and Lashaun Harris', they were not so fortunate and they acted on the commandment they thought to have received from God. Assuming one believes in God, then the courts must realize that the word of God takes precedence above all else, and if someone believes he hears God communicating with him, he has no choice but to act on this message. Someone acting under the supposed word of God, the argument goes, must be taken as delusional, the act should not be considered premeditated, and the defendant should be considered innocent by the definition of the insanity defense.

Should an extremely devout religious follower be classified as insane?

Some commentators argue that a person who is a devout follower of any religion might be considered mentally ill, perhaps legally insane. Yet, following a religion to the point where words of that religion prevent the individual from using lawful judgment may make a person mentally incapable of making the right choices. When a religion is of such paramount importance to an individual that he considers he must do everything in his power to obey its commands no matter how strange or harmful they are, then such a follower is dangerous to society because any number of things could lead a person to kill or do harm to others around him. Following a religion to the extent that Yates began to do with Woroniecki's help forced her to disconnect with the world around her because nothing else in life registered any significance or importance besides her unhealthy religious beliefs. Obviously a devout religious follower could live a life filled with good deeds, but by putting himself in a situation where he gives up discretion, and considers himself at the demands of outdated text, dreams, or prayers, may make a person a potential threat to any society which disagrees.

What are some of the difficulties that arise in mixing religion and the insanity defense?

One important problem raised by using the insanity defense for cases involving religious belief is that arguments will often presuppose that the religious beliefs were inherently flawed, and lawyers will be faced with the difficult task of trying to separate behavior from belief. A prosecutor faced with a defendant using the insanity defense must, in many cases, argue that despite religious beliefs, there was an underlying knowledge by the defendant that the act committed was legally wrong. Most significantly, as an example, adherence to extremist religious beliefs may complicate the underlying basis of the M'Naghten test for legal insanity. If the religious dogma were so deeply inculcated in the individual that it has redefined in the conscious mind his sense of right and wrong as defined by American law, extremist religious belief may be covered by the insanity defense because the individual may not recognize that he committed a crime.

In some cases, such as *U.S. v. Fishman*, the insanity defense was based on the defendant's having been brainwashed or in some way acting under the control of the religion in question, in that particular case, Scientology. The jury in such cases may also be unduly influenced by personal reactions to the religion in question and by their personal beliefs regarding brainwashing. Another concern was that if the insanity defense were expanded so as to permit adherence to certain religions or religious beliefs as indications of insanity, people could then plead insanity merely by claiming adherence to those religious beliefs.

Would it be easy for any fervent believer of an obscure or less mainstream religion to prove that he was not guilty by reason of insanity?

There are countless religions in the world today, and many of the smaller, less known religions seem to the outside world to have bizarre rituals and followers. In the days of the early Romans, it is likely that many thought the ritual of the Eucharist was insane because it was impossible for Jesus Christ's body to be eaten in the form of bread and his blood to be drunk in the form of wine. Yet today this is a common practice that most give no thought to. Many Church of Scientologist believers consider man as descended from aliens, but this idea seemed crazy to most non Scientologists. Perhaps those who belong to uncommon religions might be more likely to receive a not guilty by reason of insanity verdict because of their unconventional religious beliefs, regardless of mental illness. Judges and juries would be more likely to view these individuals as suffering from insanity because their beliefs in religion were so distinct from those of mainstream society, which could lead them to believe that something must be mentally wrong with these individuals, regardless of intent of the crime at hand.

How might defendants use religion to malinger or otherwise influence their court cases?

Society's perception of religious norms can actually factor quite heavily into how a case proceeds. Religious persuasions have obvious effects during the *voir dire* process, during which time attorneys seek to create a jury pool that holds certain views of morality based on their religious perceptions. One researcher's examination of the role of religion in twenty-five high-profile court cases dedicated a number of sections to discussing these phenomena. Specifically it outlined the use of terms like god-fearing on the part of defendants or instances in which defendants expressed their remorse in a religious context. Where prevailing religious beliefs matched those espoused by defendants during a trial, religious messages may have helped predispose juries to believe the remorse of a defendant. On the other hand, when an individual expressed outlandish or perhaps even disagreeable religious views, juries may have been more likely to view these individuals as guilty, rather than letting their professed faith be an exonerating factor in a trial. Yet it also seemed perfectly plausible that a number of the defendants described in a law review article may have dropped mention of God in order to be viewed more favorably by their juries. This could stretch to individuals who claim religious belief as an explanation for their behavior. Thus the use of religion could be a very easy, and perhaps effective, way to malinger or otherwise influence jury opinion.

What is the automatism defense and how does it relate to the insanity defense?

In order to constitute a crime, there must be both *mens rea* and *actus reus*. One of the stipulations is that the act was voluntary. If the act was involuntary, then the person who committed it cannot be blamed. The automatism defense is used to argue that the defendant did not voluntarily commit the crime. The automatism defense is different from the insanity defense. People who are insane have control over their actions but do not understand the true nature of their acts, whereas automatons do not have control over their actions. Also, an insane person must be found to have a mental disease or defect, but there is no such requirement for an automaton. This concept may apply to religiously-based insanity, because oftentimes those who are pleading insanity assert that they were commanded by God to commit the crime. There are several examples of criminals who were found not guilty by reason of insanity because they claimed to have been instructed by God. One such instance was the stabbing of the former Beatle, George Harrison, by Michael Abrahm, who claimed God instructed him to kill Harrison, who he believed to be an alien from hell.

What percentage of violent crimes are committed by people with severe mental illness?

A 2006 study found that approximately five percent of violent crimes in Sweden were committed by people with severe mental illness. This meant that nineteen out of twenty crimes were committed by people without severe mental illness. This finding would likely be surprising for the average person, because there is a conception created by the media that a large percentage of people committing violent crimes are mentally ill.

Was Andrea Yates guilty of murdering her children, the verdict in her first trial, or not guilty by reason of insanity, the verdict in her retrial?

Andrea Pia Yates was born in 1964 and raised by a devout Catholic family. She excelled in school and athletics and received a nursing degree. She married Rusty Yates in 1993, adopted the conservative religious beliefs of her new husband, and left her nursing career to fill the role of homemaker in their marriage. The Yates had five children, all named after biblical figures. The period around the birth of their first son also marked the introduction of a self-proclaimed prophet Michael Woroniecki into their lives. His zealous influence contributed to her slowly crumbling confidence in her own capabilities as a mother and wife. Her mental health began to deteriorate, and the period between the birth of her first child and her last included various suicide attempts, hospitalizations, and prescriptions for increasingly aggressive anxiety and anti-depressant drugs, many of which Yates refused to take. Though numerous treating physicians advised the family to stop having children because the increasing size of the family contributed strongly to the deterioration of her mental state, Andrea and Rusty ignored these warnings, and by the time of the killings, had five children, ranging in age from seven to one years of age.

✤ What happened on the day Yates killed her children?

On June 20, 2001, between the hours of nine and ten in the morning, Andrea Yates was left unsupervised in her home with her five children. One by one, Yates drowned the children in the family bathtub. When all five children were dead, Yates called her husband and the police to tell them what she had done. When they arrived on the scene, Yates was unemotional. Later that day, she confessed again to killing her children, saying she had done so to save them from Satan. She insisted that she was guilty of failing as a mother and should be punished for her crime.

✤ What occurred during the first Yates trial?

Initially, the defense wanted Yates declared unfit to stand trial. They brought forth her voluminous medical records, subpoenaed her family and jail employees, and brought in psychological experts. The jury disagreed and found her competent to stand trial. The defense then filed a number of motions, including letting the jury know that by finding Yates not guilty by reason of insanity, she would be placed in a hospital rather than set free. They also challenged the constitutionality of the M'Naghten test. The defense failed in both these efforts.

At this point, the defense attorneys' main goal became proving to the jury that Yates was insane under Texas law which used the M'Naghten test. They needed to convince the jury that she was not aware that she was breaking the law and that her actions were wrong. However, they had a hard battle, given that Yates herself had stated many times she knew what she did was both wrong and illegal. Instead, the defense focused on showing that her reasoning abilities were flawed.

A dozen different psychoforensic professionals were involved during the first Yates trial. Of these, Park Dietz, the prosecution's only mental health expert, was alone in testifying that Yates was sane at the time of the murders. Though his testimony was instrumental in her first conviction, it was also his false statements regarding an episode of *Law and Order* that allowed Yates a second trial. A court-appointed psychiatrist initially found her competent to stand trial, but a clinical psychologist hired by the defense argued the opposite, testifying that her delusional state made her unable to assist the defense. A depression expert for the defense said that Yates needed more time on a continuous medication schedule before she would be competent to stand trial. Six days after the competency argument began, Yates was found competent to stand trial, which began officially in February. The defense called four psychiatrists to testify that Yates did not understand the implications of her actions due to a psychotic state and was thus insane at the time of the killings. Dietz was the only rebuttal witness. On March 12, 2002, after deliberating for just under four hours, the Texas jury rejected Yates' insanity defense and found her guilty of capital murder in the drowning deaths of some of her children. The jury decided against the prosecution's death penalty recommendation and Yates was instead sentenced to life in prison with the possibility of parole after forty years.

The prosecution had charged Yates in the murders of Noah, John, and Mary but not Paul and Luke, for purely strategic purposes. Had Yates not received a guilty verdict the end of her first trial, the prosecution would still have been able to indict Yates for the deaths of her other two sons. In other words, they were keeping their options open. Additionally, the reason the prosecution did not charge Yates for one murder at a time was because Yates was charged with multiple murder, which required two or more murders. Also, a conviction for three murders would be more likely to deliver a death sentence or life imprisonment than a conviction for one or two. In Yates' case, however, despite only charging her with three murders, the prosecution chose to present evidence for all five, which may have ultimately bolstered support for the defense's insanity plea.

Yates' first jury found her guilty but voted against the death penalty. Due to Texas law, the death penalty decision could only be later overturned if the defense was presenting new evidence. At her second trial, after the appellate court overturned the first verdict, Yates' defense presented an identical case as the first trial and forcing the prosecution to come up with tactics that did not utilize the faulty *Law and Order* accusations. So even if her second jury did find her guilty of murder, they could not then also decide to subject her to the death penalty.

✡ *What occurred during the second Yates trial?*

The leading prosecutor during Yates' first trial returned to head the prosecution in her retrial. The prosecutors again did everything to ensure that Yates was convicted of capital murder. They acknowledged that Yates was severely mentally ill during the period leading up to the killings but they argued that she was still aware of the difference between right and wrong and thus culpable under Texas state law. The prosecutors used much of the same evidence that they had presented during the first trial. They cited the pre-planned element of the killings, since she had waited until she was alone with the children to act, and her immediate desire to confess to the police and her husband as evidence that she understood the wrongful nature of the killings while she was committing them. They also used their forensic psychiatrist Dietz though eliminating the testimony about the television program. He asserted that while Yates had been suffering from depression and psychosis, she still considered her thoughts about killing her children a horrendous sin, demonstrating that she was legally sane during the time of the murders. Another forensic psychiatrist testified that Yates knew her conduct was wrong. The county chief medical examiner testified that the autopsies of the Yates children indicated that they had struggled for several minutes each before drowning. The defense again argued that she suffered from postpartum psychosis at the time, unaware that her actions were wrong, and thus was not guilty under the M'Naghten test. A forensic psychiatrist and medical expert testified that at the time of the drownings Yates was severely psychotic, displayed signs of schizophrenia, and believed what she was doing was ultimately best for her five children.

Yates' second jury consisted of eight men and four women, and was much more amenable to her defense than her first jury. For example, more than twenty individuals of the jury pool from her second trial said they had already made the decision that Yates was legally insane. Additionally, nearly forty more potential jurors reported they could not be impartial because of their exposure to the case in the media. In fact, the majority of the jury pool said they were familiar with the case. The jury from the second trial was also more amenable to the insanity defense, as an institution. During voir dire, many jurors admitted that they disagreed with the state's legal definition of insanity. On July 26, 2006, after a longer deliberation than in the first trial, this jury found Yates not guilty by reason of insanity. The judge first committed Yates to North Texas State Hospital, but then moved her to a lower-security hospital in Kerrville where she received medical treatment. During her time at North Texas, she was the roommate of Dena Schlosser, another mother who killed her child, in November 2004. Rusty Yates divorced Andrea Yates in March 2005 and was married to another woman on March 16, 2006. Rusty and his new wife had a child in March 2008. Yates stated she was not distressed by the news of Rusty's remarriage and new child and that she had learned that life goes on.

What is the explanation for the different outcomes in Yates' two trials?

Yates was found guilty of murdering her children in her original 2002 trial. Due to false evidence being admitted in the first trial, a second trial was held in 2006, in which Yates was found not guilty by reason of insanity. One of the most influential reasons for the different outcomes of the two cases was the role of the media in the two trials. Despite a media gag-order for the jury of the second trial, the members of the jury had already been exposed to years of influential media that the jury in the first trial did not experience.

Many reporters and media sources claimed the outcome of the first trial was incorrect and unjust, releasing stories sympathetic to Yates' claims of insanity. A 2006 mock juror study of pretrial media bias in the Yates case concluded that individuals exposed to sympathetic, or conversely unsympathetic, media coverage of Yates' condition and the outcome of her first trial were more likely to vote for a verdict aligning with the media's view. This study suggested members of the jury, who would have been exposed to numerous sympathetic news stories following Yates' first trial, would have been influenced by the media, causing the jury's outcome to be in favor of Yates' insanity plea in her second trial.

Also, the appellate court concluded that the outcome of the 2002 trial might have been influenced by the false testimony from prosecution psychiatrist Dietz that Yates could have been influenced by an episode of *Law and Order* in which a woman drowned her children and was found not guilty by reason of insanity. The jury in the first trial may have been swayed by that testimony, seeing a clear connection between the episode and the real crime committed, and likened them enough to believe that Yates's viewing of the show was motivation for her acts. A different outcome may have emerged in the 2006 trial because, after Dietz's explanation was denounced, the insanity plea became more plausible to the new jurors than extreme theories of planning or premeditation. The jury saw Yates' insanity as a reason that she needed psychiatric help and could not be held guilty of or responsible for her acts.

Finally, Yates' defense attorney had filed many motions prior to her first case that, had they been accepted, could have had an impact on the case's outcome. One of the most important motions tried to overturn the Texas Criminal Code procedure that prohibited teaching jurors the difference between not guilty by reason of insanity and not guilty verdicts. At the time of the first trial, many jurors had not been educated that those found not guilty by reason of insanity faced mandatory hospitalization and treatment. By the time of the second trial, the public had been taught by the media that a verdict of not guilty by reason of insanity would not allow Yates to be immediately released.

What interaction between antisocial behavior and insanity occurred in the two Yates trials?

A revealing interaction between antisocial behavior and insanity occurred in the two trials of Yates who methodically drowned her five children in the hour when she was alone with them. In the first trial, Dietz's psychiatric testimony appeared influential in convincing the jury that Yates' behavior was antisocial, perhaps psychopathic, rather than the result of psychosis. He concluded that she was not out of touch with reality. In fact, he argued that she had planned their deaths, had waited for an opportune time when she was alone, had called police immediately afterwards to say she had done wrong. The jury found her guilty and she was sentenced to prison. On appeal, her conviction was overturned because of Dietz's inadvertent or deliberate misstatement concerning a television program about someone who drowned her children and then pleaded insanity which program had not even aired. On retrial, a different jury, hearing almost the same evidence and experts, found her not guilty by reason of insanity. The earlier jury had implicitly found her acts to be antisocial, perhaps psychopathic, but not the result of psychosis. The later jury found her acts to be the consequence of her psychotic mental state.

In the psychiatric literature, the American Psychiatric Association asked in its 1982 *Statement on the Insanity Defense* whether the legal standards in use concerning the insanity defense should be modified. It concluded that the insanity defense ought not to be available for persons primarily diagnosed with personality disorders such as antisocial personality disorder, which it also termed sociopathy. To do so, it maintained, would not accord with modern psychiatric knowledge or beliefs, and it concluded that offenders with antisocial personality disorders should be considered criminally responsible for heuristic reasons if for no other. The American Psychiatric Association determined that only serious disorders, such as schizophrenia or bipolar disorder, should lead to acquittals by reason of insanity.

But a different response followed Yates' second trial. In an editorial arguing for reform, the *Boston Herald* responded to the second jury's verdict finding Yates not guilty by reason of insanity in the planned drowning deaths of her five young children by advocating a guilty but insane model. It said that such a verdict would provide a balance between mercy and justice because convicted offenders could receive mental health treatment until their recovery at which time they would finish their sentence in prison. In essence, it argued that a person could be both guilty as a psychopath or antisocial personality would be, and insane as a seriously mentally ill person would be. Yet the two words contradicted each other.

This conflict between the words guilty and insane have appeared unresolvable, and in the Yates case unnecessary, for the solution the *Herald* sought was exactly what was happening after the first jury found Yates guilty of murder in 2002. Though sentenced to prison, she was spending most of the time in a prison mental health facility. In other words, the sentence imposed after the first trial found her guilty, as would the guilty part of guilty but insane, but confined her first to a mental health facility, as would the insane part of that verdict, where she would be treated until she was ready, if ever, to enter the prison setting itself. After the not guilty verdict in the second trial, she was not released into the community. Rather she was transferred to a different hospital but remained within a mental hospital setting

How might religious preaching have influenced Yates?

Michael Woroniecki preached that all men are wicked, and, according to tapes released by him, that Jesus said that whoever caused children who believed in Jesus to stumble should be drowned in the depths of the sea. Though Woroniecki acknowledged that this begged the question of whether Jesus was condoning suicide, he said the answer was yes. He believed that suicide was necessary if someone had caused children to stumble in their faith. He explained that a child's mother was accountable for teaching and training the children and that children must be not be subjected to a mundane existence, but must be trained to live a life of self-denial and sacrifice.

Following Yates' first child's birth, signs of mental illness and instability began to surface. On meeting Woroniecki, Yates found that his religious preaching struck a chord in her deepest insecurities as an inadequate mother. Plagued by overwhelming household responsibilities, violent hallucinations and postpartum depression, she was vulnerable. The initial signs of mental illness would combine with her newfound religious fanaticism to produce a deadly result. After the birth of her third child, Yates and family flew to Florida to visit Woroniecki and his family for a one-week vacation. During this time, the Woronieckis explicitly told Andrea that she was going to Hell. They exploited her great fear of her children being damned to Hell as a result of her inadequacies. Moreover, through interaction with the Woronieckis and his continued preaching, Yates was ultimately convinced of her worst fear, that she was an inadequate mother. Therefore, according to Woroniecki's preaching, Yates knew she must commit suicide. After two failed attempts, Yates concluded that she and her children would be damned to Hell. In the exact language used by Woroniecki, Yates explained to the jury at her trial that she had caused her children to stumble and both she and the children were now doomed. The only possibility for salvation existed in killing her children, who Yates believed might be spared eternal damnation by God because of their young age and innocence.

Regardless of what happened, Woroniecki continued to deny knowledge of how Yates obtained her religious ideals. In fact, he often directed the media to her husband as a potential purveyor of the religious teachings that she lived by. Video footage and Woroniecki's past newsletters existed, however, offering proof of Woroniecki's influence on her.

Was the worsening of Yates's mental health problems a direct response to the teaching, theology, and influence of her preacher?

Although the influence of the Woronieckis on Yates's self-perception remained difficult to quantify, her mental health issues undoubtedly stemmed from a deep-seated sense of failure as a wife and mother. Her dependence on parenting manuals and parenting measures such as religiously-based home-schooling indicated that Yates's spiral was intrinsically bound to her role as a mother which would appear to parallel the teachings and influence of the Woronieckis. Their theology focused strongly on the inherent sinfulness of women,

women's need to atone for original sin, and their responsibility for the salvation of their children, as well as themselves. Given how closely this theology appeared to directly relate to the mental health problems Yates was experiencing it seems clear that the two issues were connected. While the burden of culpability for the killings rested with Andrea herself, the dangerous theology which led to Yates's breakdown appeared caused by the teachings and influence of the Woronieckis.

Did Yates' religious beliefs prevent her from getting the treatment she needed?

Yates' pessimistic and disheartening religious beliefs definitely affected her decision to kill her children because she focused on the religious figures of a terrifying God and a malicious Satan, who alternatively wanted to punish and manipulate her and her children. Her religious environment also affected her acts in that it prevented her from fully seeking the psychiatric treatment she needed. While she saw many psychiatrists, psychologists, and therapists, and was even hospitalized for a period of time, she ignored medical advice to follow what her religious leader, Woroniecki, had decreed. Woroniecki preached that his parishioners should never use contraceptives and instead should have as many births as God desired. This pronouncement undeniably influenced Yates' decision to have a fifth child, despite being warned by doctors that she would develop postpartum depression and psychosis following her pregnancy. Additionally, her husband minimized Yates' disease and allowed her to be with the children unsupervised for an hour each day, in order to encourage Yates' wifely and motherly instincts, traits that Woroniecki endorsed as pious duties in women. Yates' case, therefore, exemplified the damage that religions could cause with their dismissal of mental illness and psychological and medical help.

How did instructions from Satan as opposed ✗ to instructions from God serve in determining the outcome of the Yates case?

Dietz, an expert psychiatric witness for the prosecution in the Yates case, argued for the existence of a religious component to the M'Naghten test. That test for legal insanity in Texas classified an individual as insane if he was unable to determine whether his action was morally right or wrong at the time of the crime. Dietz concluded that the idea of wrongfulness included a moral, including a religious, component, in addition to a legal component. Further he compared the Yates case to other cases where religious hallucinations provided instructions for criminal acts. Because Yates was instructed by Satan rather than God, he concluded that Yates knew her action was morally wrong since it went against God's will. Additionally, Yates believed that she would be going to Hell for her actions and was apologetic and regretful after the acts because she knew that she had committed a horrific sin by killing her children. Since Satan carried no moral authority in the state of Texas, Dietz concluded that Yates could not have been considered insane according to the moral quality of the religious instructions she received from the voices she heard.

Would Yates have mentally deteriorated if she had not ✗ been influenced by her husband's religious beliefs?

Though Yates was raised in a non-practicing Catholic family, by a father who required perfection from his daughter, religion did not play a central role in her early childhood, and it was not until her marriage to Rusty Yates that she adopted any form of zealous religious beliefs. Following the births of her five children, her mental condition steadily worsened, and she was eventually diagnosed with postpartum depression. Despite her mental illness due to this biological condition, Yates likely would not have mentally deteriorated to such an extreme that she drowned her five children without the influence of her husband's religion.

She adopted her husband's religious beliefs, eventually becoming more devout than he. Rusty Yates introduced his wife to the radical religious preacher, Michael Woroniecki, and his wife, Rachel, and the couple convinced Andrea she was a sinner, evil, a witch, and a bad mother. The Woronieckis also denounced Catholicism, Andrea's childhood religion, further labeling her as sinful and encouraging her to accept their extremist ideals. Yates claimed she killed her children to save them from Satan, an idea she would not have conjured without the influence of her husband's religion. Although there is no way to know if her husband's religion actually caused Yates to mentally deteriorate and kill her children, it was likely that without the influence of her husband's religion and its leaders, she would not have experienced the extreme mental strain that caused her to kill her children.

To what extent were her husband and her preacher responsible for the death of the five Yates children?

The religious beliefs that led Yates to kill her five children were first introduced to her by her husband. The newlywed Yates fashioned their lives after his traditional beliefs, in which the husband was the breadwinner and the wife stayed home and took care of the children. He also introduced his wife to Michael Woroniecki, who instilled in her the sense that as a woman she was a born sinner and could only find redemption through complete subservience to her husband and the Bible. Certainly these expectations influenced Yates' feelings that she was a failure as a mother, and as a result played a part in the killing of the five children. Therefore it is problematic to determine Yates alone as guilty when her husband and her preacher helped continuously instill the framework under which she performed her acts.

As her preacher provided the extreme religious beliefs that led to Yates killing her five children, should he in part be held responsible for deaths?

While Yates was the person who physically drowned the five Yates children, it is without question that other individuals played a part in the events that transpired. The Woronieckis, who indoctrinated Yates in their religious beliefs, could easily have been viewed as largely influencing her and her extreme beliefs. While it was unclear whether Yates would have suffered from postpartum depression regardless of the influence of the Woronieckis, it was more than likely it would not have devolved into postpartum psychosis without the presence of these beliefs. Yates's whole psychotic thought process, her feelings of guilt and urgency to kill her children to save them from Hell, was clearly developed as a result of the religious teachings promoted by the Woronieckis. She had previously been a non-practicing Catholic, and only turned to these extreme religious beliefs after she became involved with the Woronieckis who made her feel great guilt for her Catholicism. On an emotional level, it seemed as if the Woronieckis should have been punished for helping to lead Yates to her actions, but in a more legal sense, they could not be blamed for the events that transpired. While they may have helped her to get to the point of killing her children, Yates drowned her children herself.

Should someone who preaches religious fanaticism, as did Yates' minister, be held indirectly responsible for the criminally dangerous actions of those who plead the insanity defense citing religious beliefs?

In the Yates case, her minister, Michael Peter Woroniecki, seemed partially responsible for her actions. He preached to her that she was doomed to Hell, and Yates attempted to commit suicide on two separate occasions after receiving berating letters from him. Yates began to believe that she was a bad mother, and that it was better for her to kill her children than to let them go to Hell. Several investigative reporters and mainstream media believe that Woroniecki undoubtedly had an immense influence on Yates' decision to kill her children.

Should Yates' pastor be held accountable for the extremist religious views she claimed as the reason for killing her children?

When originally probed by her jail psychiatrist as to her reasons for drowning her five children, Yates responded with words about the seventh deadly sin. She said her children were not righteous, that they stumbled because she was evil, that they could never be saved because of the way she was raising them, that they were doomed to die in the fires of Hell. Some speculated that her extremist religious views were largely motivated by the traveling pastor she met through her husband. Woroniecki, the pastor, berated the modern Christian lifestyle in which the husband abandoned his family all day at work and the wife lacked direction. Yates likely identified with this, as her husband was employed by NASA and she stayed home with her children. The defense submitted a 2000 newsletter authored by the Woroneickis entitled *Perilous Times* as evidence of the forces which clouded her judgment, as well as videos of the Woronieckis preaching. Woroniecki was never directly implicated with responsibility for the deaths as prosecutors concluded it would be unfair to blame him for actions performed by a psychologically handicapped woman. Though his worldview was narrow and strongly worded, he did not espouse the acts that Yates would go on to commit.

Could Yates' case be considered an example of brainwashing by her religious leaders?

Brainwashing, as defined, typically consisted of intensive, forced indoctrination of political or religious beliefs, targeted at destroying a person's values and beliefs and replacing them with alternative ones. One could argue that Andrea Yates was brainwashed by the religious practices of her husband and religious leaders, the Woronieckis. The Woronieckis constantly degraded her, telling her she was evil for being a Catholic and forcing her to renounce her old religion and beliefs. They convinced her she was an unfit mother and that her role was to be the sole caretaker of her children. She eventually came to believe those doctrines, telling others she felt she was a horrible mother and that she had to save her children from Satan, which she did by drowning them. Her postpartum depression and mental illness could have played a role in making her more susceptible to this indoctrination, but it does appear she may have been brainwashed by her husband's religious leaders.

Can religious teaching influence women to kill their children?

There have been many examples of cases where mothers have killed their children as result of religious beliefs. Some have cited several passages in the *New Testament*, such as Matthew 19:14, that stated that little children always go to heaven. Some delusional mothers, well versed in religious doctrine, appeared to be motivated to kill their children while they were still young, so that their children could be guaranteed salvation and saved from a life of sin.

Yates, it could be said, was a religious fanatic who was influenced by a religious preacher. After the killings of her children, she claimed she did it to save them from Satan. Combined with her mental disorder, the religious teachings had an influence on her decision to kill her children. In another instance, Dena Schlosser, a woman who killed her baby daughter by severing her arms, followed an extremist religious leader, just as Yates did. Her reasons for killing her daughter were that she believed God wanted her to cut her baby's arms off and she wanted to offer her baby to God.

To what extent did Yates' lack of medication contribute to her acts?

Yates' lack of psychopharmaceutical drugs was a likely cause of her acts. During her third stay in a psychiatric facility, lasting ten days, she was given antipsychotic drug therapy, but returned home with new psychotic symptoms. She was taken to the hospital for a fourth time but was soon discharged and removed from her antipsychotic drug. Within weeks after this visit, her condition worsened and her husband wanted to restart the antipsychotic drug but the psychiatrist refused. He also refused Rusty's suggestion of electroconvulsive therapy because he did not believe that Yates' mental illness was severe enough to require the treatment and instead instructed her to instead think positively and that was only two days before she killed her children. Because in the past the antipsychotic drug Haldol had significantly improved her condition, it is likely that it or another antipsychotic drug would have again been useful if the doctor had followed the recommendation of Yates' husband.

What should the consequence be for an individual such as Yates who has been advised to take antipsychotic medication, has taken it and then discontinued it, and subsequently commits a serious act?

Adherence to antipsychotic medication and other medications for mental illnesses is very difficult to ensure. Many of the medications have side effects that patients may consider worse than the symptoms of their illness. Therefore, it is common that mentally ill people who commit crimes had been prescribed medication for their illness, but were not taking it at the time of their crime. Many people question an individual's personal responsibility for choosing not to adhere to their prescription, and thus their responsibility for the subsequent crime. They ask whether deliberate discontinuation of medication ought to preclude invocation of the insanity defense much as deliberate ingestion of alcohol or other substances would preclude use of that defense.

In the case of Yates, she had been placed on medications multiple times and had been put in mental facilities months before she murdered her children. She discontinued her medications, and was found guilty of murder. It remains unclear to what degree the verdict hinged on her choice to discontinue medication. In fact, many psychiatric experts and jurors supported their finding of her guilty by pointing to the fact that Yates had an understanding that what she was doing was wrong, not that she should have been held responsible for ending her medication.

If a person is placed on medication, particularly antipsychotic medication, it is highly likely that they required some sort of aid in choosing to receive treatment and in gaining a prescription.

Oftentimes aid included physicians, mental health practitioners, and family members. If a patient needed help gaining treatment based on their mental illness, then it is understandable say defense attorneys and advocates for the mentally ill that they would also need help adhering to the treatment, and therefore should not be held responsible solely because they stop medication which would ameliorate their mental illness.

In the case of Yates, her husband had brought her to mental health practitioners and she had at least two doctors who prescribed her powerful antidepressants. When she discontinued her medication, and subsequently murdered her children, many people wondered why her husband had not sought out more treatment for her or requested that she receive more medications, which had seemed to help her in the past. Also, many people questioned why her doctor had released her so quickly from the mental health institution in prior months when she and her husband had voluntarily admitted her, and why one of her doctors had himself been unclear about her medication.

Attorneys and advocates conclude that people who are ill enough to be placed on medication, particularly antipsychotic medication, cannot be held solely responsible for their own adherence. In addition, when determining criminal responsibility, jurors have not officially considered adherence to medication, though some have argued they should. Responsibility is instead determined by a person's mental state and awareness at the time of the crime, on or off medication.

Should an individual such as Yates who has ⋏ *refused medication for mental illnesses have the same access to the insanity defense as someone who has not refused such medication?*

Many argued that Yates was so mentally disturbed that she should not have been held responsible for her actions. However, she also had a long history of refusing to take the medication prescribed to treat her mental disorders. She remarked in many instances that she partly did not want to take the medicine because she was afraid of the doctors who prescribed them, but also because she was afraid that her preacher would judge her for being weak enough to need medicine.

Although the mental illness may have led to her paranoia about the doctors, her fear of her preacher's judgment as a reason to skip her medication was also significant.

Some have argued that patients who refused medication on multiple occasions should no longer have the same right to the insanity defense as those who have not refused medication. These people chose on several occasions to forego the medication, which may have prevented their crimes. While some blame may fall on the medical profession and doctors their ability to force patients to take medicine in cases of severe mental illness can be hampered by patients' right to refuse treatment. Some have suggested a contract that states that a refuser forfeits the right to claim not guilty by reason of insanity in the future if he should commit a crime.

What effect might the specific diagnosis of postpartum depression and psychosis have had on Yates' ultimate verdict?

Postpartum depression, a form of depression that affects mothers directly after childbirth, is a somewhat common mental disorder. Different studies reported prevalence rates among new mothers from five percent to twenty-five percent. Postpartum psychosis is a separate and much less common disorder, which affects about zero point one percent of all births and can lead to delusions, hallucinations, and a complete break from reality. In a very small number of cases it can lead to infanticide. These two very different illnesses are frequently associated and even confounded with one another by laypersons. Yates, who already had a history of severe depression, was diagnosed with both illnesses in the months before her acts. Her attorneys used the diagnosis of postpartum psychosis in particular to argue that she was insane during the drownings of her children. One of the reasons that this argument may have been effective in the second trial is because of this disease's association with postpartum depression. The frequency and familiarity of postpartum depression could have generated empathy and understanding from the jury for Yates, since she was identified as a normal, loving mother who was simply affected by a disease that could contaminate any one. The support from the reporters such as David Williams, who wrote editorials to further educate the American public about these diseases and demonstrate the general lack of aid for afflicted mothers, may also have produced a more sympathetic understanding of Yates' situation.

If it had been allowed, how might brain imaging of the jury in the Yates trial have influenced their final verdict?

After she was found guilty, Yates was granted a retrial because evidence emerged that faulty information had been provided by a prosecution witness in the first trial. Whereas in her first trial, the jury was composed of eight woman and four men, the jury for her second trial was composed of eight men and four women. Some speculated that this shift in jury composition accounted for her final verdict of not guilty by reason of insanity.

Proponents of brain-imaging have suggested that in the future fMRI technology may be used to assess the brain-activity patterns of potential jurors and have gone so far as to suggest that these results can allow courts to hand-pick jurors depending on whether they wish their jury to be more rationally or emotionally influenced in their decision-making. If brain-imaging had been allowed in the Yates trial, the verdict of not guilty by reason of insanity would probably have been reached in the first trial, despite the faulty prosecution testimony. Because women tend to be more emotion-driven in their decision-making, accessing the amygdala region of their brains in allotting punishment, some argued that the court's desire to have brain-activity patterns reflect more balanced rational-emotional brain activity patterns would have ultimately led to a more gender-balanced jury, that would have found her not guilty by reason of insanity instead of allowing the horrific nature of her crime to elicit a more emotional reaction.

In what way did the popular media play a significant role in the Yates appeal process?

One of the most compelling pieces of evidence against Yates was the statement by prosecution psychiatrist Dietz that Yates, inspired by an episode of her favorite television show, *Law and Order*, had premeditated the infanticides. He had been a consultant on psychiatric matters for the popular television show. But a screenwriter from that same show and a freelance investigative journalist realized that this testimony was in fact false, and that no such episode had ever aired, and gave this information to the defense. This information played an important part in keeping the first jury from sentencing Yates to death and caused the successful appeal which led to the second trial. Dietz later apologized and explained that he had fused two episodes of the popular television show. One of the episodes was based on the earlier case of Susan Smith, who killed her children by sending a car into a lake with her children in it and then pled the insanity defense on the basis that she had been instructed by God to kill them. The other episode was one depicting a teenager who killed her baby at a prom. Dietz's false testimony regarding the impact of the television show was therefore a basis for the defense's appeal. Ironically, two years after the original event, an episode of *Law and Order* based on the Yates case was aired in 2004.

Was it appropriate for prosecution psychiatric experts to draw distinctions between schizophrenic hallucinations involving God and those involving Satan, as in the Yates and Laney cases?

Two years after Yates was convicted and sent to prison, another Texas housewife, Deanna Laney, stoned her three sons to death and was acquitted by reason of insanity. Park Dietz, prosecution psychiatric expert witness in the Yates's trial, also testified in Laney's trial, but this time for the defense. The two cases were notably similar, except that Laney claimed to have attacked under God's direction, while Yates operated under the direction of Satan. In the case of Yates, Dietz testified that, because it was Satan's voice, Yates was not insane because she knew what she was doing was wrong, while in Laney's case, because it was God's voice, she thought what she was doing was right. But a law professor argued that it should not matter where the voices came from, be they from God, Satan, or a pop star. The women were responding to an extra-worldly command in a delusional state. According to Dietz, however, because the issue of insanity depended on whether the person believed they were doing the right thing or the wrong thing, a person could only be considered insane if their acts were in response to a command by God or, according to Dietz, the chief of police, both of which he considered the only authority in Texas.

What happens to religious fundamentalists such as Yates and Laney who are found not guilty by reason of insanity?

Of the religious fundamentalists found not guilty by reason of insanity, treatment was fairly consistent with the treatment of other individuals found not guilty by reason of insanity. Generally, these individuals went to a mental institution where they were treated. Examples of such instances were Yates, who claimed that God instructed her to drown her five children, and Deanna Laney, who claimed that God instructed her to crush the skulls of her sons, killing two and severely injuring another. Both of these women were very religious and strongly believed they were following the word of God. Both women went to mental institutions following their trials and remained there.

The treatment of the devoutly religious found insane was not different from those who were not religious because religious fundamentalism was not the primary cause of the insanity. Religious fundamentalists typically had some other mental disorder in addition to their religious belief that led them to commit criminal acts.

Should Andrea Yates have been placed in the same room as Dena Schlosser, another mother who committed infanticide?

Both Yates and Schlosser killed their children and were found not guilty by reason of insanity. In the North Texas State Hospital where they were held, Yates and Schlosser became close friends, and believed that they could help each other on the road to recovery. Considering Yates' and Schlosser's reports of a beneficial relationship, it seemed as if there were no negative effects to placing them together. Yet, even though the women believed that they connected with each other, one must consider the issues that arise when placing two psychotic women who committed infanticide in the same room. Although they were under medical treatment, both women committed horrific acts. Yates drowned her children, whereas Schlosser cut off her baby's arms. One can not deny that these women connected on some level, though it appeared that their connection was rooted in dangerous psychoses and delusions. In this sense, placing the women in the same room might have led them away from reintegration into society, and instead connected each with a similarly psychotic and dangerous individual.

Were fundamentalist Mormons Ronald and Donald Lafferty guilty of murder or were they insane?

The Lafferty brothers said they were following God's command when they killed their sister-in-law and her daughter. They had formerly been members of the Church of Jesus Christ of Latter Day Saints, commonly referred to as Mormons, but had become extreme in their views and were considered Mormon extremists or fundamentalists.

What were the particulars of the Ron and Dan Lafferty cases?

Ron and Dan Lafferty admitted responsibility for the killings of their sister-in-law and of their niece. They did not want to use an insanity defense as they believed that they had acted at the will of God and thus felt no shame or sense of irrationality about the killings. In fact, they thought that their religious message would be discredited by using the insanity defense. Dan was tried in 1985 before his brother and decided to represent himself. The court case only lasted five days. He was found guilty of the murders, though he escaped the death penalty because of a ten to two jury vote. The judge sentenced him to two terms of life imprisonment.

Ron was tried four months after Dan because he had attempted to hang himself during his imprisonment before the trial and had to be examined for brain damage. Ron did not represent himself as Dan had, but he did not allow his attorneys to use an insanity defense. The jury found Ron guilty and sentenced him to death. Ron, however, appealed to several different courts until finally in 1991 the United States Court of Appeals ruled that Ron had not been competent to stand trial and the conviction was overturned. The Court of Appeals declared that he had not been and still was not competent to stand trial because he did not understand the charges or legal system. He was transferred to Utah State Hospital and began a course of therapy. In 1994, he was found fit to stand trial again. In the retrial of 1996, Ron allowed his lawyers to use an insanity defense. His attorney argued that the trauma of Ron's wife leaving him had caused Ron to fall into a delusional state, which gave him a distorted view of the world during the time of the murders. Certain beliefs of Ron's did suggest a delusional disorder such as the idea that the angel Moroni was attempting to take over his body, that Christ spoke to him, that sparks flew from his fingertips. The prosecution, however, claimed that all those beliefs were consistent with the religious beliefs that he had learned as a child in the Church of Jesus Christ of Latter Day Saints. The prosecutors pointed about the similarities between his particular religious beliefs and more commonly held religious beliefs. The question was thus raised about whether if Ron Lafferty were insane, could not then any devoutly religious person be considered insane. After all, all religions contain beliefs not otherwise commonly supported by science or even common sense. In the end, the jury decided that Ron was not insane but simply guilty and he was sentenced to death. At the time of this book he still awaited execution.

Were Dan and Ron Lafferty part of a cult of two?

Ron and Dan Lafferty were Mormons with their own particular set of extremist beliefs. Dan believed that he was going to transform into the prophet Elijah. Ron thought that he had the ability to receive direct messages from God. They both rejected the world as unimportant and corrupt and concentrated instead on the rewards of the afterlife and the eventual salvation for all true Mormon believers. On July 24, 1984, the two brothers killed their sister-in-law and their niece. Dan physically committed the acts on Ron's orders, slitting the throats while Ron watched. Ron believed that God had commanded them to kill both but that Dan had been specifically appointed as the one to strike the final blow. This was an interesting case because it could be argued that Dan followed Ron in the same way that members of a cult might follow their leader. He believed that Ron was speaking on behalf of God and had to be followed regardless of the cost. It was Ron who had the grievance with his sister-in-law, since Ron believed that she had encouraged his wife to leave him, and so Dan's actions were purely based on his belief in Ron rather than any personal sense of anger or betrayal. The question arose whether the Laffertys' extremist religious views were themselves evidence of insanity. Their defense lawyers thought they were, but the brothers did not want their faith diminished by what they considered an invalid and unjust insanity plea. To this extent, their views paralleled those of both secular, like Kaczynski, and religious, like Paul Hill and Scott Roederer, killers who believed in their messages and missions and did not want them tainted by the concept of insanity with its attendant psychotic mental illnesses.

Should an insanity defense be available to religious fundamentalists such as the Laffertys?

Since the standards for an insanity defense apply equally to religious defendants as to their non-religious counterparts, religious fundamentalists should have an insanity defense available to them, but not one that is any different from that available to the rest of the population. The line between insanity on one side, and adherence to a religion in general or to its fundamental version on the other, might be a difficult one to draw at times. That does not preclude a religious fundamentalist also being insane, however. Zealous religiosity can share some traits with psychotic thinking, as for instance a belief in something unseen or a seemingly irrational obedience to a religious law which requires disobedience to society's laws. But to adjudge a belief in one's ability to talk to God, for example, as intrinsically insane is to pass judgment on many people's sanity.

The question of insanity in religious followers became most apparent when the religion was either uncommon or particularly bizarre. Ron and Dan Lafferty, for instance, subscribed to their own strange brand of Mormon fundamentalism, and their religion effectively consumed their lives. Because they believed that God had instructed them to do so, they murdered an innocent woman and her baby daughter. The Laffertys' strange take on a religion which was founded in America but had not gained wide adherents certainly raised questions about their sanity at trial, but their insanity defense was rejected by the jury, which found both men guilty. The bottom line was that the standards for the insanity defense applied equally to religious defendants as to their non-religious counterparts, with little regard for how strange that religion might seem or how much one's beliefs might vary from the core beliefs of the religion. Religious belief, even extreme or deviant religious belief, in itself did not automatically qualify someone as insane, but a religious person could, of course, suffer from a mental disorder that rendered him insane. Odd religious practices may prove to be a symptom of underlying mental illness, but it is the mental illness and not the religion itself that renders a defendant insane.

Were the killers of abortion doctors and clinic workers guilty, insane, or justified by necessity?

Why did Paul Hill refuse to plead insanity to killing the abortion provider, instead relying on a necessity defense?

In 1994, Paul Hill stood outside of The Ladies Center, an abortion clinic in Pensacola, FL, shouting pleas to mothers not to kill their children who if they did would be deemed murderers hated by God. Soon after, he shot and killed one of the clinic's abortion doctors and his escort in the clinic's nearby driveway. It was Hill's belief that he must defend the lives of the unborn by any means possible, including violent force. After firing ninety shotgun pellets, Hill immediately confessed to the crime and was arrested. He was charged with two counts of first-degree murder and one count of attempted murder of the escort's wife who was also present at the incident. Additionally, he was charged with three counts of violating the Freedom of Access to Clinic Entrances.

Once trial began, Hill decided to represent himself. He explained that killing the abortion doctor was his only choice. He said he was instructed by God to save innocent lives by killing the doctor. In a sense, Hill was employing the necessity defense. He found it necessary to kill the abortion doctor to save others' lives. In fact, in response to the prosecution's detailing of the doctor's final moments, Hill requested to show videotapes of ultrasounds of the last seconds of a fetus' life pre-abortion. The judge ruled such evidence inadmissible. Aside from Hill's necessity defense, some encouraged him to employ the insanity defense, at the least to avoid the death penalty. He refused, however, to plead insanity and instead clung to his only defense, that it was necessary for him to kill in order to save others. At the close of the trial, Hill was found guilty and sentenced to death. His last words expressed no remorse and called on fellow pro-choice activists to save innocent lives by any means possible. In recorded interviews in jail as he awaited execution, Hill reiterated the justifiability of his actions and declared that angels would await him in Heaven at his death. His statement paralleled those of Islamic jihadists who referred to the virgins awaiting them at their death in suicide bombings.

As Hill was the first person to be executed for his cause, he became an icon in the minds of some Christian fundamentalists nationwide. As a member of *Army of God*, Hill and fellow self-acclaimed soldiers pledged to prevent abortions and illegalize the actions of doctors performing these abortions and if necessary to kill the providers. In fact, *Army of God* explicitly advocated the murders of abortion clinic staffers. This ideology was justified by the fact that *Army of God*, was as its name indicates, an army under instruction by God. Hill, specifically, felt his killings were justifiable homicide. Most pro-life Christians nonetheless considered his acts illegal and said he had gone too far. In this sense, Hill's actions created an unexpected resentment and unanticipated negative reaction to his cause even among supporters of his ultimate goal. Scott Roederer who killed one of the few late-term abortion doctors was also found guilty despite his argument that he had to kill the doctor to save unborn children.

What distinguished Hill's act as one of violent Christian fundamentalism?

Hill's violent Christian fundamentalism manifested itself in three distinct ways in the murders of the doctor and his escort. First, while Hill's ideology was not drastically different from pro-life Christians, his means of achieving his ideal state were starkly contrasted. The *Army of God* preached that so long as one was working towards a pro-life agenda, he could aim to accomplish this goal by all means possible. Second was the prevalence of divine instruction within the Army. If violence was a necessary or important means in achieving their objective, then that was God's command. One must never disobey God's will simply to avert disobeying a societal law. Third, according to the Army, violence was often necessary simply because it was the most absolute means of achieving an objective.

In a plea of insanity, such as John Salvi's, for killing abortion clinic workers, how were religious fundamentalism and mental illness weighed?

Religious beliefs are not included in the American Psychiatric Association's lists of diagnostic criteria for mental disorders, but opinions on the relationship between religion and mental illness vary widely among experts. At one extreme, Sigmund Freud considered belief in religion to be a symptom of mental illness. Thus, in Freud's opinion, he would have considered all of the ninety-one percent of Americans who subscribed to a religion in 2002 as suffering from mental disorders. It would be unreasonable, of course, to have ninety-one percent of defendants plead not guilty by reason of insanity. Freud himself did not believe that religion as mental illness ought to diminish criminal responsibility. Rather, he believed it was the moral belief system of a religious follower that was ill, while the decision-making part of the brain, which decides whether to follow through on religious beliefs, remained illness-free. As an example, a person who believed that homosexuality was a sin would still be able to decide whether to murder a gay man or to leave him alone. Having a religious belief system, then, would not be automatic grounds for insanity. Yet, one could imagine a scenario in which the person's decision-making processes were sufficiently impaired as to prevent him from making rational decisions about acting on religious beliefs. In such an instance, an insanity defense would be viable, given that the defendant appeared to have no control over his actions. However, the defendant's insanity would stem not from the religious belief itself, but rather from his under-developed control mechanisms. John Salvi, who killed two employees at abortion clinics, unsuccessfully pled not guilty by reason of insanity. His attorney argued that Salvi's religious belief against abortion did not cause him to kill, but rather that his schizophrenia did. Found guilty and sentenced to prison, Salvi was subsequently discovered dead in his prison cell. Authorities said he had committed suicide.

While Freud considered religious belief to be a psychological illness, some researchers have reached the opposite conclusion, that religiosity appeared to decrease the likelihood of mental illness.

A large study discovered that non-religious people were more likely to seek psychiatric treatment than religious people, with increased involvement in the religion correlating with decreased rates of psychiatric treatment. The researchers hypothesized that this difference could be a result of the mental health promoting aspects of religion, such as its social support structure and its emphasis on marriage and the avoidance of drugs and alcohol. All of these factors have been known to promote mental health, and it may be these secondary causes, rather than religion itself, that produced the apparent decrease in mental illness among religious followers. Because the researchers examined only whether the subjects were receiving psychiatric treatment and not whether they actually suffered from mental disorders, another possible explanation for the results could be that religious people simply may have sought professional treatment less frequently but did not necessarily suffer from less mental illness. Instead of consulting a psychiatrist, religious followers may have sought the help of a religious leader, whereas non-religious people had only psychological professionals to turn to for help. Further research would be needed to understand the exact relationship between religiosity and mental health, but, whatever the underlying cause, increased religious observation appeared to be associated with decreased psychiatric care.

Did Scott Roeder who killed a late-term abortion-providing doctor succeed in portraying his act as the product of an unreasonable but honest belief in its justifiability?

Roeder admitted deliberately killing a late-term abortion doctor but he did not plead insanity. Like a previously-executed killer of an abortion doctor, Roeder considered abortion both criminal and immoral. His lawyers therefore argued that he had not committed murder, but that jurors could find him responsible for voluntary manslaughter if they decided that he met the relevant Kansas law test of an unreasonable but honest belief that circumstances existed that justified deadly force. Jurors quickly decided that that test was inapplicable to him. They found him guilty of first-degree murder, the punishment for which was a sentence of life in prison. At his sentencing, Roeder accused the judge of having presided over a trial which he termed a miscarriage of justice. He repeated his claim that the death of a few abortion providers paled in comparison to the deaths of large numbers of the unborn. He said God would avenge abortion and its providers. A friend of the victim called Roeder's act one of domestic terrorism. Some who commented on the sentencing hearing called Roeder a Christian terrorist

Should the gay panic defense, whether or not religiously motivated, be acceptable as an insanity plea or for mitigation?

What is the gay panic defense?

The term homosexual panic was created in 1920. The term referred to latent homosexuals who refused to accept and understand their sexual inclination. Its creator argued that many males who had this disorder would be attracted to members of the same sex but have a conflict between their feelings of attraction and what was considered acceptable by society. After trying to interact with females and having repeated failure, people would be depressed and anxious. He thought that panic happened in relation to a same sex member they were attracted to. Homosexual panic disorder appeared in the 1952 *Manual of Mental Disorders* published by the American Psychiatric Association, but it was omitted every year following 1952. More recently, the gay panic defense commonly has taken on a meaning much different from what was asserted in the 1920s. The defendant in the gay panic disorder as now understood is an individual who kills a homosexual person because a homosexual advance is so shocking that it produces a temporary state of panic and mental insanity. A gay man's unwanted sexual advance gives the defendant a temporary loss of self control and he therefore has no control over consequent violent actions. The panic may result from religious belief but it need not. It may result from physical concerns or it may be a residual effect of previous descriptions of homosexuality as mentally disordered. It should be noted that the homosexuality was at one time considered a mental disorder by the American Psychiatric Association and the American Psychological Association, but they both deleted it from their manuals in 1973 and 1975, respectively.

When has the gay panic defense failed?

One of the earliest high-profile gay panic defense case occurred in 1995 when a guest of *The Jenny Jones Show* announced that he was in love with his friend. Disturbed by this homosexual advance, the friend killed the guest three days after the airing of the episode. However, because success of the gay panic defense rested heavily on the violence being immediate instead of premeditated, the friend failed to show panic-based psychosis and was convicted of second-degree murder and sentenced to twenty-five to fifty years in prison.

In 1998, Russell Henderson pleaded guilty to felony murder and kidnapping and Aaron McKinney was convicted of the same crimes in the death of University of Wyoming student Matthew Shepard. Shepard allegedly made sexual advanced toward McKinney, who was later declared by friends to be bisexual. As a result of this, Shepard was robbed, pistol whipped, tortured, tied to a fence in an isolated rural area, and left to die at their hands. Though both men attempted to use the gay panic defense, the prosecutor in the case charged that both men had targeted Shepard and pretended to be gay in order to rob him. Both men's then girlfriends also testified that the defendants had planned the murder beforehand and were not under the influence of drugs as they had claimed. Both defendants were given two life sentences in prison, McKinney without possibility of parole.

In 2004, Michael Magidson, Jose Merél, and Jason Cazares used a transgender variant of the gay panic defense in a homicide case to claim that they were enraged to the point of psychosis at the discover that a transgendered teenager with whom they had engaged in sex was not biologically female. Again, the defense was ineffectual and two were convicted of second-degree murder and one of manslaughter.

Should gay panic defense strategies be categorically barred?

Most critics of the gay panic defense argued that courts should ban gay panic defense strategies from criminal trials. These strategies included using gay panic to strengthen claims of insanity, diminished capacity, provocation, and self-defense. These strategies were seen as problematic because they strengthened the negative perception of gay men as sexually dangerous and predatory. Additionally, these strategies seemed to exploit the unconscious heteronormativity of American culture. At the same time, many critics argued that banning the gay panic defense might do more harm than good. Social science research on implicit bias showed that making homosexuality salient could eliminate the otherwise automatic effect of homosexual stereotyping. Therefore, pretending that the homosexuality of the defendant was irrelevant may have allowed unconscious homophobia to operate without constraint.

How were religion and insanity joined in the film Se7en?

How was religion incorporated into the insanity discussion in the film Se7en?

The title *Se7en* came from the seven deadly sins put forth by the early Church. The list, not directly found in the *Bible*, was assembled by Pope Gregory I in the sixth century. The victims of the serial killer in the film were chosen based on their embodiment of these seven deadly sins. Each victim represented one of the sins, which are gluttony, greed, sloth, pride, lust, envy, and wrath. The movie also alluded to religious or semi-religious works that featured the seven deadly sins, such as Dante's *The Divine Comedy* and Chaucer's *Canterbury Tales*.

Aside from the title, the movie dealt with religion with regards to the motivation of the serial killer. The killer perceived his murders as fulfilling the work of God. He felt called by a higher power, at one point claiming he did not choose this task but rather was chosen. A detective assigned to the case tried to write off this postulating as delusions of grandeur, but the killer insisted that his work was the cure for society and would be replicated by those who studied his work. He compared his murders to God's destruction of Sodom and Gomorrah in the *Old Testament*, in which two cities were destroyed and thousands were killed because of the prevalence of evil. This notion of spiritual cleansing and atonement seemed a distant relic, perhaps fitting with notions of the medieval church, long since abandoned by a modern, secularized, and perhaps more civilized society. When asked outright by a more senior detective if he saw his actions as the work of God, the killer replied that the Lord worked in mysterious ways.

The killer's claim that God called him to perform the murderous acts seemed to fit with other examples of religious psychotic manifestations. Yates' case, for example, dealt with the killing of her children because of the perceived will of God. However, the *Se7en* killer challenged the notion of insanity and religious delusions for two reasons. First, his cognitive abilities seemed extremely logical and rational with regards to the crimes. Second, he demonstrated the ability to be extremely in control of his thought processes and his outward situation. Rather than allowing his religious ideation to control his behavior in an impulsive manner, he was methodical and patient in both his planning and actions.

How was the question of insanity dealt with in **Se7en?**

One of the questions raised about the serial killer in *Se7en* was whether his perception of the world was delusional and insane or whether his perception was more insightful than the rest of society. He saw the world as an evil and filthy place, where no one was innocent and everyone has been corrupted. Interestingly, the older detective saw the world in much the same way as the killer, but his reaction to it was much different. The killer committed gruesome acts in response to this sinful world, while the detective became disillusioned and attempted to retire from detective work to avoid the harshness of society. This common thread between the two worldviews showed that perhaps the killer's awareness of reality was not out of line with sanity. It was his reaction and method that were criminal, not his perception of the situation, the argument seemed to suggest.

The naïve, young detective, perceived the murders to be the crimes of a lunatic. The older detective scolded him for dismissing the killer as insane, noting with near admiration the incredible willpower and logistical ability necessary to carry out the acts murders. In a later scene, the killer pointed out that the younger detective must find it comforting to label him as crazy. By characterizing Doe as insane, Mills protected his own view of sanity. This was a common theme surrounding the insanity defense and perceptions of insanity in general. Society desired to describe unthinkably grotesque acts as insane regardless of the cognitive state of the perpetrator because of the need to rationalize normalcy and distance deviancy. The film seemed to suggest that the killer's character appeared to present the issue in greater ambiguity because of the contrast between his rational thought processes and his disturbing actions.

How did the belief in his sanity of a defendant such as Christopher Turgeon affect his lawyer's use of the insanity defense?

Defense lawyers have often planned to argue for the insanity defense even while the defendant maintained that he was sane. In cases where religious extremism and criminal acts interact, the defendant must maintain a belief in his sanity. If he admits to insanity, then he denies the connection, for example, between himself and God. Some have contended that the lawyers should be able to argue the insanity defense against the will and belief of the defendant.

Christopher Turgeon, a leader of a religious cult called the *Gatekeepers*, murdered a former member, Dan Jess, in 1998. Turgeon claimed that God instructed him to kill Jess and that he was sane during and after the crime. Turgeon's lawyer argued the insanity defense, even though Turgeon denied the claim. The insanity defense employed by his lawyer failed, and he was convicted of first-degree murder. The question remained, however, about cases in which a lawyer argued the insanity defense against a defendant's will. Could a lawyer mount a defense in which a defendant does not believe he was insane, but the insanity defense succeeds?

When dealing with the insanity defense, how has religiosity historically affected the length of sentencing in cases such as John Allen Muhammad's?

Religion has been used as apparent motivation in numerous insanity defense cases. There has been no consistency on the type of punishment or harshness of the sentence given when dealing with cases motivated by religion. Whether or not a person's actions were motivated by religion has seemed generally irrelevant in the sentencing. Yet, many argue that it has been used to increase the severity of a defendant's sentence, as in the case of John Allen Muhammad, the D. C. area sniper. He had recently converted to Islam and his trial took place in 2003, soon after the September eleventh attacks. It was thought that jurors sentenced him much more harshly based on his religion. He was sentenced to death. There have also been cases in which jurors were believed to have sentenced a defendant less severely because of a religious background, but, in general, religion seemed to be of little help to defendants.

Chapter 4.   Religion, Mental Illness, and Terrorism

How did the USA Patriot Act define terrorism?

The *USA Patriot Act* defined terrorism as a criminal act intended to intimidate or coerce a civilian population to influence the policy of a government by intimidation or coercion or to affect the conduct of a government by assassination or kidnapping.

What is the Uniform Code of Military Justice?

The *Uniform Code of Military Justice*, enacted by Congress, applies to all members of the uniformed services of the United States worldwide and provides the foundation or bedrock for military law.

What is the Military Commissions Act of 2009?

The Congressional *Military Commissions Act of 2009* changed somewhat the *Military Commissions Act of 2006*. The *Act of 2009* authorized trial of alien, unlawful, unprivileged enemy belligerents by military commission for violations of the law of war and for other purposes. The Act set out grounds on which someone might be termed an unprivileged enemy belligerent, including as a new ground, membership in Al Qaeda whether or not the individual had engaged in or supported hostilities toward the United States.

What in the Uniform Code of Military Justice *is the military equivalent of the non-military insanity defense?*

The *Uniform Code of Military Justice* stated the following about what the military called its insanity defense. According to Section 850a, Article 50a, of 10 United States Code Chapter 47, the defense of lack of mental responsibility is an affirmative defense that, at the time of acting, the military individual charged, as a result of severe mental disease or defect, was unable to appreciate the nature and quality or the wrongfulness of the acts. Beyond that defense, mental disease or defect did not constitute a defense. Burden of proof was on the defense. The three possible verdicts were guilty, not guilty, or not guilty by reason of lack of mental responsibility. As this description makes clear, the military's insanity defense employs a M'Naghten-like rule, requiring the defendant to have labored under such a defect of reason that he did not know the nature and quality of his act or did not know that it was wrong.

But a variation of the insanity defense, termed the deific command defense, could be raised when it was argued that the act resulted from a godly command. The commentator there suggested that if someone like Hasan were to use that defense, that Allah had commanded him to kill, then the verdict would result from deliberations about whether or not jihad is insane. Other commentators raised the further issue of whether the wrongfulness required was only legal wrongfulness or whether it could be moral wrongfulness as well.

Are leaders of terrorist organizations psychopaths?

A scholar argued that terrorist cells are formed by opportunistic leaders who recruit the disenfranchised to their cause using religion as a motivator for membership. However, these groups, and their leaders, in actuality dedicate themselves to garnering money, power, and attention. These leaders are charismatic and exploitative of those around them. While they espouse a certain philosophy, she asserted that they may not necessarily believe it. Moreover, these individuals may be able to easily blend into society, holding normal jobs and living ostensibly normal lives. While the members of a terrorist organization are not characterized in this manner, the leaders' personalities and exploitative strategies seem to map quite closely with the *Diagnostic and Statistical Manual of Mental Disorders* definition of antisocial personality disorder. Criterion A2 of the *DSM-IV* states that people with the disorder disregard individual rights, feelings, and desires to gain personal profit or pleasure, specifically naming money, sex, or power as three such motivations. These individuals are able to put up a superficially charming front and win over others quite easily. However, they tend to exploit these people for their own purposes. Though it may not be the case for every terrorist leader, Her conclusions about this group painted a picture of a personality type that is very similar to what qualifies for this disorder.

What is Takfir?

Takfir is an Islamic practice in which a practicing Muslim accuses another or several others of being kafir, or nonbelievers. Though some believe it is a power only a prophet can enact, others believe any individual can do it for the benefit of the greater Muslim community. This Muslim principle has proven a challenging issue for the Saudi Arabian government in their fight against extremist religious violence. Following the Saudi government's condemnation of the terrorist attacks on September eleventh, some accused the Saudis of being takfir. Further complicating matters was the fact that Saudi Arabia was founded on the concept of Jihad, when King Abdul Aziz al-Saud originally used it to unite the various tribal groups into a single nation. Thus the Saudi government has felt forced to continue to encourage Jihad as a conceptual religious principle, while simultaneously working to discourage citizens from engaging in it. The Saudi government also began targeting high-risk populations and attempting to educate them on pacific principles of Islam to make them less vulnerable to extremist propaganda.

Do most terrorists have significant psychopathologies?

Studies have found that, for the most part, terrorists do not have mental illnesses. In fact, terrorist organizations often weed out the mentally ill, fearing an unstable fighter could pose more harm to his organization than to the external enemies. While there may be a number of explanations for who becomes a terrorist and why, it could be extremely difficult, due to their general stability, to prove insanity at a terrorist's trial.

What have been considered risk factors for terrorists?

Some risk factors are psychological, as alienation, anomie, anger, perhaps even combined with depression or suicidality. Some risk factors are political, as responses to perceived oppression or actual events. Some risk factors are religious, as acceptance of instruction or exhortation by religious figures or by study of a religious text or as redress of perceived insults or as efforts to achieve martyrdom. Some risk factors are social, as efforts to join or remain in groups. Some risk factors are economic, as benefits conferred on families of terrorists. Some risk factors are cultural, as desire to maintain or advance specific cultures.

What has been termed the narrative?

A columnist argued that the theme underlying most extremist attacks constituted what he termed the narrative. In sum, he said that the narrative contended that America, conspiring with others including Jews and many Christians, declared war on Islam in order to keep Muslims down.

What is Islamic Shariah law?

Because United States law is different from Islamic Shariah law and because of the publicity given to those terrorists who are Islamic supremacists, sometimes termed Islamist supremacists, both of which can cause confusion among the public, it is important to indicate what

Islamic Shariah law is and to note its strictures. Various definitions of it concur. By those who follow it, Islamic Shariah law is considered comparable to Anglo-American common law and European civil law. Its goal in the criminal justice system is to protect religion, life, intellect, offspring, and property through punishment aimed at deterring others as well as punishing offenders.

The majority of Muslims surveyed in Arab countries and in other Muslim societies said they preferred that Islamic law be either a source, or the sole source, of legislation. By contrast, according to a report by the International Crisis Group, support for Islamic law in Turkey had never exceeded twenty percent. The vast historical differences between Turkey and the region's other countries had to be taken into account. A political party in Turkey had evolved to become more in line with Turkey's secular tradition. By contrast, it was said, secularism in the Arab world peaked in the 1950s and '60s, then stopped with the Six Day War of 1967. Some claimed that the Arabs' defeat then by Israel contributed to rise of political Islam. Political Islam has been termed Islamism. That has prospered since then.

Shariah law has been compared in at least one sense to Puritanism because it would ban alcohol, homosexuality, and what would be considered pornographic images on the Internet and in film, and those definitions would be much more restrictive than the ones provided more recently by the United States Supreme Court.

What are various types of terrorists?

One researcher identified three types of terrorists. First were idealists who wanted to alleviate what they considered oppression or suffering. Second were respondents who reacted to situations they experienced or learned about. Third were lost souls who were anomic and unconnected.

Another researcher identified four types of terrorists. First were revolutionaries who pursued a cause. Second were wanderers who found various causes over time. Third were converts who changed and adhered to new views, attitudes, values. Fourth were compliants who went along to get along.

How influential are groups on terrorists or would-be terrorists?

Many researchers claimed that the group was the most significant influence on terrorists or would-be terrorists, as gangs strongly influenced their members. Loyalty, camaraderie, identification with people or a cause, substitute parenting or familying served as strong motivators once one entered a group. Further, social psychology research demonstrated the power of two explanations of the group process. One scholar called the first process persuasive arguments. In this, those in or new to the group become aware of more arguments for a position and depending on how persuasive the arguments are, the individual may shift toward the new position. He called the second process social, though it could be religious or cultural or other comparisons. In this, an individual compares his own values, attitudes, ideas with other persons and their values, attitudes, ideas, and then depending on the individual's perception of the other persons and those with whom he would most like to identify, he may shift toward his position toward the position they hold.

What is a non-biological view of the causes of violence?

A prison psychiatrist argued that the cause of violence is not biological, but is psychological and social and economic and cultural. He contended that all violence is an attempt to achieve justice, or what is perceived by those who are violent as justice, or to gain retribution for injustice, and to maintain justice, and to undo or prevent injustice. He contended that violent acts are an attempt to ward off shame which is an absence of self-love. Terrorist violence, by extension, is goal-directed for which the motivation is psychological, political, ideological, religious. The four motivations join to produce terrorist violence.

What do white supremacists and Islamic supremacists and other supremacists share?

Many have written about white supremacists, as with the *Aryan Nation*. Others have been unclear about what to call those who are Islamic and extremists, terming them variously as Islamofascists, Islamic extremists, Islamists, Islamist militants, and the like. But parallel to white supremacists, they may well be termed Islamic supremacists or some say Islamist supremacists. They share the belief that their group is so superior that other groups should not exist. Because of many groups' claiming that sort of supremacy, some commentators have extended the term supremacist widely, even over-widely, further calling some individuals, for example, heterosexual supremacists. Just as many words besides political can precede correctness, so can many words besides white precede supremacists.

What is self-radicalization?

Some have argued that individuals, because of their personal situations, start on their own to become more radicalized, and next may seek out radicals, especially easy now through the internet, and the process then becomes a two-way process, with the radicalizer interacting with the radicalizee who becomes more radicalized. Some may seek that connection only to implement acts pursuant to their newly more radicalized self.

Are most extremists militant Islamists?

An often-stated view is that most Muslims are not extremists, but most suicide killers are Islamist extremists. Others who want to kill but not as suicide bombers may be Christian extremists as, for example, in Michigan and some other mid-western states where nine members of a Christian militia group called Hutaree, meaning Christian warriors, were arrested through the efforts of a joint terrorism task force investigation. Considered members of a religious cult, the arrested Hutarees were charged with conspiracy to levy war by arming themselves and preparing to lure police to the funeral of one law enforcement official who the militia would kill during which all of them would then be killed by homemade bombs. Led by a man who hated authority, read the *Bible* regularly, and memorized long passages from it, the members were readying for battle preparing, as they saw it, for the Anti-Christ. Such individuals, termed militant Christianists by some commentators, had only homicide, however, not suicide, as their mission.

What have the acts and trials of Muslims who engage in killing or threatening civilians suggested to the public in general?

Trials of Muslims in the United States who have engaged in violent killing acts have focused and will continue to focus attention on Islamic theology, as will such incidents around the world as the subway bombings in Moscow which killed almost forty and were thought to be by two Muslim women from the North Caucasus. When a Chechan rebel claimed responsibility for the bombings, some commentators said that the threat in the Caucasus region was part of a broader Islamic insurgency that threatened Russia's security. In response to the bombings, the president of Russia called for brutal anti-terror measures, and a political analyst said that political Islam was on the rise.

According to many reports, a significant portion of the public found itself wary of both Islamic theology and of Muslims themselves. Part of the problem was the inability to predict who would join a terrorist cause, as many reports and articles depicting the background of individuals sought or arrested for terrorist acts showed. Part of the problem was the intense, sometimes violent reaction, to actual or perceived insults, as in the killing of the Dutch filmmaker for making a documentary critical of Islam; the fatwa directed at the author Rushdie for his book *The Satanic Verses*; the attempted killing of cartoonists for their depiction of Muhammad; and the threats potentially directed at Yale University Press for its planned, then abandoned, publication of those cartoons in a scholarly book.

Still another part of the problem was the question of divided loyalties as in the instance of Hasan, a United States military officer who corresponded with a terrorist on the web, gave presentations which emphasized that division, and allegedly shouted Allahu Akhbar, meaning God is Great, as he opened fire, killing and wounding at Fort Hood; and of a sergeant who killed two fellow soldiers with a grenade a half-dozen years before. The publicity attendant upon these incidents made them more significant to the public.

In the same way, the publicity attendant upon another religion, Roman Catholicism, concerning priests' sexual relations with children, tended to make the public suspicious of Roman Catholic priests and of Roman Catholicism, just as the publicity attendant upon Muslims' killing tended to make the public suspicious of Muslims and of Islam. In the child abuse scandal, the *New York Times* reported that both the Church and the man who subsequently became Pope covered up the scandal, most significantly and with most relevance to the Pope, as it concerned the abuse of two hundred deaf boys in Germany decades before, at a time when the present Pope was leader there. The allegations concerning cover-up brought strong denials from the Vatican and a written attack on the *New York Times* and the writers who covered the story. In connecting religion with psychology, a commentator on the controversy said that the Roman Catholic Church had erred in paying attention to psychiatrists and psychologists who claimed that homosexual child abusers could be rehabilitated. By suggesting that placing the blame on religion as opposed to placing it on psychology was wrong, the commentator concluded that the Church itself was a victim of political correctness.

What is political correctness?

The term, most often applied in an accusatory way, refers to extreme sensitivity in speech, behavior, gesture, thought, demeanor, and the like, to avoid giving offense on the basis of religion, race, culture, gender, age, sexual orientation, handicap, and other similar aspects. Some commentators have more specifically applied each of, or many of, the terms in that list as modifiers to correctness to render it more particularly applicable to a specific situation than the more general term of political correctness appears to be.

Who were termed the ten significant American jihadists either arrested or still at large?

Who were John Lindh, Daniel Boyd, Najibullah Zazi, David Headley, Colleen LaRose, and Nidal Hasan?

These were six of the ten terrorists that the *Christian Science Monitor* termed American jihadists. All these six had been arrested, some of them tried and convicted, some still awaiting that. The *Monitor* characterized Lindh, captured in November 2001 and sentenced to twenty years in prison, as a convert to Islam in 1997 who had attended a madrassa in Pakistan. It characterized Boyd, arrested in July 2009 after having received Islamic radical training in Pakistan and Afghanistan, as the leader of a group supporting violent jihad movements in a number of countries. It said that Zazi, recruited by *Al Qaeda* and arrested in September 2009, was convicted of planning to bomb New York subways, and faced a possible life sentence. It said that Headley, arrested in October 2009 who pleaded not guilty and was awaiting trial in federal court, was alleged to have scouted locations for the 2008 attacks in Mumbai and to have planned to attack the Danish newspaper that published cartoons depicting Muhammad with a bomb. It said that LaRose, referred to as Jihad Jane in her internet name, the sole woman among the ten, was arrested in October 2009, and indicted in March 2010 on four counts, including charges of conspiring with jihadist fighters and pledging to commit murder in the name of a Muslim holy war. Finally, among the ten, was Hasan, a major, military psychiatrist, and Muslim, who was scheduled to deploy to Iraq, who had increasingly spoken against United States activities in war, and who was arrested in November 2009, accused in a mass shooting at Fort Hood, Texas, which killed thirteen and wounded others. Hasan's lawyer initially stated that he was considering the insanity defense for his client. None of the counsel for the others had at the time of the listing in the *Monitor* listed suggested that.

Who were Adam Gadahn, Abdul Yasin, Anwar Al-Awlaki, and Omar Hammami?

These were four of the ten terrorists that the *Christian Science Monitor* termed American jihadists. All these four were still at large at the time the list was published. The *Monitor* said that Gadahn, directly responsive to Osama bin Laden, was the most wanted American member of *Al Qaeda* and the first United States citizen in over sixty years to be charged with treason, that he had praised Hasan for his attack at Fort Hood and had considered his acts there as a model for other Muslims. The *Monitor* said that Yasin had participated in the earlier 1993 bombing of the New York World Trade Center. The *Monitor* also noted that Gadahn and Yasin were the only two Americans on the FBI's twenty-eight person list of most-wanted terrorists. The *Monitor* said that the third of the at-large jihadists, Al-Awlaki, had been in contact both with Hasan and with the Christmas Day so-called underwear bomber who had tried to blow up a flight to Detroit that day, and was often called the bin Laden of the internet. Finally, the *Monitor* referred the reader to his *New York Times* profile in an article about next-door jihadists, to learn more about Hammami, an *Al Qaeda* recruiter, who had been raised Christian and then drawn to fundamentalist Islam.

What United States born cleric said violent jihad was becoming as American as apple pie?

Anwar Al-Awlazi, linked to Nidal Hasan and to others, including the Nigerian who tried to blow up a jetliner on Christmas Day near Detroit, said of Hasan and of the American-born convert to Islam who went by the internet name of Jihad Jane and who did not appear as someone who would be profiled as such, that violent jihad or Islamic holy war was becoming as American as apple pie.

What is the purpose of the memorization process used in Islamic schools?

Many westerners believe that the memorization technique is used to indoctrinate the students into the religion, but the methodology is used extensively in Islamic schools for the pedagogical purpose of memorizing the *Koran* in its exact form. Boyle explained that the differences in western culture and Islamic culture were responsible for these diverging attitudes. For westerners, he argued, knowledge referred to understanding a text and the ability to explain the text. In the Islamic culture, the concept of knowledge referred to the ability to recite text. Although an understanding of the *Koran* was also valued, rote memorization was the first step in the learning process. The priority given to memorization stemmed from the fact that originally not all Muslims owned a copy of the *Koran* and therefore needed to keep the text in their minds. In the beginning, the *Koran* was not written down and was only passed orally. Once print editions were available, many could not afford a copy or could not read the text. Although today the higher literacy rate and new technology solves many of the previous problems, the practiced discipline of memorizing the *Koran* was a valued process in the schools. Interestingly, memorization has been found in many western religions as well. Roman Catholicism has traditionally valued memorization for many of the same reasons and has also at times faced similar criticisms.

How has the United States government's definition of terrorism evolved over time?

In a country ever more attuned to the issue of terrorism, there have been alterations and adjustments in the United States government's definition of terrorism over the years, and especially in the wake of September eleventh. The trend in general has been a move toward a more all-encompassing definition, categorizing more and more activities as terrorist activities. Compared to the attention paid to targeting terrorists today, in 1980 for example, United States immigration law did not even have a definition for terrorism. While initially defined as a premeditated, politically motivated act against civilians with the intent of influencing an audience, the definition had been expanded to include acts against non-civilians as well. In the wake of the 1996 Oklahoma City bombing, the definition was further expanded to make it crime to give any support such as food or shelter to a terrorist organization. Finally, after the September eleventh terrorist attacks, the United States government defined terrorism even more broadly, both internationally and domestically. A terrorist organization for example could be any grouping of two or more people partaking in what the government considered terrorist acts. This law had retroactive jurisdiction, meaning that people who committed past actions that might not have been considered terrorist actions by law at the time, could be prosecuted if those actions qualified as terrorist acts under current law. Some complained that the definition of terrorism had become much too broad, enabling the government to consider a startlingly wide variety of activities and people as terrorists. At the same time, however, it was understandable that the government had created a broader definition to prevent another attack like September eleventh.

Under the updated laws, actions of groups such as *Greenpeace* and *Operation Rescue* could be deemed terrorist. And past actions might be reconsidered as in the Parlak case. He was living as a respected member of his Illinois community, but when he applied for citizenship in the United States after years of residence in the country, he found himself on trial for actions he had committed years ago while in Turkey. Though these actions were not terrorist actions at the time, updated United States laws considered them as crimes. He was ordered deported to Turkey even though he felt he might be in danger upon returning. Some found it questionable that an individual like Parlak who had been in the United States for years and contributed much to his community, should be held accountable for past actions for which he had already served time in Turkey.

What is the link among religious terrorists, poverty, and education?

A researcher demonstrated in 2003 that high education level rather than low education level, and a penchant towards terrorist ideologies were positively correlated. Furthermore, in a study of two hundred fifty failed suicide bombers, widows of suicide bombers, and recruiters for suicide bombers, none was poor, uneducated, or depressed. Rather, they all held strong religious beliefs. When comparing low education levels and poverty to religious terrorism, he found no positive correlation. This did not suggest that cases did not exist in which psychopathology and religious terrorism interrelated, but research did suggest that the majority of cases did not implicate psychopathology as the major underlying cause for terrorism. Instead, strong religious conviction and group pressures seemed to correlate most strongly with religious terrorism. Also, another researcher argued that terrorists come not from poor or uneducated classes, but rather from educated, non-secular middle classes. In contrast, secular organizations, rather than religious ones, carried out roughly half of the suicide bombings in the thirty years before September eleventh. The growth of these organizations did not stem from religious bonds as approximately three-quarters of group members became a part of the group through filial or social bonds. Researchers refocused the efforts to hinder suicide bombings through a better understanding of the group psychological mechanisms involved.

How might one distinguish between religious fundamentalism and simply a strong belief in religion?

Some have suggested that several individuals should be involved in determining whether a defendant is a religious fundamentalist. They have said, for example, that while a priest or imam, an unbiased third party person educated on world religions, psychologists, and lawyers may try to reach a consensus regarding who is a religious fundamentalist the separation between fundamentalists and more ordinary strong believers of a religion is often in question. Perhaps a series of survey-type questions could determine religious fundamentalism. A caution raised is that, while distinguishing between religious fundamentalism and a simple extremely strong belief in religion, vigilance must be observed in determining the political and economic implications of differentiating the two.

Who pioneered suicide bombing?

The Tamil Tigers of Sri Lanka, a Marxist group, invented the suicide belt and have committed the most acts of suicide terrorism out of the groups studied in 2005. From 1980 to 2000, The Tamil Tigers committed one hundred sixty eight attacks, a figure that outnumbered attacks by Hamas, Islamic Jihad, and *Al Qaeda* combined. The Tamil Tigers also were the first group to use women in suicide attacks. They have fought for the creation of a separate Tamil state in north Sri Lanka.

What was the International Sikh Youth Federation?

The *International Sikh Youth Federation* was a group founded on the idea of a new nation for Sikhs, to be called Khalistan. Because Sikh persecution was rampant in India under Hindustani rule, Sikhs believed they deserved their own nation state, so as to preserve their very distinct heritage, culture, religion, and language. The Federation was borne out of this thought, and gained support in the United Kingdom, Canada, and the United States. In later years, the Federation would financially support the families of individuals who were tortured or killed by the Indian government or who simply went missing during interrogation in their fight for Khalistan. However, the Federation's operations would come to a halt in 2001, when the United Kingdom banned it and declared it a terrorist organization. Following the UK's declaration, Canada and India both declared it a terrorist group, and in 2004, the United States included it in its Terrorist Exclusion List.

What criteria were used to determine that the International Sikh Youth Federation *was a terrorist organization?*

Three criteria were used to label a foreign terrorist organization. First, it had to be foreign. Second, it had to engage in terrorist activity, or terrorism, or retain the capability and intent to engage in terrorist activity or terrorism. And it had to threaten the security of United States nationals or the national security of the United States.

What characteristics of terrorist acts make them suitable or not for an insanity defense?

Given that the individuals who committed terrorist acts have been varied, it would not be suitable to say whether an insanity defense would be appropriate in most cases. To be suitable, they would have to demonstrate a concomitant relationship between the terrorist act and the alleged underlying mental illness. With trials for Guantánamo detainees, the question of whether the insanity defense may be viable has become all the more pressing. While some who committed terrorist acts may in fact have mental illness, many were followers of particular fundamentalist religious movements that raised the issues of brainwashing and belief. Although it may be tempting to deem a belief system that provokes or necessitates violent terrorist acts colloquially insane, legal insanity holds an extremely difficult burden of proof.

One example of the insanity defense in a trial of a terrorist was that of D.C. area sniper Lee Boyd Malvo, who used an insanity plea to no avail, and who may have been linked to *Al Fuqra*, a Muslim terrorist group by association with mentor figure John Allen Muhammad. The insanity defense for Malvo was based largely on the premise that he had been indoctrinated or brainwashed by his mentor. In the case of Guantánamo detainee Salim Ahmed Hamdan, his trial was postponed for a short period due to the argument by his lawyers that the conditions at the well-known prison had driven him to mental illness. This argument may also have played a role in his sentencing, though there were other complications in that trial as well.

Are terrorist suicide bombers insane for killing themselves for their cause?

People may be considered legally insane if they lack *mens rea*, or a guilty mind. A legally insane person must not understand the act he committed was legally or morally wrong. If terrorist suicide bombers understand they are going to commit an act that will kill many people, and that killing people is wrong, then they are not considered legally insane. Regardless of whether or not the terrorists are killing themselves, they are considered legally sane as long as they understand the nature of their actions. Suicide does not imply insanity. It may be a sign of a different mental illness, such as depression, but it is doubtful many suicide bombers have the numerous symptoms required for a diagnosis of mental illness. Many religious terrorists believe they are committing violent acts for valid reasons for their causes, but as long as they understand that killing others is wrong, and still choose to do so, they are legally sane. They and those who support them view themselves as altruists in the service of a cause.

Do females have different motivations and methods of recruitment for becoming suicide terrorists than males?

The majority of terrorism research focused on male terrorists, who were the more frequent assailants in terrorist organizations. However, a study analyzed the motivations for thirty men and thirty women to become suicide terrorists and discovered significant differences between the two sexes. Female suicide terrorists were frequently motivated by personal reasons, such as revenge or key life events that affected the women personally. As an example, one of the two female suicide bombers on two different Moscow subway trains was identified as the 17 year old widow of an Islamist rebel killed in the year before her attack which killed forty and injured many more. Conversely, men were most often motivated by religious and nationalistic reasons. This data suggested different methods should be used for men and women in attempting to prevent them from becoming suicide terrorists. Despite the significant differences in motivations, the study revealed both men and women underwent similar methods of recruitment into their respective terrorist organizations. Men and women joined these terrorist groups for a variety of reasons, including peer pressure, religious group pressures, exploitation, proactive seeking of terrorist recruitment, and other unknown reasons. The only minor difference between male and female recruitment techniques was that men more often cited religious group pressure as the method used to recruit them, while slightly more women cited exploitation or unknown reasons for joining these organizations. The study suggested focusing not on the different methods of recruitment for terrorist organizations, but on the differing motivations for men and women to join terrorist organizations when developing and implementing preventive techniques.

Was it insanity or something else that motivated Major Nidal Hasan to open fire at Fort Hood, Texas, killing thirteen and wounding twenty-nine?

Who was Nidal Hasan? Nov. 5. 2009.

As the introduction to this volume indicates, Nidal Hasan was a 39 year old Army major, a military psychiatrist, a Muslim, unmarried and a loner, who treated military personnel suffering from their tours of duty in Iraq and Afghanistan, wrote and spoke favorably about jihadi, corresponded with an influential terrorist, contacted prosecutors to inform them of acts his patients had committed, had business cards printed with SoA (SWT) on them, the one referring to Soldier of Allah and the other Subhanahu Wu Ta'ala or Glory to God, gave his first name on his official email as Abduwall meaning slave of God rather than his actual first name, and was said to have shouted Allahu Akbar meaning God is Great as he opened fire killing thirteen and wounding twenty-nine at a military installation in Texas. All these made clear that discussion of the case involved all three elements in the title of this book, insanity, religion, and terrorism. In this instance, insanity referred to the mental disorders used to advance the legal defense of insanity as well as to the insanity defense itself. Further, Hasan's defense lawyer specifically indicated at the outset that he would pursue an insanity defense.

What support was there for the view that Hasan's motivation for the shootings was psychological?

On the night of the shootings, a well-known television personality with a doctorate in clinical psychology immediately concluded that Hasan's motivation for the shootings was psychological. He argued that Hasan had endured psychological stresses in his work as a military psychiatrist which were brought on by his contact with victims of the wars and by the fact that he had been unable to resign so as not to have to endure further stress during his future deployment to a war zone. Other commentators concurred with this psychological interpretation, suggesting that fear of deployment, depression attendant upon his duties as a military psychiatrist, with a kind of posttraumatic stress syndrome brought on by those duties, together with his isolation as a loner, and concerns about his academic abilities had caused Hasan to snap. Officers of the Harvard Society of Arab Students wrote that military killings in this and other cases resulted from post-traumatic stress disorder and fear of deployment, which led to his emotional breakdown, not from his religion or his jihadist comments. Also, because Hasan was a regular customer at a strip club, drinking beer and paying for lap dances with nude women there, other commentators said these violations of Islamic religion pointed to his psychological problems and to his attempts to relieve those pressures through these behaviors. These commentators suggested that Hasan was out of touch with reality, not well, perhaps psychotic at the time of the shootings, and thereby implicitly insane at the time of the acts with which he was charged. His initial attorney argued that the shootings were contrary to Hasan's lifestyle and military career and therefore provided impetus for an insanity defense.

What support was there for the view that Hasan's motivation for the shootings was religious?

Commentators pointed to the fact that Hasan had warned military physicians two years before the shootings that the military should allow Muslim soldiers' release from service as conscientious objectors. They referred to his Power Point presentation on the Koranic world view in relation to Muslims in the United States military in which he said that it was increasingly hard for Muslims morally to justify being in the military as it was engaged in operations against fellow Muslims. Many commentators pointed to his last slide in his presentation which stated the view that Muslims love death more than the military, or perhaps than the United States loves life. And they noted his listing his first name on his official email as Abduwall meaning Slave of God rather than his actual first name, and that he was said to have shouted Allahu Akbar, which translates as God is Great, as he opened fire. And one classmate recalled Hasan telling classmates and professors that he was first a Muslim who held Islamic Shariah law above the *United States Constitution*, that he was Muslim first and American second. And, on the morning of the shootings, he gave copies of the *Koran* to a neighbor and said he going to do God's work.

What support was there for the view that Hasan's motivation for the shootings was terrorist?

Some commentators pointed out that months before the shootings Hasan had tried to contact members of *Al Qaeda*, that he had expressed strong anti-American, pro-jihadist sentiments, that he had justified homicide bombings, that he had appeared to agree with anti-American hatred, that he had worshipped at a mosque led by a radical imam, that he admired and had reached out by sending more than a dozen emails to Al-Awlaki, one of those listed by the *Christian Science Monitor* as prominent American jihadists, and that Al-Awlaki had posted a comment after the shootings that Hassan had done the right thing. Further, many commented that a presentation he gave about how the war on terror was really a war on Islam and how that view when taken together with other of his comments suggested support for terrorists in their war on America's warriors. Others argued that Hasan was self-radicalized, spending extraordinarily large amounts of time viewing violent Islamic websites. In that sense, those commentators called the process one of self-imposed brainwashing. They recognized that others did not force him to view the material, to agree with it, or to act upon it. Rather, they say, he internalized the material he actively pursued and then he acted upon it.

What support was there for the view that Hasan's motivation for the shootings was ordinary, though extreme, anger?

Along with other views concerning Hasan's motivation for killing was the perception of some that the Army's refusal to grant conscientious objector status to him so enraged Hasan that his shootings were a simple act of revenge against the broad target of the Army itself as personified by those whom he attacked. Or that his anger at the failure of the Army to take seriously what he reported as criminal acts by soldiers in Iraq and Afghanistan contributed to fueling the rage which led to the shootings.

How in weighing psychological, religious, and terrorist motivations does a jury prioritize the motivations in order to render a verdict?

That essentially is the question raised whenever there is an insanity defense, or a psychological defense which would fall short of a successful insanity verdict but nonetheless lead to a verdict of diminished responsibility. For whenever there is an insanity defense there are also the more ordinary possible motivations for the acts with which the defendant is charged. In one sense the insanity defense is less a medical and psychological matter than it is a philosophical matter, for it raises the ultimate issue of the balance between free will and responsibility, and of the balance between the competing goals of the criminal justice system in distributing just desserts for past acts and in preventing future acts. This conflict between retributive and compatibilist goals is an enduring one regardless of the place of the insanity defense within the justice system.

Why was nothing done by the military about Hasan's obvious problems?

Many commentators have pointed to the reluctance of the military to take any action other than minimal efforts concerning Hasan's anti-American, Islamist jihadist, academically-inadequate work and statements, and considered that reluctance to be a result of political correctness. The military, they contended, showed extreme unwillingness to say anything negative about Islam, Muslims, Islamicism, or Islamist terrorism, especially considering the dearth of Muslims in positions such as Hasan's. In a sense, the commentators argued that the military tried to look the other way in the name of diversity, just as the Roman Catholic Church tried to look the other way concerning pedophilic priests in the name of retaining priests and protecting the Church. The ever-developing scandal in the Roman Catholic Church undid that silence just as the shootings at Fort Hood exposed the covering up of Hasan's psychological, religious, and terrorist issues.

What did the executive director of the Muslim Public Affairs Council *say about* Hasan's legal and religious options?

While the director assumed that the insanity defense was Hasan's best legal option, he argued strongly for a religious option as well. He said that Hasan should take responsibility for the illegal acts he committed and that he should seek forgiveness not only from all those individuals affected by his shootings but also from God as well. Repentance was the term the director affixed to that religious option.

Why did the Pentagon Fort Hood report not mention Islam?

Many commentators expressed shock that the Pentagon's Fort Hood report did not once mention Islam. They generally concluded that the silence was a direct result of what they thought of as brainwashing brought on by political correctness and by a misplaced emphasis on diversity at the expense of expertise, loyalty to the military and to the United States, and the necessity to protect everyone from personal, religious, or terrorist motivations that could result, as with Hasan, in harm or death.

To what extent was the Pentagon report on the Fort Hood shootings a product of political correctness?

Many commentators noted that the eighty-six page Pentagon report on the Fort Hood shootings detailed slip-ups by American military personnel but never once mentioned either Major Hasan by name or his Islamic faith. A former Navy Secretary said that fear of giving offense was a problem that had increased. He concluded that the Pentagon report's silence on Islamic extremism showed a deeply entrenched political correctness. Those who wrote the report said they did not want to explore the shooter's motives. Many noted that without a motive there would have been no killings. They also noted that Hasan was as open about his radical Islamic faith and its jihadist tendencies as he was about anything else. They referred to Hasan's proselytizing, speaking out against the wars the United States was engaged in, and shouting Allahu Akbar, meaning God is great, as he opened fire. Some in the military stated that political correctness had brainwashed the military and many others, and noted that Senator Lieberman said that the report did not recognize the specific threat that violent Islamic extremism posed to the United States military. Commentators noted that the Pentagon inquiry simply spoke in general about fundamentalist religious beliefs as if all were equivalent. Some concluded that political correctness caused jihadist extremism to be deliberately ignored.

How might interest in the insanity defense be refocused when reputed terrorists are put on trial in civilian courts, or when Hasan is tried in a military court?

While it is not yet clear how the trials of Guantánamo detainees will progress or how transparent they will be, if the insanity defense is raised in any of those trials, the potential consequences would be significant. Questions might include whether defense lawyers would argue that the jihadists were by definition insane due to their fundamentalist religious beliefs, and if so, what impact this argument would have on the American-Muslim community. Further questions would include where and how lines could be drawn in terms of what was deemed sane or insane conduct with respect to religious beliefs. If the detainees were acting in accordance with those deeply held religious beliefs, the situation would be especially difficult where compliance with those beliefs required certain conduct. Further, questions would include the extent to which America would be prepared for this question to be legally answered. The insanity defense would raise the issue of the balance among adherence to extreme fundamentalist belief, freedom of religion, and compliance with American rule of law. The complicated process of answering these questions might be enlightening to both psychology and law. Certainly the insanity defense would take on new cultural and legal significance as these questions were addressed.

Under what laws could Hasan be tried?

As a military officer, Hasan was subject to the *Uniform Code of Military Justice* for his shootings at Fort Hood and to the *United States Constitution* for his possible treasonous behavior before and during those actions. As the killings and woundings took place in Texas, Hasan was subject to that state's criminal laws. Because the laws concerning criminal offenses and the insanity defense were similar in the *UCMJ* and in the Texas statutes, there seemed to be no great difference between those two possible choices in terms of charges and use of the insanity defense. Some commentators suggested that because of the great difference between the Texas and the Federal implementation of the death penalty, that factor might important in deciding where to try Hasan for the killings and woundings.

How have Muslim extremists been viewed differently from Christian extremists?

Some have argued that it is common in the western world to perceive many Muslims as religious extremists and a much smaller portion of Christians as religious extremists. This may be due to the lack of exposure to Islam and high levels of exposure to Christianity. But it is more likely due to the world-wide terrorist incidents and continuing media reports on deadly acts and attempts by Islamist extremists viewed as terrorists. The differing views of Muslim extremists and Christian extremists also affected how their mental states were perceived. A Christian extremist who committed a murder in the name of his religion may have been more likely to be viewed as an exception as compared to a Muslim extremist who committed a murder in the name of his religion and may have been viewed as simply following the teachings of his religion.

Should a distinction be made between different religiously fundamentalist beliefs, as those of Yates and Hasan, when considering the possible use of the insanity defense?

The religious beliefs held by Yates, which led her to kill her five children, were without a doubt extreme and that case, along with the Hasan and other cases, brought up the question of when an extreme set of religious beliefs was considered an element of insanity and when the set was not to be considered so. In the case of Yates, she believed that she was acting benevolently in killing her children as this would save her children from going to Hell. In her mind, she was doing the right thing, even if afterwards she realized her error. In her second trial, this logic helped her attain the verdict of not guilty by reason of insanity. However, religious fundamentalists were not always considered fit contenders for the insanity defense. For example, if a terrorist believed he was doing the right thing in killing a group of Americans, as he likely would in most situations, the insanity defense might not be presented as a valid alternative. The Fort Hood killer Hasan's case would help address this issue.

In general, many argued that the main reason the insanity defense would not come into play in the cases of terrorists was due to the amount of stigma and hatred attached to terrorism. If a terrorist were found not guilty by reason of insanity, they contended that resulting public outrage would be inevitable, even if the terrorist truly could not understand the wrongfulness of his actions. The insanity defense would gain an even worse reputation than it already carried. A religious fundamentalist who committed an act according to their interpretation of God's will, including for the purpose of creating terror, may or may not be evaluated in the same way as Yates was. And, as more religious fundamentalists survive carrying out what they considered to be God's will, the insanity defense issue will come increasingly to the forefront. While it might be difficult to find significant distinctions between the nature of the beliefs held by someone like Yates and the beliefs of a terrorist, for the sake of the insanity defense, perhaps a distinction will increasingly be made between them.

How successful was Naveed Haq's insanity defense plea claiming jihad made him do it?

Haq, a self-proclaimed jihadist, bragged about wounding five women and killing one in the Seattle Jewish Federation office, said he was a soldier of Islam, wanted to be a martyr, and to die on the battlefield, yet did not die, was charged, tried, and found guilty of aggravated first degree murder and seven other counts. He had claimed, unsuccessfully, that jihad made him do it and that he was therefore not criminally responsible because of his insanity. His defense argued that a mental disease or defect prevented him from knowing right from wrong. But he was convicted because the jury found that his religious motivation for the attack was not a product of mental illness but rather of his terrorist ideology.

Should Farouk Abdul Abdulmutallab, a non United States citizen who attempted to blow up an airplane in flight on its way to Detroit, have been charged in a regular criminal court as a civilian criminal or before a military commission as an enemy combatant?

The twenty-three year old son of the former economics minister of Nigeria, who had led a wealthy life of privilege, attempted unsuccessfully to ignite explosives in his underwear on a flight to Detroit on Christmas Day. Apparently quiet and unassuming, he had become radicalized to extreme religious views, had received training from *Al Qaeda* perhaps in Yemen, and had evaded detection on boarding the airliner. When the explosives failed to ignite he was subdued by passengers. On landing, he was arrested and handled as an ordinary criminal. He was read his Miranda rights to remain silent and held in a regular prison setting. Arguments ensued about whether he should have been interrogated, not as a regular civilian, but as an enemy combatant in order to learn of further bomb plots, of the location and elements of his terrorist training, of the names of others he had contact with. Those who determined that he would be held as an ordinary civilian accused of criminal acts said he could be offered a plea bargain in exchange for further information. Those who argued for treating him as an enemy combatant said that time was of the essence and that a military commission was the proper way to proceed.

One commentator on the case argued for clear definitions of what qualifies for military justice and of what qualifies for civilian justice. Suggestions were that acts where there were no political or religious ties, no connection to terrorist movements, no religious fanaticism, or where there were no attempts or successes at mass killings because of those terrorist or religious motivations should be handled by the civilian justice system. Acts where there were some or most or all of those factors should be handled by the military justice system.

Beyond Abdulmutallab's effort at concealing explosives in his underwear, and as a result of his arrest, intelligence reports surfaced that plastic surgeons had inserted explosives in breast implants of some female homicide bombers and in buttocks implants of some male homicide bombers. These explosives, almost impossible to detect, raised anew questions concerning the terrorists' motivations, the responses of the justice systems to any who survive their attempts as did Abdulmutallab, and the consequences for society of issues over the mix of religion, terrorism, mental illness, and possible insanity..

Were secular, non-religious acts like students' killing large numbers in a school or a pilot crashing his plane into an Internal Revenue Service building terrorist acts or ordinary, if unusual, criminal acts?

Were students who killed others at their schools as at Columbine and Thurston High, or college professors in their home as near Dartmouth, terrorists or more common criminals like the two men who killed a family in Kansas?

When two youths killed many at Columbine High School, or two youths killed a Dartmouth professor couple they did not know, or the two men featured in Capote's *In Cold Blood* killed a family of four, one killer was generally considered more psychopathic, the other more of a follower, as is often the case when two are involved in serious criminal activity. All of these killers were psychologically analyzed. Some considered the younger ones motivated because they were victims of bullying. Others considered at least one of the killers more non-psychopathically mentally disordered than the other. But the word terrorist did not readily attach to them. Had they been Islamist or white supremacists, or otherwise religiously or politically motivated, it seemed clear that the word terrorist would have been applied.

How should Joseph Slack, who crashed his plane into an Internal Revenue Service building, have been characterized?

In February 2010, a Texas engineer crashed his small plane into an Internal Revenue Service office building injuring at least thirteen of the almost two hundred people working in the building. His motivation may have been marginally religious. He had posted a long, angry, message on the web primarily attacking the IRS, government bailouts, what he termed the plundering by corporate America, politicians. He did include the Catholic Church in his list though his rambling list appeared primarily focused on personal and larger financial matters.

Was Joseph Slack's crashing his plane into an Internal Revenue Service building a terrorist act or simply a criminal act?

Whether to define acts as terrorist or simply as criminal raises many questions and features spokespersons for each definition arguing strongly for their position. In this instance, the White House as well as law enforcement officials including the Department of Homeland Security concluded that the man's crashing his plane into the IRS building was not a terrorist act. As the local police chief saw the act, for example, it was isolated, criminal, and carried out by one individual and not part of any conspiracy or associated with others. As a director of the *Council on Islamic-American Relations* saw the act, however, it was no different from foreigners who commit political violence and are labeled terrorists. He argued that characterizing this as simply criminal led again to the conclusion that only violent acts carried out by a Muslim can be labeled terrorist. Because the perpetrator died in the crash, there was no opportunity to explore an insanity defense in the case. Examining his web comments in a manifesto, his long-simmering rage, his mixed personal and political ramblings, and his personal history all suggest that an insanity defense would undoubtedly have been sought in the case should he have lived.

How can religion affect the sentencing of those who commit terrorist acts?

How did religion affect Terry Nichols' sentencing?

During the sentencing of Terry Nichols, who conspired with Timothy McVeigh in the Oklahoma City bombing, the jury was deadlocked on imposing the death penalty, and instead arrived at life in prison without possibility of parole. A potential reason for their indecision towards the death penalty was the introduction of witnesses who demonstrated and emphasized Nichols' newfound faith and belief in God. His sister and two ex-wives served as witnesses to his faith, and his defense attorney used Nichols' faith as a key element of his closing argument. One juror in particular noted that because Nichols found religion, he could do some good in prison.

Were jurors more likely to be sympathetic, as in the cases of Terry Nichols and Ali Al-Timimi, to extremely religious defendants?

Studies showed that jurors typically were much more merciful when cases involved people who adhered to society's norms. Therefore, adherence to particular religions seemed to be important insofar as those religions were accepted by society. For example, in the 2004 trial of Oklahoma City bomb conspirator Terry Nichols, evidence of religiosity was introduced in trial to buttress Nichols' claim that he had completely changed since his crime. Citing his newfound adherence to Christianity, jurors spared his life and elected not to give Nichols the death penalty. Yet at the same time religiosity has been introduced to prosecute, as well as defend. In the 2005 Ali Al-Timimi terrorist case, evidence of his Islamic faith was introduced to prove guilt and motive. Al-Timimi was found guilty, and his jurors cited his adherence to Islam as an aggravating factor. In the final analysis, society's acceptance of the particular religiosity probably dictated its effect on jurors' decision-making.

How did Fox's 24 characterize a terrorist family in one of its seasons?

How did the creators of Fox's fictional continuing multiseason drama 24 structure the terrorist organization in one of its seasons?

The Muslim terrorists featured in Season 4 of Fox's influential television drama *24* worked under the auspices of a character named Habib Marwan. At one point, Marwan said that the terrorists were attempting to punish Americans for their imperialism, suggesting that the root of their ideological creed was power-based, rather than religious. A scholar described the general structure of terrorist cells in her book examining the reasons that religious militants killed. She explained that groups of people with a deep-seated belief may think that violence is the only way to implement their ideology, which is generally considered to be just and righteous by members of the group. Whereas this sense of justice was derived from a religious code in most cases that book described, the group in *24*, while espousing a Muslim belief system, seemed more overtly motivated by power. Marwan fit the description laid out in the book. He was a charismatic leader with the ability to blend into his surroundings, who capitalized upon an ideological mission to gather followers. Beneath Marwan, there were a number of smaller sub-groups. Some of these were centered around the family, but family ties were subordinate to those of the larger group. This was evidenced in the case of the involved Araz family. The parents and their son were part of the planning and execution of a lethal terrorist attack during Day 4. However, at one point in the season, the father attempted to have his son killed because he did not believe the son would advance the organizational cause with enough fervor. Whereas the father placed his primary loyalty with the terrorist organization, the mother realigned her loyalty, trying at all costs to protect her son. She told the protagonist of the series, Jack Bauer, that while she believed in the organization's cause, she would favor the life of her son over the group's ideology. The show's creators seemed to be drawing a distinction between right and love on the one hand and evil and power on the other hand in these two sets of characters.

What was the importance of family for religious terrorists in Fox's *24*?

Fox's popular television show *24* focused on the struggles of Jack Bauer, a special agent for the Counter Terrorism Unit, as he attempted to divert several national crises. In season 4, the national crisis was the attempted meltdown of nuclear power plants across the country by a religiously motivated terrorist group, which would result in the deaths of hundreds of thousands of innocent people. The featured Araz family comprised one sector of a religiously motivated Muslim terrorist group, consisting of the father, the mother, and their son. The family had been helping to plot this attack for years. However, the son almost spoiled the plan when his girlfriend became suspicious of his mysterious activities. His parents ordered him to kill his girlfriend, but he instead attempted to help her escape from his family. His mother therefore killed his girlfriend because she knew her son was not strong enough to do so. This suggested that although one's family was important, the fundamental mission to complete the terrorist attack was more important.

This idea was further exemplified by the father's trying to kill his son because he jeopardized the act of terrorism and was not strong enough to execute his girlfriend. The father clearly believed his mission and devotion to his religious cause was more important than his family. However, the mother was willing to abandon the mission to save her son's life. She was arrested and confessed she did not agree with Americans' values and she wanted the terrorist act to continue, but that she was willing to give up the mission to save her son. Ultimately, she was killed while trying to help the Americans and save her son. Her son proved more important to her than her religion and terrorist actions, but the father placed his religious and terrorist beliefs above his family. This analysis of *24* suggested male terrorists were more likely to place their religious beliefs and fundamental causes before their families than were female terrorists.

Did Fox's 24 suggest torture of suspected terrorists should be permitted?

One of the most popular shows on television has been Fox's *24*. The celebrated protagonist, Jack Bauer, was known fondly as America's hero, saving the country from one national disaster after another. In a post-September eleventh world, terrorism was at the forefront of many news stories, but *24* exposed the American public to a much more entertaining and riveting side of counterterrorism by following Jack Bauer for a full twenty-four hours each season as he handled different crises. One of the most common scenes presented in the show was Bauer torturing a suspected terrorist, or being tortured himself. Throughout the show's seasons, Bauer tortured countless individuals, including religious and political terrorists, White House aides, coworkers, the wife of a suspected terrorist, his own love interest, and his brother. Bauer used a wide variety of torture methods, including gunshots, knives, chemicals, electrocution, threats to other family members, and sensory deprivation. The most interesting fact was that Bauer's torture of other individuals did not always provide useful information, though in most cases, he was successful at procuring information from a suspect. However, there were several instances in which the torture merely proved the suspected individual knew nothing about the terrorist acts Bauer was investigating. There were a few incidents in which, even after extensive torture, Bauer was unable to learn anything new from his suspects.

Despite the potentially negative consequences of torturing innocent people, as well as torturing terrorists who simply failed to offer any valuable information, *24* still portrayed torture in a necessary and positive light. Coworkers of Bauer's were often tortured after being suspected of working for enemy agencies, but these individuals, even after shown to be innocent, merely returned to work to help save the country. There was often anger and occasionally a request for a salary increase, but the tortured individuals seemed to understand it was for the good of the country. This seemed to be the message the show was portraying. In the instances in which actual terrorists were tortured, it often provided fruitful information for Bauer and his team, which allowed them to successfully divert a national disaster. This outcome also suggested *24*'s message was in favor of torturing terrorists because it would potentially save American lives. Even Senator McCain, despite undergoing extensive torture when held as a prisoner of war, watched and had appeared in the program. Despite many Americans being against torture, the popularity of *24* and its pro-torture message may have suggested that many people believed torture should be used against terrorists to help prevent possible attacks on America.

Chapter 5. Brainwashing, Deprogramming, Reeducating, and Deradicalizing

What is brainwashing?

The term brainwashing was first used in English in the 1950s, although practices that are now considered brainwashing have been used for hundreds of years. Brainwashing involved the imposition of certain beliefs and attitudes in an individual, even if these beliefs contradicted the person's current beliefs. Some common techniques to brainwash an individual included dehumanization, sleep deprivation, partial sensory deprivation, psychological harassment, inculcation of guilt, and group social pressure. The best known instances of brainwashing have been cases involving prisoners of war and religious cults.

What is the difference between negative and positive persuasion?

The term negative persuasion was considered synonymous with brainwashing, since cases of brainwashing almost exclusively dealt with negative acts. However, it seemed likely that forms of positive persuasion, which might also be considered brainwashing, have occurred in more subtle fashions. The question is how one distinguishes between the two, and to what end.

Cases of negative persuasion have often been termed brainwashing. A well-publicized instance involved Patty Hearst, who was said to have been coerced by the Symbionese Liberation Army to commit felonious acts. Kidnapped, deprived of food, blindfolded, and confined to a closet for nearly two months, Hearst eventually seemed to accept the ideology and actions of the Symbionese Liberation Army, and work with them in several of their larger crimes, such as the robbery of the bank in San Francisco.

Cases of positive persuasion have not garnered the type of media attention afforded to the Hearst case. Although they might seem rarer, one could think of actions that a person would not typically carry out, but might under the influence of positive persuasion. The difference inherent in these two types of persuasion seems to be the methods of indoctrination. A woman, for example, would not be held in a closet for two months in order to get her to accept an ideology of donating to charitable organizations. In that sense, severe indoctrination towards a positive end seems improbable.

Is it only considered brainwashing because it takes place over a relatively short period of time and is meditated by specific individuals?

During Hearst's trial, psychiatric expert a psychiatrist argued in her defense that the tactics used by the Symbionese Liberation Army were enough to cause her to undergo a drastic personality change. The SLA's tactics included limiting Hearst's communication, constantly hammering her with their ideology, convincing her that the group had a higher purpose, and making her experience shame and guilt. Some scholars argued that these can have a large effect on personality, even to the extent of firing a weapon at innocent civilians as Hearst did. But the question might arise as to what the differences are between the brainwashing that occurred in Hearst's case, within the relatively short period of fifty-seven days, and the forces that mold personality more generally, over the course of entire lifetimes. For example, a teenage gang member might, by virtue of his situation, have his communication limited only to the criminals he grows up with and then works with. Whether based in brotherhood, fame, power, or money, the group's ideology and higher purpose might be applied more steadily over a long period of time, but they are still applied and have an effect on the gang member. Supporting any group other than the gang could be rewarded with shame and guilt as well as physical abuse. In short, the teenage gang member is placed in a similar personality-shaping environment to the brainwashing victim, and yet the brainwashing victim is more likely to have our sympathy, because the tactics used were more overtly mediated by other individuals and were employed over a shorter period of time.

What makes brainwashing different from other forms of social influence?

In psychology, the study of brainwashing has fallen into the category of social influence. Social influence is the collection of various ways in which people can alter other people's attitudes, beliefs, and behaviors. If brainwashing falls in the same category as advertisement or religious education, then why is brainwashing given so much attention and consideration as a criminal defense? Some psychiatrists have stated that what distinguishes brainwashing from other forms of persuasion is its severity as a form of social influence. With brainwashing, the change in the victim's way of thinking comes without the person's consent and often against his will. Also exclusive to brainwashing is the victim's complete isolation and lack of control over sleep patterns, eating, bathroom use, and fulfillment of other basic human needs. In the process, the victim's identity is systematically broken down, at which point the agent, or brainwasher, replaces it with another set of attitudes, beliefs and behaviors that fall in line with those of the agent. It is this level of invasive influence that distinguishes brainwashing from even the most coercive forms of social influence and propagandistic methods.

Do certain factors make an individual particularly susceptible to being brainwashed?

The process of brainwashing is one in which an individual's self-identification is systematically torn down and rebuilt; in the process. In the process, the object of reliance is shifted from the self or previously established social supports to the brainwasher. As such, people with certain personalities might be at an increased vulnerability to brainwashing techniques. Those who demonstrate high levels of self-doubt and weak senses of self or who might think in absolute moral terms could be at such risk. In the military, soldiers have been taught mental detachment techniques as part of prisoner of war survival training. Detachment requires people to psychologically disengage from their physical surroundings through meditative techniques. Some prisoner of war accounts have said that previously strong religious belief helped them detach from the brainwashing process. Soldiers have also been taught the stages of the brainwashing process, since knowing the different parts can weaken the impact of the techniques.

What is the relationship between hypnosis and brainwashing?

Hypnosis is controversial as a psychological means for extracting truth. Its reliability has been discredited by the ease with which patients can fake hypnosis as well as in cases where psychologists have asked misleading questions during hypnosis that led to serious and faulty accusations. Brainwashing happens in a controlled environment where a subject is susceptible to suggestion or manipulation through pressure that can be sensory, physiological, or the feeling of authority, or through peer pressure which also results in severely disrupted individual autonomy and independent thought. These open the way to compliance with the new connections formed, not to those of the past. Malleable thought, or the inability to think independently, appears related to the dissociated state that occurs when under hypnosis. A deceptive false belief is important in causing brainwashed people to join or remain in an extreme group, replicating the suggestibility that occurs under hypnosis. Some have strongly rejected the view that coercive persuasion can result from hypnosis, but still agree that defective thought can strongly influence changes in behavior or beliefs in fully conscious individuals.

What issues of identity might arise when considering brainwashing and the perpetration of a crime?

Brainwashing has been used on several occasions as a defense in criminal proceedings. Lawyers argued that the individual charged with an act was rendered unable to distinguish right from wrong because of the new belief system he now followed, a belief system he adopted most likely under severe duress. In this state, the individual may indeed have adopted a skewed moral system, one that the original individual would not have. Indeed, it was argued that it was not the original individual who committed the act. But the question of whether that person changed fundamentally as a result of the brainwashing was at issue. On a less extreme level a major book featured patients who concluded that their true personality only emerged after they started taking anti-depressants. Their true self was not withdrawn or anxious, but rather sociable and friendly. This raised the question of the extent to which personality is a construct of biologically determined factors and whether when these factors change, the individual changes. If so, as is the case during brainwashing, the issue becomes whether the criminal justice system can ignore the idea that the brainwashed individual, rather than the original person, is the one on trial.

Such an individual might indeed be considered legally insane because of the psychological trauma he has undergone, but in many cases, it did not seem that this issue of identity was even called into question. Further, the question arises of whether courts should be able to hold this new individual responsible without directly considering what the old individual may have thought or believed. Hearst might never have done the things she did before her psyche was manipulated by the Symbionese Liberation Army, but after the brainwashing had occurred, it might not be reasonable to ignore the fact that the person who committed crimes was not in fact the Hearst who had been kidnapped. It might be prudent to force any individual who uses a brainwashing defense to undergo mandatory deprogramming and then serve some sort of prison sentence. Whether the length of the sentence might be shortened due to obvious extenuating factors is an issue. But the new individual might remain culpable unless deemed legally insane, which should be a separate consideration.

What experiments should be evaluated in deciding whether or not to include brainwashing as a mental disorder?

The synonyms for brainwashing are persuading, conditioning, convincing, programming, indoctrinating, molding, and talking into. Working under this interpretation of brainwashing, everybody is brainwashed to some degree. However, there ought to be a distinction between brainwashing in the everyday sense, such as viewing commercials and being tempted to buy a product, and brainwashing that drastically alters a value system, thoughts, behavior, which then prompts individuals to join cults and commit crimes, as in the Hearst case.

The American Psychiatric Association has not listed brainwashing as a mental disorder. In evaluating the claims for brainwashing, it is important to look at psychological studies that essentially examined brainwashed individuals. For example, Milgram's famous though now ethically questionable psychological study found that despite a participant's false belief that he was delivering a real electric shock to a learner, sixty-five percent of the participants obeyed the principal experimenter to deliver the maximum four hundred fifty volt shock even when the learner was vocalizing pain. In another famous now also ethically questionable study, the prison experiment, Zimbardo randomly divided Stanford subjects and put them in a simulated jail. Some were guards and others were prisoners. The study ended after six days, because the results showed that the guards began to devise humiliating and sadistic rituals for the prisoners, and the prisoners in turn complied with the rules and became severely depressed. It is interesting to note that in this latter study, the students knew they were part of a psychological study, and it was only an experiment, yet they were effectively brainwashed. Before abandoning the very real effects of brainwashing, all bodies of literature that might give better insight into brainwashing need further investigation.

9. *How do the notions of brainwashing differ between American and European cultures?*

Some commentators advanced the claim that European culture seems more embracing of religious brainwashing discourse than does the United States culture. This is interesting considering that the majority of brainwashing research and definition comes from the United States. Part of the argument has been that the United States has rejected brainwashing rhetoric because of the religious implications accompanying it. Brainwashing by religious cult indoctrination seems to imply that all religious institutions are capable of mind control to a certain degree, and this notion of coercion is at odds with religion based structures common in the United States. Europe, appearing more secular in nature, seems much more receptive to the notion that religious groups possess the ability to control the beliefs and actions of their congregations. The characterization of European nations as more paternalistic, as opposed to the more libertarian American government, is another possible aspect of European acceptance of claims of brainwashing. If European society is in fact more paternalistic than the American, then more responsibility would be placed on society's pressures than on the actions and free will of the individual. This belief system has allowed European governments to implement more policies to protect the individual from himself or from social coercion, whereas in the United States the emphasis is on less government intervention and more religious and personal freedom, for the most part.

There is also the American sentiment that the power of individual free will is stronger than group influence. This sentiment appears not to be held with equal weight by European culture. One commentator argued, however, that these claims were exaggerations and stereotypes that did not truly reflect attitudes of either culture. He noted that the United States had allowed disruption of cults' rights to autonomy and freedom. During the seventies, parents often were able to obtain court orders to remove their children from cult-like religious sects and enroll them in courses of deprogramming. The evidence suggested that more recent cases of religious related incidents might lead to less tolerance of cult-like activity. One scholar cited *Molko v. Unification Church* as an important United States case where the courts found that under certain conditions brainwashing claims are not in opposition to *First Amendment* claims of freedom of religion.

Another possible reason for perceived differences in attitudes between the United States and Europe is the overall levels of crime in the two cultures. Some scholars have argued that the United States, with its higher levels of homicide and violent crimes, is less shocked by religious based acts of extremism than Europe because violence in various circumstances is more common and normal. This analysis seemed to make some sense except that Europe has tended to have a higher level of suicide than the United States. Religious cults, such as *Heaven's Gate*, often manifested their extreme behavior in suicidal rather than homicidal actions. Surely Europe is not more shocked by cases of suicide than the United States is, considering the rate of suicide in Europe is greater.

What is the relationship between popular depiction of political brainwashing and reality?

Many of the films involving brainwashing have centered on the political ramifications of its use. *The Manchurian Candidate* in 1962 and its remake in 2004 both explored how brainwashing may be used in political situations to manipulate soldiers and gain control of power. While *Time* in 1957 published an article discussing the applications of Pavlov's training with dogs to human brainwashing, as recently as 2008, *Wired* published an article about the current research on the potential uses of brainwashing for the military in terms of mind control and mind enhancement. In particular, that article examined how the military could make use of mind control to excite and energize those enlisted.

The article also raised ethical questions involved in mind control, including the oppositional relationship between mind control and free will. If the military used brainwashing on its soldiers, how then could any soldier be held responsible for his actions, though under the Geneva Convention, it would seem that such soldiers would be responsible. It appeared that brainwashing should be explored as a legitimate impediment to individual responsibility. It has seems that as more is discovered about the way that the human mind works, and as advances are made in what can be done to control or enhance the human mind, brainwashing may be more likely to emerge as a realization of the fictional concerns.

Were there certain characteristics that made a person more likely to be susceptible to recruitment by a cult?

A variety of individual characteristics contributed to a higher likelihood of recruitment by a cult. Emotional vulnerability, weak or non-existent family relations and support systems, and difficulty attaining the basics needed for human survival all led to a greater susceptibility to recruitment by cults. Furthermore, psychological history was an important factor as well, as a childhood of abuse or neglect, exposure to abnormal family patterns, and a tendency to use and abuse controlled substances had all been found to be associated with an increased likelihood of joining a cult. High levels of stress in the individual at the time of recruitment could have also contributed to a successful recruitment. Studies found that cult recruitment methods such as coercion, intimidation, and brainwashing were especially effective against people with a combination of those characteristics. Not everyone who fell into one of these descriptions joined a cult of course, but these descriptions nevertheless did provide an indication of what types of people might have been most likely to fall prey to a cult.

How did the term brainwashing come about?

During the Korean War many of the American prisoners of war seemed to adopt the belief system of their captors. The press at the time believed that these Americans lost the ability to think for themselves and abandoned their free will. These techniques of mind control were termed brainwashing by a journalist. He collected a large amount of Chinese Communist propaganda and he used this along with the American prisoners as his basis for the term. He believed that brainwashing was not a version of intrinsic mental coercion like religious or political conversions, but rather an extrinsic mental conversion where a person is in a sense turned into a type of robot. He envisioned brainwashed people to have forced thoughts and beliefs in a captive body and to basically be a slave to their controllers. His model of brainwashing was quickly accepted by society and in the mid 1970s by other journalists.

How has brainwashing historically been viewed by courts?

The American legal system has had very little sympathy with those claiming to have been brainwashed. Brainwashing first garnered attention during the Korean War. After being subjected to many psychologically destabilizing tactics such as starvation and isolation, soldiers captured by the Chinese or North Koreans publicly made Communistic, anti-American, and often treasonous statements while in detention. Some went so far as to refuse being repatriated to the United States when the war was over. When the rest did return to America, many were charged in military tribunals and used indoctrination as an affirmative defense, but the courts disagreed and convicted them.

The federal civilian courts have also taken a low view of the indoctrination defense. No federal court accepted an expert witness' testimony on indoctrination. Federal courts rejected experts' testimony, saying that it did not have a significant enough following or acceptance to be permitted.

State courts have also not accepted indoctrination as a defense. A case which garnered significant attention was that of John Allen Muhammad and Lee Boyd Malvo, who were known for their shooting spree in the District of Columbia Metro area. Malvo, 17, and Muhammad, 42, terrorized the area by sniping people seemingly at random. When caught, Malvo pleaded an affirmative defense of indoctrination, stating he was taken in by the older man and was effectively brainwashed. While Malvo was convicted, he was not sentenced to death, as Muhammad was.

Can brainwashers be brought to trial?

The question of the extent to which the state can involve itself in regulating religious movements that utilize brainwashing is tricky. Religions are protected by the *First Amendment*, and their validity and authenticity cannot be questioned by the state. However, there is a growing field that contends the *First Amendment's* protection does not extend to religions which utilize brainwashing. The proponents of state action argue that the *First Amendment* presupposes that people freely and voluntarily join religious movements. However, groups that brainwash individuals generally do so in a very crafty manner that disguises their true intentions. Cult members do not give their informed consent when joining the movements because the cults have hidden their true agenda from their followers. A religious group that uses psychological tactics to win over members' allegiances is not inherently culpable. If that were the case, many youth groups would be shut down and their leaders imprisoned. However, there have been successful civil cases against group leaders for fraud and intentional infliction of emotional duress.

How has the legitimacy of expert testimony about a brainwashing claim been monitored in the courtroom?

Originally, testimony by experts in brainwashing cases had to adhere to the *Frye* standard. That standard held that testimony to be admissible had to be generally acceptable to the scientific community. The purpose was to guarantee that an average juror would not be misled by testimony just because a supposed expert in the psychological community said it. Because brainwashing is a complicated subject and there was concern that many apparently credible social scientists with eccentric theories could be convincing, the *Frye* rule ensured more protection from pseudo expertise. That standard remains in some states. In 1993 that standard was supplanted in federal courts and in the majority of state courts by the *Daubert* standard. This standard more specifically termed the judge the gatekeeper of evidence, required that expert testimony be both relevant and based on scientific methodology from the scientific method, and set forth factors for determining what was indeed the scientific method.

Is there a credible scientific procedure to accurately determine whether someone has been brainwashed?

Though brainwashing has been used as a defense primarily in civil cases involving religions, it has proven unsuccessful in many other cases, most famously *United States v. Hearst*. Ultimately this defense failed in that criminal case because, although new values may have been imposed on that individual, the ability to determine right from wrong was not lost. Legally, the individual still committed the act knowing that it was against the law, even if the desire to commit the act came from another source. The scientific community's opinion on brainwashing has been ambivalent for years. In the 1980s, the scientific community realized it needed to take a position on brainwashing because trials were calling in mental health professionals to speak as expert witnesses in cases involving brainwashing. The American Psychological Association formed a committee to investigate the psychological effects of brainwashing. Initially the committee reported that the theory of brainwashing was not acknowledged by the scientific community, but then withdrew its ruling to report that there was not sufficient evidence to take a position on the issue. Even more recently, the scientific community as a whole has not come to accept the theory of brainwashing. The inability of the scientific community to accept brainwashing has created a burden for any defense attorney attempting to remove culpability from his client as a result of brainwashing. The Hearst trial proved that American jurors need an expert opinion on the matter before they can forgive a defendant's actions. The theory of brainwashing seems not to work until supporting scientific proof is presented.

What is the history of using brainwashing as a defense in cases of crimes against humanity, acts of genocide?

The Nuremberg trials, which resulted in the executions of various high-ranking Nazi officials after World War II, featured various attempts by defendants to claim lack of responsibility for their actions because of a form of brainwashing established by the Nazi regime. Several officers claimed that, while they had carried out executions, raids, and mass killings, they had done so without ever questioning the authority of their superiors due to a deeply-ingrained sense that what they were doing was correct. They argued that they were not supposed to think for themselves and that their military and ideological training led them to accept as fact that Jews were to blame for everything wrong. This claim that the officers could not have disobeyed orders because of the effective brainwashing did not impact the outcome of the trials as major officials were tried and convicted of crimes against humanity.

Are there anti-brainwashing laws in the United States?

Many people have argued that state statutes have not provided adequate remedy for victims of brainwashing. Proponents of anti-brainwashing legislation pointed to France, where anti-brainwashing legislation provided the state with sufficient means of providing justice for its victims. Proponents also argued that because brainwashing caused great harm it made no sense that the state could prosecute those who committed assault, but not those who brainwashed. Opponents argued that it would be difficult to draft legislation which drew a clear line between brainwashing and political persuasion, for instance. Even though proponents of laws said civil suits were insufficient, opponents argued that the civil court system was one way to effectively remedy the ills of brainwashing. Another possible proposal was to restrict anti-brainwashing laws to minors and disabled persons only, so as to avoid overuse. Even so, no state in America had laws forbidding brainwashing.

What are some of the issues concerning brainwashing raised in such legal cases as one involving the Society *popularly known as* Hare Krishna?

It has been argued that many of the cases brought to the higher courts in the United States, in which a defendant used a brainwashing defense or in which a plaintiff levied a complaint of brainwashing against a religion, were used by the general public to bolster negative opinions of new religions. Through the examination of the particular case of *George v. ISKCON*, the International Society of Krishna Consciousness popularly known as Hare Krishna, a commentator took a critical look at the experts involved with the case, including the well-known psychologist Margaret Singer, who tried to establish the scientific basis for brainwashing. *George v. ISKCON* was a case in which a young woman, after being a member for several years, sued ISKCON once she had left the organization and converted to fundamentalist Christianity. She sued for emotional distress and imprisonment, saying that she had been brainwashed into joining the group. The main issue identified in the article was that these cases could be problematic for two reasons. They facilitated the avoidance of personal responsibility and choice and they added to the bias against minority religions. Both of these outcomes could lead to a further misunderstanding and mistrust of minority religions by the general public, exacerbated by the popularization of films such as *The Manchurian Candidate*, creating less tolerance for freedom of religion, an important part of the *Bill of Rights*.

Is brainwashing considered a legal defense for committing a crime?

Brainwashing has not been recognized as a formal legal defense. However, it has been used in trials as a mitigating factor in extreme cases of cult, terrorist group, and religious indoctrination. Two legal defenses that brainwashing might play a role in are duress and battered woman syndrome. Both of these defenses allowed individuals to be excused for their crimes because they were coerced to commit the crime and did not do so of their own free will.

What is forced deprogramming and how does it relate to brainwashing?

Forced deprogramming referred to the attempt to force individuals to give up their allegiance to a religious or social group. This typically involved preventing the person from participating in their religious or social organization. There was no standard deprogramming procedure and techniques for deprogramming varied, but common techniques included isolating the subject and using evidence to show they were manipulated. Forced deprogramming was often utilized when the relatives of a person suspected he had been brainwashed by a religion or social group, usually viewed as a cult. Forced deprogramming was seen as a counter to the mind control tactics used by religious cults. It employed many of the same methods that brainwashing did and as a result, there was a fine line between brainwashing and deprogramming. Deprogramming was widely accepted in the United States in the 1970s and 1980s, but since then became less accepted. This was due to concerns that deprogrammers were actually manipulating people.

What is exit counseling?

As methods of force used during deprogramming were criticized over the years, the voluntary process of exit counseling for removing extreme or controversial beliefs held by individuals gained popularity. As opposed to the verbal assaultive techniques used in deprogramming, exit conversations were structured as a dialogue between the believer, his or her family, and the counselor. Often times, families went through extensive preparations to make sure that this program was effective. The dialogue was structured to fit with the value systems of the group the believer attempted to remove himself from, and individuals were empowered through increasing levels of influence over how counseling sessions were carried out as time went on. Individuals were further able to walk out of counseling at any time they wanted and were not criticized in the way that individuals were in deprogramming. Counselors practicing exit counseling often agreed to a code of ethics and only engaged in discourse with other counselors who had also agreed to follow this same code positioned against force and coercion. In general, the process was one that gave individuals a chance to express and evaluate their beliefs in a non-confrontational, non-critical environment. These methods were found to be effective in helping people discard their beliefs.

What practices could be used to reverse or reform the beliefs of a religious fundamentalist or terrorist?

Deprogramming or reeducation has described the process used to make someone discard political, social, or religious beliefs. Often times, family members were the ones who forced the person into a deprogramming or reeducating regimen, as naturally the beliefs and actions of a religious fundamentalist could be troubling to an individual's relatives. Though deprogramming frequently involved force, when it did not and a person voluntarily accepted a program designed to cause him to abandon his beliefs, this process was known as exit counseling. This non-coercive method gained popularity over the years.

Traditional deprogramming methods often consisted of an abduction followed by an assault on the views promoted in the cult or organization the individual was a part of. Often times this was an emotionally traumatizing process as the strongly held views of the person were debunked and shown to be delusional or at least false. Nonetheless, verbal assaults on the believer and his beliefs appeared to be a necessary part of the deprogramming process, just as they were important in the initial brainwashing. Outside of their organization, individuals eventually realized the misguided nature of their beliefs. In some extreme cases, violence, in the form of beating or sexual assault for example, had also been implemented as a part of deprogramming.

The methods of force used in deprogramming, especially in religious or quasi-religious groups generally considered cults, came under fire with questioning whether it was legal to forcibly remove and deprogram someone from a group that he apparently voluntarily agreed to join. A 1977 case in California, *Katz v. Superior Court*, declared that in order for a person to be forcibly detained the person had to be deemed gravely disabled. This ruling was implemented in many other states as well. At the same time, however, police and courts often sympathized with families. For example, in some instances a court case on the legality of deprogramming began without notification to the deprogrammed individual, allowing him only to add his perspective once the case had been going on for some time. Furthermore, judges often explained the choice of evil rule to juries, which asserted that families should be excused for their use of force in the deprogramming process if there was legitimate evidence that involvement in the cult or other group was injurious to the individual. Regardless of the controversy over the methods, however, deprogramming was found to be quite an effective process for removing unwanted beliefs.

Did civil suits as brought against Rick Ross for his effort to deprogram Jason Scott provide an effective alternative to criminal trials on deprogramming claims?

Many people argued that state statutes did not provide adequate remedy for victims of brainwashing and of deprogramming. Without anti-brainwashing laws, many argued that the state could not adequately prosecute people like Rick Ross. Yet the Jason Scott case represented an instance in which a civil suit provided an alternative to criminal responsibility for deprogramming. Ross abducted eighteen-year-old Scott and attempted to deprogram him from his Pentecostal church. Scott was handcuffed, gagged and bound, thrown in a van, and taken to a beach cottage where he was subjected to a weeklong interrogation about his religious beliefs, forced to watch movies about the evils of Christianity and conservative Protestantism, and was often struck in the head during theological debates. In the end, Scott was released upon his feigned admission that he had completely given up his previous religious beliefs.

In the 1993 criminal trial, unlawful imprisonment charges were brought against Ross and his associates. And while it was clear that Ross had attempted to deprogram Scott, Ross was acquitted, since there was not adequate evidence that he was responsible for the actual imprisonment, which was the only actionable portion of the claim. With the possibility of conspiracy to deprive one of human rights and religious liberty, the civil arena gave Scott much more ability to hold his abductors responsible. A jury unanimously held Ross accountable, concluding that he acted intolerably, indecently, and atrociously.

The case sparked a debate about the inadequacy of the criminal law to deal with deprogramming claims. Some believed that emotional abuse should be treated just as physical abuse. Others believed the Scott case provided a perfect example of the adequacy of alternative forms of liability, including but not limited to the civil suit. After all, the civil suit offered the right to sue another for the deprivation of the right to be free from force, violence, or intimidation about the choosing of his religion. In the end, it seemed that the civil law could be an effective alternative to criminal prosecution in the case of religious deprogramming.

Were there any negative effects associated with deprogramming efforts directed at those who had previously been brainwashed?

As brainwashing can have dramatic effects on people, distressing others who knew them before their indoctrination, it is natural that there have been many attempts to try to deprogram the brainwashed and remove the newly implanted beliefs. It was not known what the full effects of deprogramming were, however, though there was evidence that the process might entail adverse effects on the individual. For example, a study in Japan revealed that forced deprogramming resulted in post-traumatic stress disorder and major depressive symptoms in a patient forced into an intense deprogramming regimen by her family. The motive of the Japanese deprogramming initiatives was to regain control over the minds of those who had become adherents to religious cults by way of brainwashing. Though this case may have represented a rare occurrence, it still suggested that deprogramming might have had adverse consequences. In the context of having a brainwashed family member however, it could be deemed preferable to deal with these potential negative psychological effects rather than the brainwashed state.

Is it constitutional for the government to involuntarily deprogram cult members?

The central question to this debate is the extent to which the *First Amendment* protects religions. If it protects all religious beliefs, then it is illegal for the government to deprogram any cult member, for the government cannot intrude into any religious matters. People on one side say that it is unequivocally unconstitutional for the government to deprogram cult members. They point out that it is a state-caused loss of religious belief and that it forces the state to criticize certain religious practices and beliefs. These, critics point out, are all in opposition to the *First Amendment*. Some scholars, however, argue that the *First Amendment* holds an exception in certain circumstances. Cults, for example, often mislead or withhold information when people join them. Thus, the argument goes, people are not truly giving their informed consent when joining such a cult. As members learn more about the cult, their ability to leave it decreases because they may have been brainwashed. This school of thought posits that the First Amendment protects only free and willing religious practice. If deprogramming removes the brainwashing without actually removing the member's religious faith, then the state may do so. However, there is a caveat. If brainwashed members understand that they have been manipulated and choose to stay with the cult anyway, all parties agree that forced deprogramming is unconstitutional.

What were the elements of the Saudi Arabian program for reeducating or deradicalizing terrorists?

The program has been summarized as containing forgiveness, theological reeducation, psychological counseling, prison time, and cash. A course included such topics as jihad, relations with non-Muslims, fatwa or religious decision issuing authority, and proper understanding of takfir, the practice of declaring other Muslims to be apostates. The aim was to correct radicals' thoughts and to make them more mainstream Muslims. Cash included monthly stipends, as eight hundred dollars to one Guantanamo prisoner returned to Saudi Arabia along with a new Toyota Corolla and twenty thousand dollars to finance his marriage. All such programs included intellectual education components; emotional redirection components, and social group support components.

Were various Islamic deprogramming or reeducating efforts successful at countering extremist behavior?

After the terrorist attacks on September 11, 2001, researchers looked for methods of deprogramming or reeducating Islamic terrorists. Deprogramming operations took place in many countries, including Saudi Arabia, Egypt, Singapore, Yemen, and Algeria, and the United States. Furthermore thousands of former militants successfully completed voluntary reeducation programs the aim of which was to persuade them to renounce Islamic terrorism ideologies.

Some compared the process of deprogramming or reeducating terrorists to that of twelve-step programs like Alcoholics Anonymous. Some indicated that former terrorists met with psychologists, and with Islamic scholars who acted as religious advisers. Many programs, such as those in Saudi Arabia, used financial incentives to supplement the spiritual counseling and academic instruction. For example, many graduates of the Saudi program received monthly stipends, cars, and money to pay for marriages. The theory was that this helped returnees avoid the need to enter terrorist organizations anew. Many programs also implemented terrorist halfway houses.

The programs were generally considered very effective. Not only would former jihadists have to pass an examination, they would also have to sign a pledge that they had abandoned their terrorist leanings. Financial incentives and assistance from government social workers also ensured that the lure of extremism was countered even after the program's end. In fact the administrators of the Saudi program reported in 2008 that less than five percent of its program's 3,200 graduates reverted to extremist practices. And while scholars argued about the morality of the Saudi financial incentives, psychologists agreed that in most cases imprisonment was not sufficient to adequately address extremism. Some investigators, however, did point to those who, despite the reeducation and ancillary benefits, had rejoined terrorist groups.

To what extent have deprogramming, reeducating, deradicalizing, and rehabilitating meant the same thing?

Deprogramming was a term usually applied to the method of returning those who had joined cults to their pre-cult ideas, attitudes, and views. Reeducating sounded more positive and less forced and was applied to those whose ideas, attitudes, and views were considered in need of reform or mainstreaming. Deradicalizating appeared more similar to deprogramming in that it attempted to undo whatever radicalization had taken place, and was often applied to those who had taken up with supremacist extremists. Rehabilitating was a term often contrasted with punishing as competing goals of the criminal justice system.

Did Patricia Hearst, Hedda Nussbaum, Lee Boyd Malvo, and Theodore Kaczynski attempt to use brainwashing as an insanity defense?

Brainwashing can and has been used as an insanity defense. For example, in the case of the Washington, D.C. area snipers, seventeen year old Lee Boyd Malvo alleged that he had been brainwashed by forty-two year old John Muhammad. And Patricia Hearst alleged, unsuccessfully, that she had participated in criminal acts as a result of brainwashing by the Symbionese Liberation Army. Though Hedda Nussbaum was never charged, largely because he needed her testimony against Joel Steinberg, he declared she was insane at the time of the child's death, presumably because she had been brainwashed and physically and psychologically severely abused by Steinberg. Kaczynski stopped the proceedings before he could be tried.

Was Patricia Hearst brainwashed into remaining with a secular terrorist organization and therefore insane rather than guilty of aiding them?

Who was Patricia Hearst?

Patricia Hearst was born February 20, 1954, in San Francisco, California. Granddaughter of publishing mogul William Randolph Hearst, she enjoyed an affluent upbringing outside San Francisco and eventually moved to Berkeley, California with her then fiancé Steven Weed. On February 4, 1974, Hearst was kidnapped at gunpoint from her apartment by the Symbionese Liberation Army, a neo-revolutionary group led by escaped convict Donald DeFreeze. For the next two months, Hearst was kept in a closet and, according to Hearst, brainwashed by the group of radicals who targeted wealthy capitalists in order to obtain funds to help the underprivileged. Initially, the Hearst family agreed to demands made by the Symbionese Liberation Army, including two million dollars worth of food for the poor, but eventually negotiations reached a stalemate. During this time, Hearst made the transformation from victim to apparently willing and active member of the Symbionese Liberation Army. She took the name Tania and drove the getaway car in the robbery of a San Francisco bank. After escaping a 1974 police assault, Hearst spent a year running from authorities and was eventually arrested and convicted of bank robbery in 1975.

What influence did Hearst's social identity have on her experience with the Symbionese Liberation Army and her subsequent criminal case?

The Symbionese Liberation Army targeted young wealthy individuals to hold hostage in order to acquire money to support their mission of aiding the underprivileged. In light of this, Hearst's status as heiress to the Hearst fortune made her the perfect candidate for abduction by the Symbionese Liberation Army. Additionally, Hearst's status as a rich, white female may have made her more susceptible to the brainwashing tactics exercised by the Symbionese Liberation Army, which included berating, shaming, and guilt-inducing. It was reported that most of their verbal abuse targeted her privileged background. After her arrest in 1975, Hearst's social status also played a large role in her trial. Her family's fame brought an undue amount of media attention to the proceedings and their wealth enabled them to hire the famously successful attorney F. Lee Bailey. In addition to all of this, it has been argued that Hearst's social status was what led to her guilty verdict. Instead of viewing Hearst as a victim, the jury saw her as another rich, white, socialite indulging normal teenage rebellion.

In the Hearst trial what was the argument for insanity based on brainwashing?

The defense brought in several experts in psychiatry, psychology, and mind control to build a case for insanity based on brainwashing. Psychologist Singer argued that the conditions of abduction lowered Hearst's IQ, and psychiatrist West emphasized the physical abuse and stress of the kidnapping. Others were research experts on mind control, and three argued that Hearst had been indoctrinated into the extreme ideals of the kidnappers through brainwashing. Two other experts also gave opinions for the defense, arguing that Hearst's belief system had broken down and her personality had been altered by the events. They gave examples of Hearst's behavior that pointed to brainwashing including inappropriate laughter or crying during conversation as well as instances of memory loss. Her situation was also compared to the Stockholm syndrome, in which hostages sympathize with the cause of their kidnappers. The prosecution countered with only one expert psychiatric witness.. He argued that Hearst willingly involved herself in the operations of the Symbionese Liberation Army, and he described her as a girl with little direction, looking for a cause. There was some objection from the defense as to whether he was qualified to testify in court.

What happened to Hearst?

On March 20, 1976, a jury of seven men and five women rejected Hearst's brainwashing defense and found her guilty on all charges. This was actually quite shocking, since jurors reported that before any testimony began, they believed that Hearst was innocent. Though the sequestered jury was shielded from the publicity of the trial, they did see many movies during the five-week trial, including *One Flew Over the Cuckoo's Nest*, *Swept Away*, and *Taxi Driver*, three movies which involved varying degrees of psychopathic characters. That aside, the jury reported having been swayed by a few key elements of the trial. First, members of the jury reported that they ultimately found Hearst's story simply unbelievable. A female juror, for example, thought Hearst was undoubtedly lying, and that it seemed implausible for Hearst to keep a love token given to her by a man who supposedly raped her. Other jurors described Hearst as remote, and compared her in court to a robot of sorts. Jurors also wondered why Hearst chose not to take the stand in her own defense. In all, the jury took only twelve hours to find Hearst guilty of armed bank robbery and use of a firearm in the commission of a felony. She was originally sentenced to thirty-five years in prison, considered a harsh punishment given the circumstances of the case, but only served two years before having her sentenced commuted by President Carter. She was given a full pardon by President Clinton in January 2001. She later aided in the conviction of one of her Symbionese Liberation Army accomplices, testifying for the prosecution.

What happened to other members of the Symbionese Liberation Army?

In the midst of the Hearst trial, the public and the prosecution forgot the group who coerced Hearst into her role and conspired with her in the crimes. Only after Hearst's sentence was commuted by Carter and she was pardoned by Clinton did charges arise for other members of the Symbionese Liberation Army. In 2002, Sara Jane Olson, William Harris, Emily Harris, and Michael Bortin were indicted for a murder which occurred during the same bank robbery in 1974 that sparked Hearst's trial, although charges were only brought in 2001. All four pleaded guilty to the charges, and were given the maximum sentence under their plea bargains. James Kilgore, the last member of the Symbionese Liberation Army to be prosecuted, was also found guilty and sentenced to fifty-four months in prison. Besides him, the remaining members of the Symbionese Liberation Army who committed the bank robbery alongside Hearst were living normal lives, except for Sara Jane Olson, who was already in prison. Kilgore was living in hiding, and was not found until a year after the charges were brought against him.

What relation did Jonestown have to religion, brainwashing, and terrorism?

What was the Jonestown cult?

Jonestown was the location of the *Peoples Temple* community in Guyana in South America. The *Peoples Temple* was a religious cult led by Jim Jones that formed in the United States and had several branches throughout California. After receiving criticism in the United States from the media and the police, Jones decided to move the group to Guyana with the goal of forming a socialist paradise. Several hundred Temple members moved to Jonestown in the summer of 1977 and the population of Jonestown reached its peak in 1978 at about one thousand members. The members of the group were forced to work during the days and attended scheduled activities at nights. There was frequent use of communist propaganda, including the constant broadcasting of recorded readings by Jones over tower speakers throughout the community. The group had very little communication with the outside world except for a radio and those living in Jonestown were forbidden to leave, a rule that was enforced by armed guards. The quality of life in Jonestown quickly deteriorated. The conditions of the buildings grew worse over time and food had to be imported due to the poor soil conditions. Those who disobeyed rules were subjected to various punishments including being imprisoned in a plywood box, and members who attempted to escape were drugged for extended periods of time. Jones held White

Nights intermittently where he would declare there was an emergency and residents had to decide on a course of action, which generally consisted of fleeing to the Soviet Union, committing mass suicide, staying in Jonestown to fight attackers, or running into the jungle. Before the actual mass suicide, there were a few White Nights where the community members were made to believe they were poisoning themselves but no poison was actually contained in their drinks. On November 14, 1978, Congressman Leo Ryan visited Jonestown due to concerns raised by the *Concerned Relatives*, a group with connections to members of the Jonestown community who advocated the United States investigate the community. Although Ryan viewed Jonestown as fairly successful, a few families opted to leave the community while he was there. Jones viewed himself as a failure as a result. Congressman Ryan and others were killed by gunmen from the cult at the airstrip as they were attempting to leave Guyana. Ryan was the first Congressman to be murdered in the line of duty in the history of the United States. On the same day, Jones told the community members that Congressman Ryan was going to be killed and that they needed to commit suicide. *Flavor Aid* was mixed with cyanide and other poisons and distributed to the community members. This resulted in the deaths of over nine hundred Peoples Temple members, the greatest single loss of American civilian life in a non-natural disaster until September 11, 2001.

How might the Jonestown cult have included elements of brainwashing?

The Jonestown community was instructed by Jones to drink cyanide and commit a revolutionary suicide. While many of the members of the community did so voluntarily, or because of the urging and coercing of their leader, others did not willingly engage in the mass suicide. Those who did not willingly commit suicide with the group were forced to drink the poison or were shot. The fear of being shot as other members had been may have caused members to select a more peaceful death by poisoning. Before the mass suicide, it was likely that many members of the community were displeased with their lifestyles of slave-like labor and no longer wished to follow the beliefs of Jones' Peoples Temple. The people of Jonestown in Guyana were not allowed to leave the community which was under constant armed security patrol so that there was no way to escape. Under the constant threat of violence, it seemed that the people of Jonestown were brainwashed in their gullibility and naivete in following a strange leader with hopes of finding a better life. They unfortunately found a horrible and inescapable life instead.

What is the cultural legacy of Jonestown?

Probably the most common cultural reference to the events in Jonestown has been when people refer to drinking the kool-aid. Although the phrase refers to the method of mass suicide and murder used by the followers of Jones in Jonestown in drinking cyanide-laced beverage, the phrase has now been routinely used for any situation in which a person has accepted a questionable set of beliefs. In particular, drinking the kool-aid has referred to blindly following any precept with which the questioner disagreed. The popular wisdom that emerged from the Jonestown tragedy was to distrust the charismatic leader or demigod. The Jonestown massacre and cult received extensive media attention when it occurred in 1978, and continued to play an important role in the popular understanding of religious cults. Ironically, Jones moved his followers to Guyana in part in order to escape media scrutiny. When the congressman went to investigate the resettlement in Guyana, bringing media attention, some Jones's followers killed him and four others on the airstrip. This in turn led to the mass suicide by poison and homicidal killings.

The events at Jonestown have been re-imagined and revisited in several documentaries, as well as incorporated into many works of fiction. One particularly striking cultural legacy of Jonestown was the fictional account of its events in Armistead Maupin's novel *Further Tales of the City*. A wealthy socialite, her lesbian lover, and their Eurasian twins escaped Guyana via Cuba and Jones stalked them home to San Francisco. Obsessed with being the father figure for the twins, Jones followed them to Alaska and back to San Francisco, where the socialite's loyal housekeeper killed and buried him in the backyard. For purposes of the novel, written four years after the massacre at Jonestown, Jones was imagined to have had a look-alike who died with the others while the real Jones returned to San Francisco. As a figure for the cultural imagination, Jones remained a disturbing and mysterious character.

Were some of Hitler's closest military commanders and personnel who were with him at the end still as loyal to him as cult members are who engage in suicidal or homicidal behavior?

Both his surviving personal secretary's book and the film *Der Untergang* based on it demonstrated the loyal behavior of some of Hitler's closest military commanders and personnel even after Hitler committed suicide in his bunker and the end for them and the Nazis clearly was at hand. Their behavior showed the same cult-like loyalty to him as had been shown by the followers of Jones at Jonestown or the followers of many other leaders in other secular and generally religiously-oriented cults.

Was Unabomber Theodore Kaczynski brainwashed, a secular terrorist, a psychopath, a seriously mentally disordered paranoid schizophrenic, and/ or an extremely angry isolated individual?

Theodore Kaczynski was born May 22, 1942, in Chicago. He claimed that his mother and father were verbally abusive and his family was considered lower-middle class. Kaczynski was accepted to Harvard at sixteen and received his masters from the University of Michigan at age twenty five. During his time in school, Kaczynski exhibited reclusive behavior and although he was always very smart he never succeeded socially or with women. His behavior in college was described by many as being psychotic. After Michigan he almost got a sex change operation to remedy his sexual and social frustration, but he left the appointment embarrassed and dropped the idea.

Becoming disgruntled with teaching after two years at the University of California Berkeley, he decided that he desired a life of solitude. Denied a plot of land in Canada he settled in Lincoln, Montana, where he lived off his own land. After a few years there, he began researching bombs and practicing constructing them. He was fed up with society and what he saw as materialism and technology corrupting the world. He felt that bombs would be a perfect way to get out his message. Kaczynski sent bombs through mail packages to various people he identified as part of the problem. During a seventeen year period, his activity was very sporadic and overall he killed three people and injured twenty three.

Kaczynski was eventually caught after publishing his manifesto entitled *Industrial Society and its Future* in the *New York* and *Los Angeles Times*. They published it because he said if the papers did not publish his work then the Unabomber would strike again. The name was derived from his being the university and airline bomber. When his brother saw the piece, he recognized it was Ted, and turned him into the authorities after they agreed not to seek the death penalty. He was arrested in his home on April 3, 1996, where the authorities found enough evidence including his journals in Spanish and English detailing his victims and thoughts over a twenty year period. Kaczynski was self represented in court and he pled guilty. He did not use the insanity defense because he thought this would deny credibility to his manifesto and his beliefs. Kaczynski was sentenced to four consecutive life sentences without parole and then appealed but it was denied in 2002. Many have believed he will continue his appeals as he is adamant about the correctness of his thoughts.

Was Kaczynski brainwashed by the experiments he underwent at Harvard?

A scholar argued in his book that Kaczynski's murderous streak was greatly exacerbated if not sparked by the experiments that he underwent during his time at Harvard. He contended that Kaczynski was subjected to a form of mental torture that essentially unbalanced him. While the case demonstrated the care that must be taken to protect subjects during psychological experiments, many others concluded that the experiments were not comprehensive enough to be thought of as brainwashing nor did any think they removed culpability from Kaczynski. First, the experiments did not happen in isolation. Kaczynski was surrounded by many kinds of influences at Harvard and later in life, any of which could have influenced his later behavior. Second, the experimenter's purpose was not to indoctrinate his subjects into a particular belief system, but merely to attack the beliefs the subjects already had. While that may have counted as a kind of trauma, which could led to anger, hostility, and violence, it was not considered brainwashing which would have forced Kaczynski into thinking from which he could not break away, thus potentially freeing him from responsibility.

What happened in the prosecution of Kaczynski?

Though the prosecution initially intended to seek the death penalty, they agreed to drop the death penalty in exchange for a plea of guilty from Kaczynski. The defense attorneys originally wanted to use the insanity defense in an effort to obtain a verdict of not guilty by reason of insanity, but Kaczynski refused to allow them to use it because he thought it would discredit his manifesto. Instead, the defense followed a strategy of eliminating damaging evidence from the trial in an effort to avoid the death penalty. Nonetheless, the defense team, without his permission, filed documents from psychiatrists describing his mental state in order to convey his instability and to prevent him from receiving the death penalty. Before the trial began, however, he asked to replace his attorneys with a celebrity lawyer, but this was not allowed by the judge. Then he asked for permission to represent himself, though, following a psychiatric test that showed he was competent to stand trial, the judge refused to allow him to represent himself. An hour later, both sides came to an agreement on a plea bargain.

Who served as expert witnesses in Kaczynski's trial?

The defense hired an expert to evaluate Kaczynski before the start of the trial. After the completion of a review of his writing, and interviews with Kaczynski and his family, the doctor came to the conclusion that Kaczynski was suffering from paranoid schizophrenia.

A psychologist also met with Kaczynski twice for the defense and concluded that though he had great intellect, his mind was clinically abnormal and that he was in denial of his mental illness. His denial of his mental disorder and his deeply ingrained fear of being considered sick, however, led to his resistance to psychological evaluations by the prosecution and the defense once it was clear that his lawyers considered him mentally sick. Kaczynski refused to be evaluated by government experts, which led to a motion by the prosecution to not allow the use of any expert testimony in the trial. This motion was approved, though lay evidence could still be used by the defense to establish their case on his mental fragility.

Later in the trial, when Kaczynski asked to represent himself, the judge ordered that he be given psychological evaluations to deem whether he was fit to do so. The psychiatrist from the federal correctional facility in Butner, NC, was chosen by the judge to evaluate Kaczyinski's level of competency. She had previously completed similar tests in such high profile cases as the attempted assassination of President Reagan by John Hinckley. She found Kaczynski fit to stand trial, but the court did not allow him to represent himself based on the untimely nature of such a change. A plea bargain was soon reached by the two sides, ending the case without the use of expert witnesses in the courtroom.

How did the jury affect Kaczynski's case?

Due to the massive media involvement at the time, the jury was subjected to innumerable accounts and interpretations of the case that were difficult to ignore. Although the judge specifically directed them on several occasions to ignore all news regarding the case, the jury likely viewed and absorbed some of the media's take on it. The jury selection task itself also came riddled with problems including the protracted, five week jury selection process. The final jury was composed of nine women and three men. It included people who reported religion to be a strong factor in their decision-making, and people who had family in law enforcement. After the jury was chosen, delays occurred in part due to Kaczynski's attempts to represent himself, which forced the judge to hold off the trial. As it turned out, however, because the trial ended in a plea bargain, the jury had no effect on the actual outcome of the case.

What was the disposition of the Kaczynski case?

Kaczynski pled guilty to all charges, thirteen counts for attacks in three states, which killed three people and injured two others. He was sentenced to serve life in prison without a chance for parole. As of spring 2009, he was in a maximum-security facility in Florence, CO, though he remained active in courts to some extent, battling over the auction of his journals and other correspondences as well as the exhibition of his cabin, though his efforts in these matters had been unsuccessful.

Had Kaczynski gone to trial, would he have been found fully criminally responsible for murder, partially criminally responsible for manslaughter, guilty but mentally ill, or not guilty by reason of insanity?

Most commentators thought he would have been found guilty of murder because of the planning involved, the non-psychotic nature of his manifesto, and the danger he posed.

To what extent was brainwashing involved in the death of a child of Hedda Nussbaum and Joel Steinberg?

What was the series of events leading to the child's death?

Hedda Nussbaum and her partner Joel Steinberg had two daughters, one of whom was illegally adopted. Though their household seemed happy from the outside, Steinberg was abusive towards Nussbaum. She was very subservient to him to the point that she asked for permission to use the bathroom and thought he had godlike powers. Nussbaum had a personality and upbringing that would make her susceptible to a man like Steinberg. She had always taken a subservient role. As a child, she was always second best to her sister and she attempted to emulate her in many regards. As Nussbaum's relationship with Steinberg progressed, he became increasingly more abusive. He physically and emotionally battered her. He came to rule her life. On the evening of November 1, 1987, Steinberg came to Nussbaum with their daughter Lisa unconscious in his arms, and Nussbaum claimed that Steinberg confessed to knocking Lisa unconscious. Nussbaum tried helping the young child and wanted to call 911, but Steinberg would not let her. They continued on with their evening plans, and she ignored her daughter believing Steinberg would care for the child. The two even used cocaine until the early hours of the morning. It was not six-thirty in the morning that Steinberg finally permitted Nussbaum to call the police after Lisa stopped breathing.

What happened to Joel Steinberg?

For Steinberg's trial, her counsel ensured that Nussbaum would testify before the grand jury against Steinberg and convinced the jury that Nussbaum was a victim too, which showed the jury that she was beaten senseless and so was unable to call emergency services about Lisa's condition. Steinberg did not give interviews or testimony for the grand jury, but Nussbaum told the jury about cults and hypnotic powers and the night of the incident. The jury was also swayed by expert testimony concerning Nussbaum's lack of energy to deliver a fatal blow. In midst of television coverage and media attention, the jury received the case for deliberations and spent eight days reviewing testimony. Since it was so important to prosecute Steinberg, and since Nussbaum's testimony was seen as crucial for that matter, Nussbaum was never charged with any crime. The jury never had to decide if Nussbaum herself was guilty of any crime in the case. Many believed that Nussbaum should have faced prosecution so that a jury could have decided her guilt or innocence or insanity. While Nussbaum was originally arrested and charged in the death of Lisa, charges were eventually dropped and Nussbaum was free. She toured the country as an activist for awareness of battered woman syndrome, giving talks and appearing on shows such as *Larry King Live* and

Oprah. Nussbaum published her memoir in 2005, entitled *Surviving Intimate Terrorism*.

What made Nussbaum's case unique?

The Nussbaum case was unique in one important respect. She was never brought to trial. The Manhattan District Attorney at the time called for the murder charge against her to be dropped. After hearing that she had no active role in the murder of her daughter, the judge agreed to drop all charges. The reasons that motivated dismissal of the charges almost certainly included the need to use Nussbaum as a key witness for the prosecution in the case against Steinberg, as well as Nussbaum's extensive abuse at Steinberg's hand, and her lack of physically abusive action against her daughter. Immediately after her arrest, Nussbaum did retain defense counsel who campaigned for the media to focus on Nussbaum as a victim rather than as a culpable party.

Since Nussbaum was never tried for the murder of her adopted daughter, there were no expert witnesses. The District Attorney claimed that Nussbaum's visibly unstable condition was enough to not prosecute her, but he still sent her to Four Winds Hospital for evaluation. Although treated at the facility, she was never tested for competency to stand trial or for criminal responsibility, in other words for insanity. Since Nussbaum was not on trial, there was no reason for the defense or the prosecution to obtain an expert witness to determine her mental status. Steinberg's defense was not based on the insanity defense and therefore it did not require an expert witness to determine his mental state.

What is the relationship between Battered Woman Syndrome and brainwashing?

Battered woman syndrome first came into the public consciousness following the work of a psychologist in the 1970s as she attempted to understand domestic violence. She argued that victims of chronic abuse eventually became depressed, and began believing the abuser's repeated assertions that the abuse was the fault of the victim. This cycle eroded the victim's self-esteem, which explained why victims often did not seek outside social support. Some considered the syndrome a type of brainwashing, in which women are deluded into believing that they are worthless and are deserving of their abuse, and that there is no way to improve their situation. When the psychologist began to testify at trials of women who had been accused of killing their abuser, she evoked the syndrome as an explanation for their behavior. It became a legal defense to cases of deliberate killing.

The concept of the syndrome is somewhat contradictory, as it is used both to explain the victim's prolonged inability to change her own circumstance, and the final decision to kill her abuser. The syndrome is thought both to be a form of brainwashing and a variant of the traditional self-defense argument. The government investigated the syndrome when it published the Violence Against Women Act of 1994, an expansive piece of federal legislation dealing with intimate violence. Though it included extensive testimony from victims of the syndrome, who cited the verbal abuse as the primary source of brainwashing, the Act ultimately concluded that there was not sufficient psychological evidence supporting it. Still, it has occasionally been invoked in legal cases to defend battered women. Yet a simulation indicated that if a battered woman endured emotional rather than physical abuse, she was more likely to be judged guilty by an experimental jury.

What were the verdicts in the Nussbaum and Steinberg cases?

Because the prosecutor agreed not to charge Nussbaum due to her diminished capacity as a frequent victim of abuse, she was never legally implicated as responsible for her child's death. Interestingly, this conclusion was not one reached in court, but rather one agreed upon between her lawyer and the prosecutor prior to the trial. The jury did convict Joel Steinberg, Nussbaum's partner, of the most serious charge he was eligible for, first-degree manslaughter. The judge then accompanied it with the maximum penalty of eight and a third to twenty-five years in prison.

Did Nussbaum believe she was brainwashed?

Nussbaum agreed to several public interviews after Lisa Steinberg's death. In 2005, she appeared on *Larry King Live* where she spoke about her relationship with Steinberg and the brainwashing she endured. She explained that because of her history of shyness, Steinberg's helping her gain much-needed confidence ultimately led to her dependence on him. She said she placed him on a pedestal. This dependence became so deep-seated that when he hit her for the first time, after spending three years together, she sloughed it off as a fluke. She explained that she was fascinated and obsessed with Steinberg, who would talk to her for hours as she listened intently. She later realized that these long talks were periods of manipulation and brainwashing, to the point that he could then completely control her. She reached a point where using the bathroom required his permission. He kept her from seeing family and friends for the years they were together. Eventually, the beatings became so common that she had to avoid contact with family and friends simply to prevent them from becoming aware of the abuse. The night of Lisa's death, she asked his permission to call 911. She said that the brainwashing process was gradual. This led to her being unaware of the reality of the situation, as she slowly but certainly was losing her sense of self. It was for this reason that when Lisa was hurt, Nussbaum was helpless. Looking back, she explained that she was not a whole person at the time of Lisa's death. She was not capable of protecting herself or her daughter.

Following Lisa's death, Nussbaum spent a year and a half in psychiatric hospitals. The individual and group therapy she received there coupled with support from family and friends set Nussbaum on her road to recovery. With time and deconditioning, she eventually realized the brainwashing she had been subjected to and the fatal repercussions of this. In 2009, she said she saw herself as an entirely different person from the woman totally under Steinberg's control. She explained that the brainwashing she endured destroyed her sense of identity, but that she had since rebuilt and recovered it.

What techniques did a United States convert to Islam, Jamie Paulin-Rodriguez, allegedly use to brainwash her six year old son?

According to a report, a United States mother converted to Islam over the course of a year. It was alleged that she was in contact via the internet with two of the American jihadists the *Christian Science Monitor* wrote about, LaRose and Zazi. Arrested in Ireland as part of a plot to kill the Swedish cartoonist who depicted Muhammad as a dog, she was at least temporarily released from custody. More related to some of the issues in this book, it was further alleged that she brainwashed her young son by enrolling him in a radical Islamic school in Ireland. There, according to his father and his grandmother, the boy said the students were building pipe bombs, learning how to fire guns, saying that Christians would burn in hell, and forbidden to associate with non-Muslim children. Though brainwashing and educating refer to the same goal, the former has a pejorative connotation while the latter has a more neutral, even beneficent, connotation. Brainwashing connotes total immersion, though many education institutions also practice total immersion. The end toward which the training or learning is directed tends to separate the use of one of the words from the use of the other.

Chapter 6.   *Neuroscience and the Law*

What is neuroscience?

According to the *Law and Neuroscience Project*, neuroscience is the study of the brain and nervous system, and how they enable behavior and learning.

What is the Neuroscience and Law Project?

The *Law and Neuroscience Project* was an official initiative of MacArthur Foundation to explore how the findings of neuroscience should and should not be dealt with in the law. The team was headed by a group of five psychologists and one former United States Supreme Court Justice. The initial goals of the panel were to ascertain the neuroscientific discoveries that were germane to law, to develop a list of recommendations for reforms for a variety of legal issues, and to create a primer for judges explaining the essential information about neuroanatomy and neuroscience. One of the issues the group hoped to advance was how to deal with neurological findings and their application to guilt, innocence, and truth telling. The work of the team sought to create better standards for the use of neurological information in the courtroom and to add greater legitimacy to this type of evidence.

How might the prior experience of the initial chairs of the Law and Neuroscience Project *affect policy decisions?*

The initial chairs of the *Law and Neuroscience Project* were former Supreme Court Justice Sandra Day O'Connor and professor Michael Gazzaniga of the University of California, Santa Barbara. O'Connor, was a Justice from 1981 to 2006, served as the honorary chair of the Project. Gazzaniga, well known for his research on how the physical structure of the brain affects the mind, co-chaired the effort, and also served as the director of the project, maintaining day-to-day operations in the central office at the University of California, Santa Barbara. Other acting members on the board included Steven Hyman, the Provost of Harvard University and Professor of Neurobiology at Harvard Medical School who formerly worked as a chair of the National Institute for Mental Health, Marcus Raichle who penned the original and definitive study in 1988 on how to properly interpret fMRI scans, District Court Judge Jed Rakoff who had declared a proposed federal death penalty unconstitutional, and Professor Frederick Schauer of Harvard Law School who had published over 200 articles many dealing with the nature of legal sources in court.

At the outset some raised the question of whether the governing board, though extremely gifted and knowledgeable in the field, might find their prior beliefs clouding the project and raising the issue of the subjectivity of some of its conclusions. In particular, the district court judge who declared the federal death penalty unconstitutional might cause concern around issues concerning sentencing given neurological evidence. While his logic may have been sound at the time, the United States Court of Appeals reversed his decision in 2002.

What is the relation of neuroscience to the law?

This answer and all those in the subsequent questions concerning psychology, law, and the *Law and Neuroscience Project* are taken directly from the website where it stated that the legal system incorporates assumptions about behavior that, in some cases, are centuries old and based on common sense and culture. For example, it tends to assume that people make deliberate choices and that those choices determine what they do. However, recent breakthroughs in neuroscience research indicate that such choices may sometimes be based upon electrical impulses and neuron activity that are not a part of conscious behavior. These actions can include not only criminal activity, but also decisions made by police, prosecutors, and jurors to arrest, prosecute, convict, or mandate treatment. Therefore, as neuroscience increases understanding of what influences human behavior, how this knowledge is applied can have a major impact on the future of the legal system.

What did the Law and Neuroscience Project *indicate were its research interests about criminal responsibility and prediction?*

At the outset it should be noted that a successful insanity defense negates criminal responsibility. A successful insanity defense means the charged individual is not guilty. Not guilty and lack of criminal responsibility are equivalent. In order to explore criminal responsibility, the project's official website listed a number of questions for study. The following excerpts were taken from the *Law and Neuroscience Project* website. What does it mean to hold a person criminally responsible for his or her actions? Do advances in neuroscience provide assistance in determining if certain individuals who suffer from mental illnesses, brain abnormalities, or other causes of potential diminished mental capacity deserve to be excused from responsibility? Further, do those advances help predict if people with abnormalities will behave dangerously or if they can be helped with new interventions? The excerpts continued with a number of more specific questions. Among them were these. Persons suffering from addiction, psychopathy and other forms of brain damage make up a significant proportion of accused and convicted criminals and of those at risk for criminal behavior. Their brain conditions raise the critical questions identified above about responsibility, prediction, and treatment. Answers to such questions will doubtlessly have implications for assessing criminal responsibility in individuals who do not have abnormal brain conditions. So called normal individuals exist at various points on a continuum of brain and behavior categorizations, making distinct categorization difficult. A transcendent question is whether neuroscientific based on group averages or behavioral diagnoses, can properly be applied to a particular individual before the court.

The project's goal, as stated on its website, was to assist attorneys, judges and legal experts make accurate assessments of responsibility and accurate predictions about future dangerous conduct and potential for treatment. Accuracy in both types of decision is crucial to just outcomes. That determination will lead to scientific research to address those areas identified as both critical and lacking in information. More generally, new neuroscientific discoveries might well undermine many of the laws assumptions about human behavior that implicitly and explicitly guide legal policy. For example, if neuroscience can demonstrate that an addicts behavior is not fully under the addicts control, it may be unfair to hold the addict legally accountable for that behavior. At present, the criminal law does not excuse or mitigate the conduct of addicts, but neuroscience will unquestionably put increasing pressure on the moral and legal model of addiction that portrays it as within the addicts control and it may motivate a more medical response. As a further example, if psychopaths cannot appreciate moral wrongfulness, is it just to hold them accountable for the harms they inflict? Finally, if a patient with frontal lobe damage is prone to behavioral disinhibition, should he or she be blamed for impulsive, criminal actions? Further, the project, again on its website, said that the goals for research with addicts, psychopaths and people with brain damage are to understand the relation of their abnormal states to criminal behavior and risk, to develop reliable diagnostic procedures that courts may rely upon in assessing such individuals and predicting their future behavior, and to encourage the design of therapies and other interventions that might restore non-criminal functioning and thus benefit the individual and society. .

How have the findings of neuroscience been incorporated into the courtroom?

Though the technology was rather new, neuroscience began to be incorporated into the courtroom, and will likely be increasingly so in the future. Neuroscientific findings called into question one of the foundational principles of the United States legal system that in most all cases humans were rational decision makers, responsible for and conscious of their actions. Some decisions however, the research suggested, might have been based on unconscious electrical impulses and neuronal activity, which questioned the notion that humans were deliberate decision makers in control of their actions. This issue came out in the 2005 Supreme Court case, *Roper v. Simmons*. There neuroscientific findings on the development of the adolescent brain were addressed by the court.. Specifically, court briefs cited that a lack of development in the frontal lobes of adolescents, associated with self-control problems, reduced this defendant's responsibility for the crime. And this case was a sign of things to come. As the findings of neuroscience became more and more prominent in the courtroom, it was important to consider just how they should be incorporated.

Until the technology of neuroscience was improved, however, its findings were not able to take on as prominent a role in the law. The accuracy of fMRI lie detector tests, for example, was less than the necessary standard for evidence, though some said that devices able to produce the required level of accuracy were potentially only five years away. And, with the impending improvements in technology, the uses of psychological experts in the courtroom were likely to change greatly. Cases had generally involved multiple experts testifying for the defense and prosecution and potentially giving conflicting conclusions about defendant's mental status and its impact on defendant's behavior. This effort at understanding the psychological state of defendants, it was suggested, would give way to scientific brain scans for instance. While they would appear more objective, they would nonetheless still require interpretation. In that sense the functions of expert witnesses would be unchanged, though what they were interpreting and the way in which judge or jury perceived the evidence might be significantly different. Deciding whether someone was in control of his actions or able to tell the difference between right and wrong as in the case of the insanity defense would remain contentious in the adversary system of justice. Many hold out the hope or expectation that as technology improves, the determination of insanity will become more of a hard, objective science, that the subjectivity will be removed once experts have less leeway in interpreting the scientific facts as they present themselves in the images of an fMRI scan for example.

Others argued, however that though individual parts of the brain may potentially only be interpreted in one way, it is possible that different psychologists might pick out different parts of the images to attach significance to. Subjectivity would thus remain as a part of expert testimony. In the case of the use of fMRI lie detector tests there would also be the factor of inaccurate readings, as the technology has not been perfected to the point of producing total accuracy. In general, it is hard to predict exactly how expert testimony will be affected, but the availability of hard scientific evidence to back up the claims of expert witnesses will likely add to the credibility and weight that their testimony holds in the course of trials.

How might functional Magnetic Resonance Imaging affect the insanity defense?

Functional magnetic resonance imaging, or fMRI, might have aided psychologists in cases where the defendant pled not guilty by reason of insanity. This concrete evidence would have been useful during the trial of Kenneth Bianchi, who was believed to be malingering. The use of fMRI might be helpful to determine whether the defendant was malingering when psychologists' opinions vary. Furthermore, many juries are skeptical of the presence of mental illness, especially when defendants have received treatment by the time of the trial and do not then appear to be mentally ill. Currently, the juries only have the opinions of psychologists as to whether a defendant was mentally ill or not. Especially with the burden of proof on the defense, fMRI evidence might be helpful for jury deliberation.

Some scientists have also believed that they may be able to use fMRI to determine whether an individual is a psychopath or not.

There is an abnormal flow of blood in the brain of a psychopath when viewing pictures of fearful faces. Researchers believed this directly related to the lack of empathy felt in psychopaths. The introduction of fMRI scans in the courtroom to determine whether someone is a psychopath would not help a defendant's case if he were employing the insanity defense, however, since psychopaths are not legally excused by their mental illness.

Why would the introduction of neuroscientific evidence in courts be controversial?

The main problem with the introduction of neuroscientific evidence in courts has been that neuroscience is still a nascent field. Even a neuroscientist and professor expressed great doubts about place of neuroscience in the courtroom. The amount of information known is much less than that still remaining to be ascertained. Given the reverence bestowed upon neuroscientific knowledge, and the difficulty of understanding the way cellular and molecular interactions cause behavior, its incorporation into the courtroom would be complex, particularly since neuroscientific evidence may be difficult to cross-examine or even to properly judge. A misunderstanding or erroneous conclusion based on these issues could result in an unjust verdict. Some have been extremely concerned with the potential for misuse of neuroscientific evidence prematurely introduced in the courtroom as legal evidence. On the other hand, some neuroscientists have contended that they could tie a particular part of the brain to thought about crime and punishment. In some initial studies, one particularly striking result was the discovery of how emotional the mind is in weighing evidence. The researchers saw future use of fMRI in selecting a jury with lower emotion readings in how decisions are reached. Their underlying assumption was that a better verdict would be reached based upon reason rather than emotional reactions.

Since neuroscience continues to develop its understanding of what new technologies like fMRI mean in a practical manner, many argue that it seems problematic and even dangerous to introduce fMRI into the courtroom at this time. One extreme example of the uncertain relationship of the law and neuroscience is the Weinstein case in the early 1990s. The judge in the case chose to compromise, permitting brain scans showing the arachnoid cyst affecting Weinstein's brain, but not allowing the explanation of what correlation the cyst might have with violent behavior. That the judge would permit the images with no explanation suggested that the use of neuroscience in the courtroom can be cause for great concern.

Whereas some of the more indefinite forms of testimony permitted into the courtroom such as eyewitness and expert testimony can be questioned, the main issue with neuroscience is that by its very nature as a discipline, neuroscience tries to explain human motivation, intention, and action. While neuroscientific testimony can be disputed like the other forms of testimony, it presents more difficulty because the discipline tries to explain the basic foundation of human action. This is a newer scientific field, more complex, and less capable of being understood and properly evaluated, so undue weight may be given to an expert witness whose conclusions may be nothing more than the most current hypothesis and may be far from scientifically definitive or even accurate. Until neuroscience has found more answers to the questions it proposes to answer, many argue it should not be used in the courtroom beyond the facts that may be agreed upon.

How could neuroscience influence jury selection?

Jury consultants might opt to use fMRIs on prospective jurors, to see what parts of their brain were activated when they were shown tapes of lawyers and witnesses. Such tests might help illuminate hidden biases that the juror would not admit to or might not even be aware of. These tests would provoke ethical concerns, however, regarding the degree to which such deep-seated prejudices might actually influence behavior, or whether it would ever be possible to find someone without them. Subjecting jurors to these tests might also stilt their responses as they overcompensated to seem less prejudiced.

How might lawyers use neuroscience during jury selection in insanity defense cases to yield more impartial decisions?

Functional magnetic resonance imaging in a 2008 study revealed that emotion did in fact play a role in the decision processes of juries. This strongly corroborated and began to provide an explanation for the fact that juries' personal feelings shaped their ultimate verdicts in insanity defense cases. In a questionnaire-based experiment with a pool of prospective jurors, researchers observed that personal attitudes about the insanity defense itself strongly predicted trial outcomes in insanity defense cases. Thus, when empanelling a jury, defense lawyers were often focused on securing jurors who would be least emotionally opposed to an insanity defense.

Thus, if the aim of *voir dire* was to secure jurors who were least emotionally charged against the insanity defense, it seemed fMRI could have been used effectively on prospective jurors. This was especially so given the complicated and often confusing nature of the law in insanity defense cases. After all, the aforementioned study revealed that the large majority of the public holds a negative view of the insanity defense. Furthermore, studies showed that these preconceived notions might be so strong that many legal instruments meant to safeguard against them, such as judges' instructions and insanity standards, were ineffective. In *voir dire*, lawyers attempted to secure jurors who would be amenable to the insanity defense. It seemed, therefore, that actually analyzing the brain of potential jurors would have moved the legal system one step closer to impartiality, or at least objectivity.

What are the pros and cons of using brain imaging in jury selection?

Some proponents of brain imaging suggested that new fMRI technology may actually aid lawyers in selecting jury members. Hypothetically, lawyers could assess the different brain-activity patterns of potential jurors and decide, based on these results, who would make the best deliberators in a specific case. For example, perhaps the defense would prefer to have jurors who make decisions based on maximum rationality and minimum emotion, whereas in other cases, maximum emotional reaction would be preferable. However, if courts were to judge members of the moral community, it would seem they should be held to the standards and expectations of a random sampling of that very moral community. While brain imaging may be beneficial in eliminating jurors who are wholly incapable of judging criminal responsibility, it seems more just for the pool of individuals to reflect the broad spectrum of brain-activity patterns within the moral community regardless of the case at hand.

Does emotion play a significant role in the ultimate decisions of juries?

To more fully understand the basis of juries' conclusions, researchers used fMRI to examine the brains of subjects who were contemplating fifty hypothetical situations of criminal responsibility. Researchers found that at least two regions of the brain assess guilt. The right dorsolateral prefrontal cortex, which was associated with analytical reasoning, was highly active. Yet at the same time, the emotional circuits of the brain were also activated. This indicated that when assessing guilt, people used emotion as well as reason to make their decisions. Researchers found the emotional factor surprising. After all, the law was meant to be objective and impartial. Yet the fact that humans used emotion in making decisions suggested that the law was administered less objectively. This led some to conclude that safeguards should have been implemented, including possibly fMRI's on prospective jury members.

Can neuroscience be used to determine mens rea?

Positron emission tomography has been reported to have the ability to differentiate between premeditated killers and impulsive killers using patterns of neural activity. These findings have not played an important role in a United States criminal trial. However, a woman was found guilty of murder in an Indian court based on brain wave oscillations that showed evidence of guilty knowledge.

Can functional Magnetic Resonance Imaging serve as a reliable lie detector?

A study by a psychiatrist and a psychologist showed that fMRI was able to detect lies correctly up to eighty-five percent of the time. The fMRI allowed the researchers to see that the activity in the brain's frontal lobe increased dramatically when one lied. Although eighty five percent was a high number, the fMRI did not catch all lies. The fMRI did not catch spontaneous or repeated lies, since these were likely lies that did not require much thought and therefore did not stimulate the brain as much.

Are brain scans a reliable form of identifying criminality?

The quick and simple answer to the question is no. Research has found that the different regions of the brain are encoded for different things. The dorsolateral prefrontal cortex is responsible for planning, strategizing, formation and executive function. The anterior cingulated cortex is responsible for reward anticipation, decision-making, empathy and emotion. The ventromedial prefrontal cortex is responsible for the processing of risk and fear in decision-making. However, the evidence for what region of the brain encodes for what is all very inconclusive. Critics argued that depending on the methodology used, the color coding scheme, the areas examined, and the emotions examined, results could vary significantly. In addition to the potential inaccuracy, brain scans, many philosophers and ethicists argued, were wrong in principle. Brain scans invaded privacy, and blurred the line between what courts could admit as permissible or not. Additionally, brain scans, some argued, would free criminals of responsibility if lack of both free will and decision making can be proven by the brain scans. Aside from brain scans, companies are beginning to invest in various lie detector tests. These tests only have an eighty to ninety percent accuracy range so far, the same as a polygraph test, and polygraph tests are not admitted into courts. These companies hope to create a ninety to ninety-five percent accuracy range for the lie detector tests, so that this evidence can be admitted into courts. Yet, the same problems that arise with using brain scans also arise when using lie detector tests. These tests also blur the line between how heavily the evidence should weigh in, when the accuracy is not one-hundred percent, and issues of privacy are also still very much prevalent.

The material on neurolaw may reinforce the current legal system when admitting evidence such as brain scans. Or allowing brain scans entered as evidence into the courtroom or to be used for screening or other purposes may drastically undercut the current legal system causing an entire paradigm shift. The law seeks to hold individuals responsible for their criminal actions. But new technologies, on the one hand, might diminish that notion of responsibility. But equally challenging, new technologies might uncover thoughts preceding actions and might make possible the punishing of thoughts rather than behaviors. Questions of monitoring thoughts, of how to punish thoughts which might or would lead to offending behaviors, and of when to begin looking at thoughts would all emerge. Some would argue that juries and judges alike would continue to want to punish criminals only for their actions. But other might want to go beyond, really before, behavior and action and punish the thoughts which would lead to prohibited behavior and action. Considering much of the neurolaw evidence has so far produced inconclusive results, the current legal practice may continue. But continuing neuroscientific research may suggest that individuals have no free will. How specific the coding of the brain will be remains uncertain, especially considering that many studies have shown that many parts of the brain work together to complete any given task making it all extremely complex to present in a legal context. But efforts will continue to be made to expand neurolaw with more sophisticated technology that might shed better light on the inner workings of the brain. Until then, however, the judge's, jury's and society's continuing methods of influence on determining punishment for criminals will continue to prevail.

Should a defendant's fMRI be admissible during trial?

Neuroscience presents the opportunity to use fMRI technology on defendants, to provide them with images of the crime to find which sections of the brain are activated. From this, one may be able to deduce a guilty reaction, which could indicate his relationship to a crime. This technology is not dissimilar to the lie-detector technology which is currently available. But that technology is not admissible in court. Although it also uses a person's physical reaction to sense if he is being dishonest, the heightened circumstance and nervousness associated with taking the test may make its results inconclusive. Similarly, it seems unlikely that a person's reaction to a violent crime, especially one he or she is accused of perpetrating, would be able to elicit a simple enough reaction to determine guilt or innocence.

How do psychopaths' neural deficits interact with the different tests of insanity?

Psychopathy alone will not excuse one from criminal responsibility. Under the M'Naghten rule, the defendant must not be able to understand the difference between right and wrong. However, psychopaths have an outstanding ability to understand the difference between right and wrong. Their problem lies with their inability or unwillingness to conform their behavior to society's standards. Psychopaths fare no better under the American Law Institute test for insanity. While one could argue that their neural deficits are a mental defect, an essential part of the test, the American Law Institute makes an exception for psychopaths. That defect cannot manifest itself solely as repeated criminal or antisocial behavior, yet one of the criteria for a diagnosis of psychopathy is repeated criminal or antisocial behavior. Accordingly, insanity due to psychopathy is not an accepted defense even if its underlying cause is as chemically-based as any other mental defect's.

Do brain scans reveal murderers who use the insanity defense to have different neurological activity than non-murderers and psychopathic murderers?

According to a study, individuals charged with murder who were found incompetent to stand trial or not guilty by reason of insanity had different neurological activity than non-murderers. Positron emission tomography scans were conducted on a sample of murderers who fit this description, and their results were compared with those from a group of control subjects of similar ages and genders who had not committed murder. The scans revealed the murderers to have significantly decreased activity in their prefrontal cortexes compared with the control group. The prefrontal cortex is responsible for regulating one's aggression, risk-taking behaviors, argumentative behaviors, impulsivity, self-control, maturity, and problem-solving skills. Significantly decreased brain activity in the prefrontal cortex compromised these behaviors and characteristics of a person, arguably making him or her more likely to engage in violent, and potentially murderous actions.

Not only did this study reveal differences between neurological activity in murderers and non-murderers, but it also discovered neurological differences between different types of murderers. An initial study demonstrated that individuals considered to be incompetent or believed to be insane when they committed their murders had decreased prefrontal cortex activity compared with non-murderers. However, criminals who committed cold-blooded murders with little or no emotion, such as psychopathic serial killers, had neurological functioning more similar to the control group than the theoretically insane murderers. The controlled, predatory murderers exhibited high prefrontal cortex activity, suggesting they were fully capable of regulating their own behavior, in these cases to commit violent homicides.

This study suggested individuals who may be found incompetent or legally insane after committing a murder may have neurological evidence to prove they have a brain abnormality that could serve as a mitigating factor in their sentencing. Juries often struggled to determine whether a person pleading not guilty by reason of insanity was actually insane, and definitive evidence of brain scans could have helped validate an individual's plea of insanity. This research also suggested there may be neurological differences among psychopathic murderers and other murderers, which could help end the debate about whether or not psychopaths suffer from a psychological disorder and should therefore not be held legally responsible for their actions. Currently, psychopathy is not considered a viable diagnosis for use in the insanity defense, and this research suggested this was the correct decision since psychopathic murderers have neurological activity similar to non-murderer humans, while insane or psychologically incompetent murderers have significantly different brain activity.

What are the implications of neurological scans detecting brain abnormalities in violent offenders?

A study of contrasting neurological activity among insane murderers, cold-blooded psychopathic murderers, and non-murderers suggested differences in prefrontal cortex activity were a correlation, and perhaps a cause, of violent activity. The study suggested insane murderers had decreased prefrontal cortex activity, while psychopathic murderers and non-murderers had higher levels of prefrontal cortex activity, allowing the sane individuals to control their actions for peaceful or violent activities. This implied that psychopathic individuals were not legally insane. A great debate involves whether psychopathic individuals should be held legally responsible for their actions when they seem to exhibit abnormal behaviors, such as lack of remorse and empathy. The study supported the argument that psychopaths should be held legally responsible for their actions because their neurological scans suggested they had the capacity to control and plan out their own actions. However, there was contrasting neurological evidence that suggested all murderers, regardless of their sanity or antisocial tendencies, had increased levels of subcortical activity. This subcortical activity predisposed individuals to exhibit more aggressive temperaments than non-murderer control subjects. If this research was able to prove an individual insane and therefore should not be held responsible for his or her actions, it seemed logical that neurological evidence showing brain abnormalities in all murderers that predisposed them to violence should be considered a mitigating factor and prevent these offenders from being legally responsible, as well.

This argument showed one of the potential problems with neurological research. If the majority of the population is found to have some sort of brain abnormality, should those who qualify not be held legally responsible for their actions? This would severely undermine the legal system, likely allowing numerous individuals to be released or civilly committed against their will. Neurological research like this could become a preventive measure against violence, requiring all individuals to be screened for brain abnormalities that have been linked with an increased predisposition to violence. These brain scans could then be used as evidence that individuals were likely to commit harm to themselves or others, which could be grounds for civilly committing them to prevent them from committing violent acts. This would be an attack against individual's human rights, suggesting it was solely brains that determine actions. This would suggest that humans lack any free will and are not responsible for actions because they were caused by brain activity beyond control. Other mitigating factors have influenced behaviors, such as environment. Therefore, exploring the influence of neurological imaging on criminal responsibility should proceed with caution.

Do psychopaths have different brain structures from non-psychopaths?

Psychopaths have impairments in many brain areas related to moral judgment. Such individuals have deficits in the dorsal and ventral regions of the prefrontal cortex, amygdala, hippocampus, angular gyrus, anterior cingulated, and temporal cortex, as was found in 2006. The researchers also noted that many of these areas overlap with brain areas known to influence moral judgments: the dorsal and ventral regions of the prefrontal cortex, the amygdala, and the angular gyrus are activated when making moral judgments and emotions. The research gave further credence to the view that psychopaths' bad behavior was due at least in part to their diminished ability to feel the emotional component in moral decisions. Though they knew the difference between right and wrong, they were not able to emotionally feel the difference. In fact, psychopaths in particular had outstanding abilities to make socially-acceptable moral decisions when asked hypothetical questions. Their problem stemmed from being unable to follow through in their personal actions.

Why might one consider making the insanity defense available to severe psychopaths but not making it available to less severe psychopaths?

A scholar argued that severe psychopaths lack moral rationality meaning they do not have the capacity to empathize with their victims and therefore do not understand the point of morality. Because they lack moral rationality, severe psychopaths only have the threat of punishment to deter them from committing crimes, whereas normal people have both moral rationality and the threat of punishment to deter them. He argued that because severe psychopaths do not have the same resources as normal people to deter them from committing crimes, the insanity defense should be expanded so that severe psychopaths can be found not guilty by reason of insanity. Less severe psychopaths, however, should not be protected under the expanded insanity defense, because they still retain a weak moral rationality and therefore have more deterrence available to them than severe psychopaths.

What is the difference between psychopathic behavior and that caused by psychosis?

In the Yates trial, psychiatric expert witness Dietz initially convinced the jury that Yates behaved in a manner characteristic of psychopathy, rather than psychosis. The distinction between these two states had important legal ramifications, as the former suggested an understanding of reality, and really implied *mens rea*, while the latter was characterized by delusion and separation from reality, making *mens rea* somewhat impossible, as the mind is separated from the actual world. It is this state that can be successfully used in pleading insanity. The *Diagnostic and Statistical Manual of Mental Disorders*

-*IV* listed nine formal psychotic disorders which were schizophrenia, schizoaffective disorder, schizophreniform disorder, brief psychotic disorder, delusional disorder, shared psychotic disorder, substance induced psychosis, psychosis due to a general medical condition, and a not otherwise specified psychosis. These categories demonstrated the central idea that psychotic individuals were expected to have mistaken or otherwise false representations of the world. Psychosis rarely causes violence, whereas psychopathic behavior is characterized by aggression, competitiveness, and lack of empathy. As the first Yates trial demonstrated, an individual characterized as a psychopath, rather than as suffering from psychosis, would fare much worse employing the insanity defense.

Given that severe psychopaths are likely to commit more crimes that are more heinous than less severe psychopaths, would it be fair for severe psychopaths to be eligible for the insanity defense and less severe psychopaths not to be eligible for the insanity defense?

A scholar argued that severe psychopaths do not have moral rationality to deter them from committing crimes, and therefore they should be eligible for the insanity defense. By implication normal people, who do have moral rationality, should not be eligible for the insanity defense. Less severe psychopaths, however, fall in the middle of the spectrum. They possess higher levels of moral rationality than severe psychopaths, but lower levels of moral rationality than normal people. Less severe psychopaths' capacity for moral rationality, while not entirely absent, is certainly impaired, and yet the scholar argued that this residual moral rationality is sufficient to qualify less severe psychopaths as members of the moral community. As members of the moral community, less severe psychopaths would be ineligible for the insanity defense. This arrangement, in which severe psychopaths are excused for their crimes and less severe psychopaths are not excused for their crimes, is likely to appear counterintuitive and unfair to the outside observer. The individuals who are least compassionate after committing a crime and most likely to commit a crime in the future could be found not guilty by reason of insanity, whereas the individuals who are somewhat compassionate after committing a crime and less likely to commit a crime in the future could be found guilty. The law, however, sees insanity as black and white. Either one is legally insane or one is not legally insane. But in reality, the mental conditions that underlie legal insanity fall along a spectrum with many shades of gray. There are not just psychopaths and normal people, or even severe psychopaths and less severe psychopaths. Rather, there are many gradations in between, and therefore many levels of guilt. Only the person with the purest moral rationality could ever be considered truly guilty for committing a crime. The truth, however, is that no one has a flawless moral capacity, and as a result it has been argued that none deserves full blame and punishment for crimes. As long as society continues to prop up a legal system based on free will in a world increasingly understood to be deterministic, many contend it will be confronted by the problem of assigning guilt to people who do not have full control over their actions. The scholar attempted to create a boundary of moral culpability between severe psychopaths and less severe psychopaths, but instead he illustrated the arbitrary nature of any such boundary of moral culpability in a world where people may not be responsible for their actions.

What characterizes the neurobiology of post-traumatic stress disorder?

Post-traumatic stress disorder is characterized by the usurpation of normal fear conditioning by an overwhelming trauma in a vulnerable person. Vulnerability can be conferred by genetics, prior experience, or by diminished hippocampal volume, some studies say. In PTSD, the amygdala becomes hyper-responsive to fear-related cues and have more difficulty habituating to fear faces. Moreover, the medial prefrontal cortex, responsible for cognitive control, is unable to suppress the normal fear response. PTSD individuals can undergo normal fear conditioning and extinction, but they have an increased recall for already extinguished fear. The disorder is difficult to diagnose, as the symptoms are often characteristic of a normal response to traumatic events, essentially, though, the difference is that they fail to abate. PTSD is basically excessive activation of the normal fear-conditioning paradigm.

What does this mean for the use of post-traumatic stress disorder as a basis of the insanity defense?

The rationale for the insanity defense is that an individual is unable to form criminal intent for a crime or does not understand the wrongfulness of his actions because of a preexisting mental condition. PTSD could very well prove a convincing basis for this defense. Individuals with the disorder essentially experience pathological fear conditioning. This may make them hyper-responsive to dangerous situations, predisposing them to react as though a situation poses more of a threat than an unaffected individual may judge is appropriate. Though this does not force them to act violently, PTSD could explain a response that would otherwise have been deemed excessive. It is important to note that PTSD, like all psychiatric illnesses, is on a spectrum-symptom severity varying quite substantially between patients. How one PTSD individual responds to a situation may not be the same as how another patient responds. Nevertheless, in certain cases, a strong argument could be made that a PTSD individual does not have the ability to accurately judge the threat posed by a situation and thus may overreact to it. If this led to criminal actions, the disorder may prove a mitigating factor.

Should a coercion defense be used for defendants who act under an irresistible impulse?

The coercion defense is generally used when a defendant had been forced to harm the victim by someone else, as, for example, if a gun had been pointed at the defendant's head. A scholar raised the question of whether addictions, undesirable sexual desires, or any so-called irresistible impulse could be considered a type of one-party coercion because the defendant could not help or control himself. He also pointed out, however, that the one-party coercion defense would be very hard put to prevail in court as it would be almost impossible to define when a person truly could control himself. The criterion for a successful two-party coercion defense is that the defendant acted as a reasonable person would, such as prioritizing his own life over someone else's. This criterion, however, cannot apply for a one-party coercion defense as reasonableness is already excluded with the idea of an irresistible impulse.

There are a few issues with allowing irresistible impulses, such as addictions or innate and perverse sexual desires, to be part of a coercion defense. There is no definitive way to decide what counts as irresistible. Every behavior is caused by a variety of internal elements including genetic disposition, past experiences, hormonal fluctuations, and so on. And people who perform awful acts as a result of irresistible impulses are dangerous to society and need to be confined, although it is possible to have that confinement be based in a psychiatric institution rather than in a prison.

How can neuroscience be used to assess future dangerousness?

A strong motive for discontinuing the use of neuroscience as evidence in criminal trials is that it relies on a specific abnormality in the brain to assess if one were insane at the time of the crime. However, neuroscience could also find an abnormality that could sway judges or jurors enough to convict or sentence a criminal if they thought that the abnormality indicated a higher likelihood of recidivism and a lower possibility of being rehabilitated. For instance, an individual on parole might never be freed if a permanent abnormality was shown in his brain. Many argue that restrictions should be placed on predicting violent and sexual crimes from neuroscientific evidence. A defect in the brain should not automatically cause detention, but could perhaps merit counseling, surveillance, and other forms of monitoring to watch a person whose brain abnormality increases the chance that he will reoffend.

Is neuroscience an effective tool for assessing future dangerousness?

It seems that any sort of brain evidence is not very helpful in assessing future dangerousness at this point. While brain scans can point out abnormalities, a criminal's behavior cannot be entirely attributed to the defect though there is a relationship between brain biology and environmental factors that influence behavior. In the event that one does have a brain abnormality, it is not always the case that that person should be considered dangerous due to that single fact. Additionally, many times too much credit is given to an enlarged amygdala or a tumor that adds pressure to some part of the brain, but it is possible that when these abnormalities do exist they have no direct connection to one's behavior at the time of a crime.

How could transcranial magnetic stimulation be used to treat the insane?

Transcranial magnetic stimulation is a technique that can be used to stimulate or inhibit precise regions of the brain using weak electric currents. It is a noninvasive procedure that can trigger brain activity with little discomfort. Triggering one area of the brain can essentially shut that area off and prevent it from contributing to brain processes like decision making. Transcranial magnetic stimulation has been suggested as a potential way to treat damaged brains in the future. A mental disorder could be treated by inhibiting the regions of the brain that cause that disorder. This could apply to the treatment of those found not guilty by reason of insanity and could be used as a way to rehabilitate them. It could also lead to changes in the way the mentally ill are perceived in the legal system, because if there were a proven treatment for criminals with mental disorders, juries might be more willing to find criminals not guilty by reason of insanity. Transcranial magnetic stimulation could also be used to make jurors more or less emotional when making decisions, which could greatly affect the outcome of trials. TMS has also been developed to suppress the areas of the brain involved in lying in order to make people less capable of lying and could act as a lie detector.

What are the moral implications of using transcranial magnetic stimulation to treat the insane?

There are many moral implications of using transcranial magnetic stimulation to treat the insane. Its use alters the brains of people in a way that leads them to act differently from the way they would naturally act. The alteration of the brain, while it could prevent criminals from committing future crimes, could also inhibit the criminals in other unforeseen ways. The technology is still very young and side effects of transcranial magnetic stimulation are not well known. Critics have argued that there is also the potential to abuse the power of transcranial magetic stimulation. There is no clear definition of what makes a normal brain, but brains that do differ substantially from the average brain may be subject to preventative treatment, even when the person has not committed any crime.

Should castration be used to help rehabilitate sex offenders?

In the past decade, the Czech Republic provided castration for ninety-four violent sex offenders, removing the tissue that produces testosterone. Castration, the Czech Republic claimed, is the most effective way to ensure that violent sex offenders will not harm any new victims. Other countries have considered adopting forms of castration including chemical castration, in which testosterone is suppressed chemically instead of physically. Many people, however, argue that castration infringes on the rights of sex offenders, and others see castration as tied in with eugenics. The question of whether not society should be able to impose castration on violent sex offenders becomes, for some, a question of whose rights are more important in the eyes of the law, the rights of the criminal or the rights of the criminal's potential victims. And yet the question is more complex than that, because the criminal's attitudes are changed by castration. They experience diminished sexual urges, and they may no longer pose a threat to society or risk imprisoning themselves. Some violent sex offenders ask for and are thankful for the release brought to them by castration. It is hard to argue that their selves are being harmed when the changes they undergo bring them healthier, safer, more enjoyable lives. Allowing sex offenders to choose between keeping their dangerous sexual urges while remaining in jail and decreasing their sexual urges while on release from jail, many argue, is not coercion. Rather, it is providing criminals with an option they did not have before. In a way, it is expanding their rights, not impinging upon them.

How would improvements in neuroscience technology have affected the use of psychological experts in the courtroom?

With the impending improvements in technology, the use of psychological experts in the courtroom was thought likely to change greatly. Under the long-standing criminal justice system, for example, multiple experts could testify in insanity cases for the defense and prosecution and potentially give conflicting conclusions on the mental status of defendants. In most cases, an expert was put on the stand because lawyers knew that he would provide testimony that accorded with their arguments. Overall, with the current resources available to psychological experts, it was quite a subjective task to decide whether someone was in control of his actions or able to tell the difference between right and wrong as in the case of the insanity defense. Some argued, however, that once technology improved, the determination of insanity would potentially become much more of a hard, objective science. Much of the subjectivity would be removed, as experts would have less leeway in interpreting the scientific facts as they presented themselves in the images of an fMRI scan for example.

Others argued however, that though individual parts of the brain might potentially only have been able to be interpreted in one way, it was possible that different psychologists might have picked out different parts of the images to attach significance to. Subjectivity would thus have remained a part of expert testimony. In the case of the use of fMRI lie detection tests there would also be the factor of inaccurate readings, as the technology had not been perfected to the point of producing total accuracy. In general, it was hard to predict exactly how expert testimony would be affected, but the availability of hard scientific evidence to back up the claims of expert witnesses was likely to add to the credibility and weight that their testimony held in the course of trials.

How did Roper v. Simmons *involve neuroscience and the law?*

The United States Supreme Court in *Roper v. Simmons* declared capital punishment unconstitutional for offenders under the age of eighteen. The case saw the submission of many neuroscience briefs. The Court used those briefs to bolster its decision that it was difficult to tell whether a youth's crime was the result of immaturity or more permanent antisocial tendencies. The leading brief was filed by the American Medical Association and partner organizations and argued that youths' brains are not fully developed in the prefrontal regions until one's early twenties. Therefore, adolescents have limited capacity to control their impulses. It wondered how then a juvenile could be held accountable for the neurological immaturity of the brain. While this specific brief was not mentioned in Justice Kennedy's majority opinion, the Justice did mention the general immaturity of youth. He mentioned that both scientific and sociological studies supported this claim. While an offhanded acknowledgement of neuroscience, clearly the filed briefs had some influence on the decision as well as Kennedy's particular opinion. *Roper v. Simmons* raised many questions about the intersection of juvenile delinquency, law, and neuroscience. The question of whether the neuroscience of the juvenile brain should perform as a mitigating factor in adolescent culpability rose to the forefront during this case.

How much should neuroscience be used in the courtroom compared to psychological testimony?

Evidence gathered from brain scans and other neuroscientific data may become critical when evaluating testimony related to the insanity defense. Scientists' knowledge of the brain may be somewhat limited, but there is valuable information. Some argue that when a defendant undergoes a brain scan and lesions or other damage is identified, that provides meaningful evidence to help a jury come to a decision. Interviews and testimony by psychologists and psychiatrists have provided a wide variety of conclusions. Yet similar to psychological testimony the current state of technology within neuroscience means a brain scan can be variously interpreted as well. The best way to approach any case may be to combine the current best practices in neuroscience and psychological expert opinion to diminish subjectivity and guess work as much as is possible.

How is the application of neuroscience to law similar to the application of the insanity defense to law?

Neuroscience findings are closely linked to the idea of the insanity defense because both seek to establish common ground between the scientific or psychological world with the legal world. The scientific or psychological world sees people's decisions as a result of complex interactions between stimuli, past experiences, and cognitive functions. The legal world explains individuals as culpable and in control of their decisions. While the legal system holds people responsible for their actions, the scientific or psychological way of thought believes that people are not wholly in control of their actions. Neuroscience research and the insanity defense are similar because they propose explanations outside of personal conscience for someone's criminal behavior.

How are religious psychotic manifestations linked to general psychosis or schizophrenia?

Imaging studies found evidence that the inferior parietal cortex plays a substantial role in both schizophrenic misattribution in psychotic patients and common religious experiences in healthy individuals. Researchers found a link between religious delusions and overactivation in the left temporal lobe and underactivation in the left occipital lobe. These findings were controversial as they pointed to a common cause for both psychotic delusions and religious experiences. However, this neurological link between schizophrenia and religious belief, along with the prevalence and frequency of religious imagery from a cultural standpoint, helped to explain religions presence as a consistent theme in schizophrenic delusions.

What are some of the recent breakthroughs in neuroscience?

Through functional magnetic resonance imaging and other methods of electrophysiology scientists know which regions of the brain are active for specific types of activities. For example, scientists have been aware of exactly where the brain does work during behavioral monitoring and emotional regulation and what happens to human emotion and reasoning if networks in these regions malfunction or become disconnected. A well-known expert in the field told of interviewing a woman with a lesion who was positive that she was being interviewed at her home in Maine, although the interview took place in New York City. Scientists have claimed to know which networks of brain regions might be responsible for inferring the thoughts of others and the important role that these processes have in social interactions. Scientists made strides in understanding how the brain maintains attention, plans actions, detects cheaters, and perceives objects and many other critical daily activities. Research continues to explore the brain's role in moral decision making and religious experience.

Have there been cases in which treatable neural deformities have been the main underlying cause of illegal behavior?

Two professionals described a case where a man's neural deformities seemed to lead directly to illegal behavior. An otherwise normal man developed a brain tumor and became addicted to sex. He collected child pornography, visited prostitutes, and made sexual advances toward his prepubescent stepdaughter. During treatment, he was unable to stop himself from making sexual advances on the nurses and female workers around him. He was perfectly aware that his actions were immoral, and he said that his desire for pleasure was greater than his ability to control himself. A brain scan showed he had an orbitofrontal tumor. The orbitofrontal cortex has been linked to hedonistic pleasures and self control. Upon its removal, his symptoms disappeared and he was allowed to live with his stepdaughter again after successfully completing a sex addicts program, which was based on Alcoholics Anonymous. A year later some of his symptoms reappeared. He began collecting pornography again. Another brain scan showed the regrowth of his tumor, which was subsequently removed. The authors did not note whether his symptoms reappeared as the study was published soon after his second tumor was removed.

Chapter 7. Free Will, Determinism, Psychology, and Legal Responsibility

Can free will as a legal assumption coexist with determinism as a psychological assumption?

As neuroscience advances and imaging studies make clear marked and significant differences in the brains of the mentally ill, it becomes increasingly clear that an assumption of equal cognitive footing that underlies free will may not be entirely sound. Psychopaths, for instance, have been found to display significant grey matter reductions in the prefrontal cortex, a region of the brain that is highly involved in social perception, explaining psychopaths' inability to empathize, for example. That said, brain science has also shown that there is a difference between proclivities and compulsions. Addictive behaviors, for example, contain a physical component as well as a psychological component, which is reflected in neural connections. Nevertheless, willpower does seem to have some influence on people's ability to stay clean and sober. It seems that neuroscience, at least for the foreseeable future, may be able to provide a deeper understanding of why mental illnesses manifest themselves the way that they do, and it may even give some clues as to the difficulty or ease of controlling behavior, but this legal and philosophical debate will still remain salient.

What is the difference between the religious belief in predestination and the principle of biological determinism?

On the most obvious level, the former is a solely religious concept, while the latter is solely biological. They both, however, espouse a force governing behavior and events in life that is not individual cognition. The religious concept is based on a belief that in creating the world, God determined its fate and the fate of the individuals who live in the world. Different faiths have variations on this concept. Some say that the fate of individual, while perhaps not determined temporally in advance, is at the whim of whatever divine power governs the world. Biological determinism, on the other hand, is based on the idea that all of our actions are rooted in our genetics. Individual differences in decision-making are seen as originating in anatomical differences. Unlike religious predestination, it is possible to alter behavioral patterns in this philosophy if physical states can be altered as with medication. Nevertheless, these two concepts can intersect and be used together quite easily, especially when genetics are seen as determined by some divine power.

Do the fMRI experiments demonstrating brain signals preceding conscious recognition of free will make free will implausible?

In several experiments regarding free will and decision-making, a signal in the brain precedes a conscious recognition of will by the actor by several seconds, demonstrating that the notion of free will is highly implausible. The signal in the brain can be seen as far as ten seconds before the conscious recognition of will, which demonstrates the failure of conscious will as a process in making decisions. Although the experiments describing the failure of free will provide examples of moments when free will can fail, the experiment contains several lapses in logic that fail to explain the intricacies of free will and decision-making.

The strongest criticism of the experiment comes from the type of decision demanded from the subjects. In the experiment, subjects are asked to push a button with either their right or left hand. The decision to push the button with a certain hand can be predicted by the fMRI several seconds before the subject consciously recognizes that the decision took place. However, this experiment only delves into simple decision-making. Choosing between the left and right hand in pushing a button hardly describes the types of decisions made every day by humans, especially in social situations. If the experiment involved more complex decisions, then the experimenters could safely posit the implausibility of free will.

Beyond the failure to recognize the simplicity of the decision, the researchers ignored the possibility of the brain signal acting as a simultaneous nomic equivalent. In other words, the brain signal could be the decision itself, even if it is unconscious. In this view, the deterministic argument for markers in the brain preceding actions of the body can be countered by arguing that the markers in the brain are the same as the decisions made by the mind.

What were the earliest clues that free will may not exist?

Many people point to the works of an American scientist as the first indication that human actions may be predetermined. His experiments were the first to tie the idea of a readiness potential, pre-motor planning of movement or action, to human volition. Essentially, his experiments suggested that the human brain determined action significantly prior to human conscious awareness of it. Thus, it is a person's brain that decides action and not his or her conscious action. Still, though his work may have been the first to provide scientific evidence against free will, determinism has been around for centuries. Many religions rely on a notion of a higher power that predetermines human action. Philosophers have long grappled with human free will. Schopenhauer famously explained that while humans can select what they want, they have no ability to manipulate their wants.

Can free will and determinism co-exist?

Studies have shown that the brain becomes aware of decisions up to ten seconds before the conscious mind registers these decisions. Many researchers have used these findings to argue that humans are deterministic beings and that free will is an illusion. However, humans also possess the sophisticated ability to veto these natural urges and, in this sense, are also governed by free will. Because the human brain is preoccupied by the notion of causality, and is equipped with the ability to imagine the future outcomes of a decision, the mind is systematically weighing its choices in order to make the most advantageous decisions. It is this perpetual anticipation of future outcomes that gives the impetus to veto the natural urges humans are unable to prevent emerging. Except for the small margin of severely handicapped individuals in which this veto power is perpetually impaired, everyone is born with the ability to foresee consequences of their own actions and exert free will over their deterministic impulses. In this sense, although human beings are subject to determinism, they still must be considered sovereigns of their own minds, free willed individuals, and held morally and legally responsible in a court of law. In the debate over whether free will or determinism guides human behavior, the conclusion is that the two are indeed co-existent and ultimately render the human mind autonomous.

What are the implications of the ability for free will to coexist with determinism?

The theory of compatibilism argues that free will and determinism both exist and are compatible with each other. The theory depends on the definition of free will. For example, a free act can be defined as an act that does not depend on compulsion by another person. Therefore, actions that are predetermined by physics and the laws of nature can still be free acts if they are not forced on someone by another person. Many philosophers believed in compatibilism. Compatibilists do not think that free will should be viewed as the ability to make a decision regardless of past experiences, beliefs, and desires, because past experiences, beliefs, and desires are essential to the decision making process. Opponents of the theory of compatibilism argue that the definition of free will used by compatibilists does not go far enough. They agree that free will implies acting without coercion, but they do not think an act that is not coerced is necessarily free. Free will for determinists is defined more strictly to imply alternate possibilities for beliefs and desires rather than fixed beliefs and desires. Some compatibilists view addiction as an internal compulsion, and thus, acts that come about as a result of this compulsion are not free acts. Insanity could also be viewed as an internal compulsion in this sense that takes away free will. If one's free will is taken away and he is compelled by some force, this limits the amount of responsibility he has for his actions. Therefore, the theory of compatibilism could imply that the insanity defense is legitimate, as long as one is being compelled by an internal force that takes away free will.

How did readiness potential affect an understanding of free will?

In the 1970s, a researcher, a pioneer in the field of consciousness, demonstrated that the brain fires electrical potentials in the motor cortex, reflecting an impending behavior, markedly before conscious reporting of a decision is possible. Essentially, this sparked questions about whether unconscious processes are the basis of what people consider volitional acts, a debate that hit at the heart of the free will versus biological determinism debate. The argument for determinism as reflected by this particular experiment is relatively clear. Actions are apparently determined by unconscious neural processes. While this may form the basis of a good argument for people on the determinism side of the debate, it is important to note that this is highly contentious. It is important to note that conscious processing may occur downstream from motor processing. It may not be the case that the decision was not made by the individual, that it was somehow the product of random electrical patterns, but rather that the process of reporting that decision takes more time. Moreover, neural connections and subsequent neural response mechanisms are shaped by previous behavior and learning situations, both of which comprise the concept of identity that people commonly espouse. Thus, even if it is in fact not cognitive control that is directly responsible for every decision, it may not mean that it is not the individual who is making a certain choice. Furthermore, this experiment did not look into the ability of the cognitive system to override an initial impulse, so this experiment really made no conclusion as to whether or not people can choose to act apart from predispositions, which is an important consideration to make when considering criminality.

In the face of determinist claims, should the ultimate aim of the justice system be deterrence, rehabilitation, or retribution?

Determinism meant that individuals could not be held morally responsible for their actions because all events were determined by causes external to the will. In other words, since individual action was determined by some externality, and not by the conscious choosing by the individual, people could not be held responsible for those actions. Some have argued that this proposition should have been extended to the justice system. They said that the ultimate aim of the legal system should have accepted determinism as a true principle and designed a system based on it. The system they therefore advocated was consequentialist, and it relied on rehabilitation of criminals, as opposed to retribution, as the ultimate aim of the justice system. Proponents of this claim argued that punishment was legitimate only insofar as it rehabilitated criminals. Others said that this argument was flawed. The ultimate aim of a justice system could not have been rehabilitation, as illustrated by a classic example. In a system wherein governments paid convicted criminals not to commit future crimes, governments could have taken the tax revenues they would otherwise be spending on prison security, for example, and instead could have redistribute that tax money to rehabilitative efforts for convicted criminals. This system might have ensured that people would not commit crimes, yet it was fundamentally flawed from a moral point of view because rehabilitation was never the ultimate end of the justice system. Yet even determinists have acknowledged that punishment can achieve deterrence. If one lived in a world where one knew the punishment for murder was a vacation, one might be more likely to murder. On the other hand, if the punishment were life imprisonment, one would be less inclined to kill. This basic proposition, the idea that pure punishment effectively deterred, was one that went uncontested by even the strongest proponents of determinism. The significant consequence of this revelation was that society had other ways to justify retribution, even in the face of determinist claims.

What are the implications for the criminal justice system if human behavior appears to be governed solely by deterministic principles?

Research seemed to suggest that human beings' sense of free will is merely an illusion. Analysis of brain scans have shown that signals are sent by the brain to begin a specific action before the conscious part of the brain is even aware that a decision to perform that action has been made. Brains in effect are determining actions instead will. At first this seems to complicate the idea that the justice system is based on the principle that each person is culpable for his or her actions. Because the brain is not an external force but the most integral part of a person, persons must claim responsibility for their decisions.

Should the law incorporate the idea of determinism?

While it may be the case that certain motor actions are governed only by a series of neurons firing, the same cannot be said of actions that require premeditation. In those situations, someone must have thoroughly contemplated the idea, giving him enough time to stop the action. Furthermore, the accuracy of predicting an action lies at about seventy percent, not nearly enough to prove that all actions are deterministic. There is still much to prove about the higher governance of actions before anyone can concretely declare that all actions are determined.

What might a more consequentialist legal system look like?

If there were no free will, then retribution as a justification for punishment would be outmoded because no one would be responsible for their actions. Accordingly, punishing someone or giving them their just deserts, would be ethically problematic, for no one morally deserves anything. Most legal systems, including the American legal system, use retribution as a reason for punishment. For instance, prisoners being executed must be able to understand the reasons why they are being killed. Only in a retributive system would the condemned need to understand why. In a consequentialist or utilitarian system, however, punishment is a tool to improve society rather than wreak vengeance. Punishment could, instead, be directed to deter future offenders, to prevent the current offenders from re-offending, and to reform as much as possible. Accordingly, a consequentialist system would dole out punishments differently. It could go in several different routes. One would be a scheme that focused on deterrence. Punishments would be severe and public to ward off other would-be criminals. Another could focus on rehabilitation and train prisoners to have marketable skills and psychologically counsel them instead of locking them in cells. The Saudis have tried this when working with terrorists. Though their motives were not related to determinism, they tried retraining and reeducating and rehabilitating former terrorists. In this light, the Saudis were practicing a consequentialist rather than retributive system, with mixed results.

What are some of the concerns related to responsibility that a lack of free will as evidenced in neuroscientific findings would raise?

The main concern has been how moral responsibility could be assigned if humans did not have free will. Recent studies have shown that the unconscious brain may form decisions as much as ten seconds before the individual becomes conscious of having made his choice. Given the heated debate surrounding issues of assigning responsibility to drug addicts, establishing as fact that neuroscience undermined the possibility of free will would no doubt have an impact on the anxiety around absolving humans of all responsibility for actions. In particular, this kind of scientific base could have ramifications in courtroom as neuroscience was incorporated into the legal system and permitted as evidence.

Assigning moral responsibility has been one of the ways in which societies function. Without responsibility, fear of chaos would loom, with the idea that all is permitted if humans were purely vehicles of a predetermined fate close at hand. The idea that responsibility cannot be assigned because all choices are predetermined would seem counterintuitive or at least counterproductive. In everyday life, whether or not an illusion, free will certainly has made each decision an individual makes seem freely made. Perhaps even if free will has been an illusion, it has been important to assigning responsibility.

In considering the consequences of such questions of free will and responsibility, the insanity defense could be destabilized. If a defendant argued that he had no free will to choose not to commit the act, a defense of my brain made me do it could be established. Crimes of passion having already been distinguished from coldly calculated crimes, the impact would be important if science asserted that no crime could be planned out exactly because the unconscious mind made its choice before that choice was consciously recognized. Further, if no one were in control of his actions, then responsibility could not be considered. Many have argued that for a time it seems best to maintain at least the feeling of free will in thinking about responsibility until there has been more substantial proof against this world view.

How do the studies on decision making and free will affect the potential incorporation of neuroscience into the legal system?

Neuroscientists have asserted that almost all decisions made about assigning moral responsibility were largely emotionally based and that furthermore gut reactions have often been in fact better than the most carefully pondered decisions. In this light, the idea of screening jurors' brains to avoid those individuals who make emotional decisions in order to achieve a more rational decision process and verdict may actually be counterproductive. In addition, the debate about free will is an important example of why the assimilation of neuroscientific evidence into legal proceedings at this time would be premature. Scientists have not agreed on how to interpret the results of the experiments being completed on the decision making process, a process critical to questions of responsibility. Without solid practical applications, the science could not be trusted for evidence because of problems with interpretation.

What effect might new findings on human capacity for free will have on the insanity defense?

The insanity defense and the court system in the United States have relied on the notion that humans had free will and control over actions as they decided to commit them. However, new research threw into dispute the idea of free will, suggesting that perhaps determinism overrode free will. Maybe humans were not demonstrably responsible for their decisions, even though in general they liked to believe in free will. Original studies on this issue revealed that a split second before a conscious decision was made, there was a brain signal that could be detected indicating the decision had been made though the decision maker was not aware of this. Later research showed that a decision in the circuitry of the brain could be detected up to seven seconds before a person said they had consciously arrived at a decision. Researchers asked participants to choose to press a button with their right or left hand, letting them freely choose when to decide, but noting when they consciously made this decision. Researchers found they could see decisions were actually made seconds before participants indicated and in a great number of cases, they could actually predict the decision as well.

These studies did not necessarily suggest that humans had no control over the resulting action and thus that people committing heinous acts should not have been able to qualify for the insanity defense. Rather, though research showed psychologists could predict the decisions of participants at a greater likelihood than chance, they could not attain one hundred percent accuracy, which suggested that decisions might have been reversible at the point of the conscious decision even if the brain has subconsciously acted before. This discrepancy between predicted decisions and actual decisions could also have been due to technological deficiencies. Perhaps with better technology, decisions could have been completely accurately predicted from these impulses coming multiple seconds before the recognition of conscious decision-making.

Some worried that this would absolve people of responsibility for all their actions, similar to the way in which the insanity defense did so in extreme cases in which a lack of control could be found in the perpetrator. Other research however suggested that even people with completely normal brain functioning, might not technically have been responsible for their actions. However, it might not have been so bad to gain an understanding of the circuitry that lead to horrible actions by individuals. This might have helped change the focus of the American law system from one that centered on punishment to one that emphasized ameliorating the actual causes of these actions. The insanity defense allowed those who were severely mentally ill and unable to demonstrate a deliberate understanding of their actions to get help. With new findings, however, perhaps a greater move would have been made to help those who make criminal decisions, focusing on the unconscious brain functioning that preceded their actions. The use of the insanity defense would not have necessarily increased, but potentially, some of the psychological aspects of treatment following a positive insanity defense verdict could have been applied to a wider variety of cases.

Is it likely that a functional legal system can be based exclusively on determinism?

As a scholar has argued, free will is only necessary in a retributive legal system, a legal system in which the goal of punishment is to give guilty people what they deserve. If instead there is a consequentialist legal system, that is, a legal system in which the goal of punishment is to have positive effects on society, then free will is not necessary for a legal system to function. Accepting the premise that there is no free will and imagining a consequentialist legal system based on determinism, then the deterministic ideas that form the foundation of the insanity defense will expand and play a larger role in how society thinks about criminality. It is more likely, however, that free will is a necessary fiction on which the retributive legal system relies, meaning that the deterministic ideas that form the foundation of the insanity defense will remain an anomaly in the legal system.

What might be one practical way to adjust the legal system under a consequentialist framework?

The insanity defense is the result of questions about whether individuals with specific mental disabilities, individuals unable to control their actions, and individuals unaware that committing a crime is wrong can be considered not guilty when they commit what would otherwise be crimes. When one begins to question whether these individuals should be considered not guilty, one might go on to question the system of law as a whole. If these individuals can be considered not guilty, other people whose actions were influenced by other forces beyond their control should arguably be considered not guilty. And since every aspect of existence as humans, from climbing the stairs to the thoughts that take place in brains, follows the physical laws of the universe, everyone is influenced, in all actions, by forces beyond control. One could argue from this that none should be considered morally responsible or guilty for his actions.

If determinism nullifies personal guilt, it seems that society must question the retributive law system. It does not seem right to punish criminals for crimes when guilt can ultimately be diffused across the entire universe or, very minimally, to the other individuals in the criminal's life and their socioeconomic status. Perhaps it should not be a retributive system which punishes people based on what they have done in the past, but rather a consequentialist system, which also takes into account the effect their punishment will have on the world in the future. A retributive system is, in many ways, implicitly consequentialist in that it punishes people for the good of society. Perhaps it would be more fair to individuals to make the system more explicitly consequentialist, relieving them of personal guilt and adjusting the way in which they pay restitution to society for their crimes.

One mechanism for this consequentialist payback to society might be restorative justice. Restorative justice is based on the concept that crimes are committed not against the state, but against the community, and therefore instead of being jailed even executed, criminals should be made to heal the harm done to the community. This begins in many cases with a face-to-face mediation between the criminal and the victim of the crime in which apologies are made and accepted and both criminal and victim are humanized in each other's eyes. In some cases victims can make the choice between jail time and direct service to the victim. Restorative justice has been shown to increase rates of victim and criminal satisfaction with the justice system as well as reduce recidivism rates for criminals. This is just one way to envision a system of law that does not ignore the events of the past but also considers how those events might best be understood to improve the future.

In order to create a penal system that reflects the absence of free will, is it necessary to convince all people of the absence of free will?

Many say it is not. Even if, as is likely, most people continue to deny full determinism in the face of increased scientific evidence, the penal system can still be altered in ways that respect that not all criminal behavior is the result of free choice. People unwilling to accept full determinism may be willing to accept the importance of situational factors such as education and socioeconomic status in determining whether or not a person commits a crime. As evidence of the strength of these situational factors increases, people may be willing to consider ways of dealing with criminals that not only punish them for their crimes, but also attempt to address the underlying situational factors that may have led them to commit their crimes.

When situating juvenile delinquency in the debate between free will and determinism, should juveniles be tried as adults in court?

The *Frontline* documentary, *Juvenile Justice,* provided accounts of the conflicting opinions of members of the legal system regarding whether or not to try certain juvenile offenders in adult or juvenile court. In its essence, the debate hinged on whether juveniles were fit for rehabilitation in the juvenile system. Therefore, in confronting the question of whether a particular juvenile belonged in adult court, the juvenile underwent a fitness hearing. Probation officers evaluated whether the juvenile could be rehabilitated and prepared a fitness report, which was then presented to the judge. Whether the juvenile was fit to remain in the juvenile justice system was contingent on a number of criteria. First, the degree of criminal sophistication of the juvenile was considered. Second, the success of past attempts at rehabilitation by the juvenile justice system was assessed. Next, the judge considered the sufficiency of the jurisdictional time that the juvenile court had as well as the juvenile's history of delinquency. Last, and most important, the circumstance and gravity of the offense the minor was charged with was taken into account. If the juvenile was charged with a violent crime, being found unfit under one of the criteria automatically deemed the juvenile unfit for juvenile consideration. The minor was transferred to the adult court. If, however, the juvenile was not charged with a violent offense, all criteria were weighed and the judge considered whether the juvenile was fit to remain in the juvenile justice system based on a holistic analysis. After such consideration, the judge decided to either move the juvenile into adult court or allowed the child to remain under the supervision of the juvenile justice system.

The most extreme proponents of determinism argued that all juveniles should be tried in adult court as their actions were not only determined but also reflective of crimes to come. If free will was eradicated, than so too was the hope for offenders to rehabilitate and overcome their determined life paths as career criminals. However, those who accepted free will would argue that all juveniles should remain in the juvenile justice system. There, if one had free will, rehabilitation was a necessary and possible correction for antisocial behavior. Altering criminal behavior was convincing youth offenders to exercise their free will in safer and more appropriate ways. In sum, the determination of whether a juvenile was fit to remain in the juvenile justice system or should be transferred to the adult system, was largely contingent on whether one believed in the concept of free will or the philosophy of determinism.

When does one individual's responsibility for an event end and another person's responsibility for that event begin?

Questions arise about the standards in law used to determine how far back one must follow a chain of events in order to determine who is guilty and about how the, law limits the number of different parallel or interlocking chains of events that are considered in a case. The conception of a chain of events is itself flawed as an explanation of causation for causation is more like a web of infinitely interconnected events that all influence each other. Law must filter out the many small factors that affect a crime from all sides and at many different points in time. Finally, the question arises as to whether it is fair to assign guilt to one individual whose actions are the product of so many endless influences.

Did a description of the lack of free will point to a substantial change concerning the culpability of criminals?

It has been argued that the theory of free will should not be removed completely because of neuroscience discoveries that implied that the unconscious brain has already begun carrying out an action before the conscious brain made the decision to do so. Instead, it has been contended that free will needed to be redefined, to a definition that retained moral responsibility for actions because the notion that no one has personal control of his ultimate actions was absurd. Some have noted that the subconscious brain reacts before the brain has consciously made a decision, but nonetheless determinism and free will can coexist. In that sense free will has veto power. Some have argued that free will was present when some decided to either continue the action that the unconscious brain started or decided to veto it and alter the action, thus consciously deciding on a course of action. That kind of description did not remove culpability from criminals. Although criminals might not have been consciously in control of their actions when the initial synapses began, researchers argued that the individual had a point at which he consciously decided to continue the illegal action. Since there was a point when the criminal could have either gone down the right path or the wrong path, and knowingly chose the wrong path, he would still be found culpable since he consciously knew the difference between right and wrong.

To what extent can addictive drugs affect free will?

Some researchers argued that addictive drugs have neurological effects that disallow individuals to make conscious choices between one course of action and alternatives. In studies of people under the influence of an addictive drug, dopamine marked the experience as highly enjoyable and guided future behavior towards using the substance again to obtain the same feeling. After extended use, drug-seeking became an individual's priority, above making normal rational choices. They argued that free will is eliminated under the influence of addictive drugs because the brain redirected behavior to seeking more drugs at all costs. In terms of insanity, the limits of free will could be evident because many criminal offenders who pled not guilty by reason of insanity were users of addictive drugs, including alcohol which can limit rational behavior. Additionally, many criminal offenders had mental disorders that required strong medications which could lead to additional drug seeking behavior beyond normal behavior, even if acquiring a drug involved criminal activity. So, to some extent, the actions might not be attributable to free will when under the influence of addictive drugs or while performing drug seeking behavior, one has failed to see the seriousness of his crime or to know the difference between right and wrong. Others, however, especially a psychologist and a psychiatrist, strongly argued that what has been termed addiction is actually a disorder of choice. In attacking the medicalization of substance use, abuse, and dependence, they reintroduced concepts of free will and of voluntariness.

If what is experienced as free will is an illusion, then how should society reform the way it punishes people for their crimes?

If what is experienced as free will is an illusion, then individuals are not morally responsible for their crimes. If they are not morally responsible for their crimes, then a lack of moral responsibility for crimes can no longer justify the punishment received for crimes. If moral responsibility for crimes can no longer justify punishment then it seems there are but two just options. One is to cease to punish for crimes. The other is to continue to punish for crimes, but to justify that punishment for crimes on a basis other than moral responsibility.

Choosing the first option and ceasing to punish individuals for their crimes would remove disincentives to commit crimes and remove opportunities to reform criminals. If the law removes disincentives to commit crimes and removes opportunities to reform criminals, then crimes will increase, and it is probable that overall utility will decrease. Using a utilitarian framework, a decrease in overall utility is undesirable and therefore the first option, that is, ceasing to punish for crimes, is an undesirable response to the fact that moral responsibility can no longer justify the punishment individuals receive for their crimes. Choosing the second option and continuing to punish for crimes, then the law must justify the punishment of individuals for crimes on a basis other than moral responsibility for crimes. Using a utilitarian framework, the law can justify punishment for crimes on the basis of increased utility. The punishment for crimes increases utility by providing disincentives to commit crimes and opportunities to reform criminals. However, justifying the punishment for crimes on the basis of increased utility requires that the law reform the way individuals are punished for crimes. The law must view punishment not as the just reward for criminal behavior, but rather as a tool with which to address the conditions which led to the current criminal behavior and prevent future criminal behavior. When punishment is not an end in itself but rather a means to an end, the law is forced to evaluate which punishments most effectively reform criminals and provide sufficient disincentives for would-be criminals. Further, if what individuals experience as free will is an illusion, the argument over capital punishment ceases to be an argument about whether criminals deserve to die for certain crimes and becomes solely an argument about whether criminals dying for certain crimes decreases the incidence of crime. Numerous studies have debated whether or not capital punishment significantly deters crime, and the results are unclear. Because the results are unclear as to whether capital punishment significantly deters crime, it is unclear whether capital punishment should continue to exist. The law should examine whether the extremely large amounts of money spent on capital punishment could be used in other ways, for example, criminal rehabilitation, youth job training, even early childhood education, that would decrease the incidence of crime more than capital punishment.

How is juvenile delinquency a product of both free will and determinism?

Some criminologists have argued that adhering to solely the free will view or solely the determinism view overlooked the possibility that juvenile delinquents were committing crimes as a result of the interaction of free will and determinism. Free will itself, according to those criminologists, was influenced by a multitude of factors including societal laws, social norms, and economic incentives. Moreover, free will was undoubtedly influenced by the individual characteristics of the offender. However, while offenders would, through free will, choose to commit crimes, situational factors would also influence criminal actions.

Some criticized hard determinism, which deemed all criminal behavior to be pre-determined. Moreover, such hard determinism presented criminal activity as a merely unavoidable consequence of the youth's upbringing and other circumstantial influences such as biological, sociological and psychological factors. The major criticism of hard determinism was in the philosophy's tendency to essentially overpredict real delinquency rate. Therefore, it was said, such hard determinism distorted the rate of youth offending as well as the behavioral nature of the offenders. Juvenile offenders did exhibit patterns of rehabilitation that explicitly clashed with the idea of criminality as a permanently determined characteristic. Youth who exhibited sporadic offending were a prime example of the problematic nature of determinism in juvenile delinquents. In place of the rejected hard determinism some offered the philosophy of soft determinism. That account of determinism allowed for a degree of free will or control over one's criminal actions, while stating that juveniles were neither entirely able to act on free will alone nor entirely determined in their actions by the past or current circumstances. The philosophy of soft determinism rendered the juvenile offender adrift. In effect, the juvenile's delinquent acts were not entirely determined or entirely chosen on account of free will, but instead adrift between the two states.

Is conscious deliberation in decision making always preferable?

Researchers discovered that individuals tended to make smarter consumer choices when distracted and thus unable to consciously deliberate and thoroughly inspect their choices beforehand. Researchers noted that the more multi-faceted a problem, the better the unconscious brain determined the solution. This research suggested that the unconscious human brain may be a better decision-maker than the hyperanalytical conscious mind. Moreover, common experiences have shown that oftentimes overthinking can induce stress and be ultimately more detrimental than helpful in such tasks as driving, playing music, and competing in sports. However, though the benefits of conscious deliberation may be somewhat illusory, this theory cannot possible apply to all decision-making. Social psychological research has shown that under the same distracting conditions in a study, stereotyping of strangers increased by a significant degree. Without time to consciously deliberate, individuals were more likely to oversimplify, exaggerate, or demean another individual based solely on unconscious prejudices about that person's race, gender, religion, ethnicity, socioeconomic class, disability, occupation. Therefore, while the unconscious brain may outdo the conscious mind in the choosing a vacation destination or riffing on a guitar, this research cannot be generalized to interpersonal decision making. Accepting the theory in this arena would essentially encourage racial, gender-based, and religious stereotyping and decrease the moral responsibility of individuals to consciously veto these deterministic impulses.

Chapter 8. Jurors and Psychologists and Lawyers in Two Mock Trials

What were the mock trials which were based in some part on the real case of Brett Reider and of his mother?

Members of the seminar who contributed to this volume participated in two mock trials based on the case of Brett Reider. The basic facts of Reider's killing his mother, as presented in his sister's *Family Video Diary* on HBO, were preserved, but for mock trial purposes some fictional materials were added to allow for two trials, two sets of psychological experts, two sets of lawyers, and two jury deliberations.

What were the basic facts of Brett Killed Mom?

Brett Reider, fifteen at the time, stabbed his mother to death after she began hitting him because of a low mark he had received that day on a quiz in school and after he first stunned her with a stun gun he had brought home with him. A boy who had befriended Brett and sympathized with him and who, with Brett, had talked about killing her and who encouraged Brett's use of the stun gun testified against Brett. Charged with first degree murder, Brett was convicted of second degree murder, involuntary manslaughter, and sentenced as an adult to eleven to twenty years in prison. Three years afterward, his older sister, Alissa, made a documentary she called *Brett Killed Mom*, which was shown on HBO as part of its *Family Video Diary* series. In discussions with him at the institution where he was confined, and with her father, their Mom's sister, and a few of the boys who were his friends and knew of the abuse but said nothing, all those interviewed agreed that his Alissa and Brett, but especially Brett, had suffered constant abuse for many years from their Mom, Claudia. Not only did Mom verbally and psychologically demean Brett despite his great academic and athletic and personal successes, but she often hit and kicked him. At Brett's first opportunity in 1999, he was paroled. The documentary is often shown on HBO.

What were the procedures followed in the two mock trials?

In the seminar, to allow for two different trials, one focusing on a possibility of civil commitment for Mom if that topic had arisen and the other on criminal responsibility of Brett, some fictitious elements were added to the case. Everyone in the class participated in either a legal or a psychological capacity. Those who legally argued and psychologically testified for Mom's commitment in the first trial then legally argued and psychologically testified for Brett's lack of criminal responsibility in the second trial. Those who argued and testified for Mom's freedom in the first trial then argued and testified for Brett's criminal responsibility in the second trial. After both trials, all contributors were assigned to two six-person juries, one to deliberate each case. Each jury included members from both sides of the case. As much as possible, jurors served with different members for each jury. The six-person juries were comprised of three from one side of the case and three from the other. Juries were then remixed for the second trial.

What materials were added to Mom's case to permit a trial for her civil commitment to a mental hospital?

To permit the first trial on whether Mom should be involuntarily civilly committed to a mental hospital, some psychological diagnoses and materials were added to show her suffering from borderline personality disorder, others to show bipolar disorder, still others to show schizophrenia. Most of the mock trial psychological experts additionally testified that she referred to religious themes and images in many of her demeaning comments about Brett, constantly referring to Brett as the Devil, saying he was not really her son but the son of Satan. It was also added that Mom mentioned a religious figure she had been reading about and had met at gathering in the town who spoke of damnation and of her need to chastise her children. Mom's lawyers in her trial argued she was not civilly committable. Lawyers for the hospital where she had been initially evaluated argued that she was dangerous by reason of mental illness and should be committed. They added that her religious preoccupations and her talk of death and resurrection made the situation even more perilous. Finally, some psychological experts testified that she was religiously preoccupied and troubled but not seriously mentally ill. The standard for civil commitment used in the mock trial was the Massachusetts General Law which permitted commitment of an individual where there was a likelihood of serious harm, to himself or others, by reason of mental disorder. Lawyers had material supporting their initial questioning and their cross examining.

What materials were added to Brett's case to permit possible verdicts of not guilty by reason of insanity as well as of murder and of manslaughter and of not guilty?

To permit the second trial to include the possible verdict of not guilty by reason of insanity, which was not argued in the actual trial, in addition to the possibilities of guilty of murder, guilty of manslaughter, or not guilty, some psychological experts were added who diagnosed Brett at the time of the stabbing as suffering from post-traumatic stress disorder. Others were added who testified that he was suffering from battered child syndrome, others that he was suffering from psychotic depression, and others that he was acting in self-defense based on his mother's past battering of him. Some experts testified that he was not mentally ill but simply in a rage at the time of the stunning and the stabbing, and that he felt he had a pact with the other boy to carry through on their plan though the other boy was not present at the time. His lawyers argued for a verdict of not guilty by reason of insanity. The prosecution argued for a verdict of murder or at least of manslaughter. The standard for insanity used in the mock trial was the M'Naghten test.

What were the jury deliberations in the two cases?

After both trials concluded, the six-person jury deliberations began for each of the two cases. Everyone participated on two juries, one to decide whether Mom should be civilly committed, the other to decide Brett's criminal responsibility for killing his mother. Jurors were instructed on the law and were told not to take a vote immediately but to give everyone a chance to discuss the case before tallying the jurors' votes. Comments after jury deliberations provided a useful perspective on the group processes that were at work and on the verdicts that were reached. Unlike real juries, everyone knew that all the jurors had been taking the same course on *The Insanity Defense*, that all the jurors were Harvard students though from different backgrounds but with similar institutional experiences, and that all had studied the same materials and examined the same psychological and legal issues. And yet, what surprised almost everyone was that the juries reached different conclusions. Students reflected their surprise at this development in their written comments following the trials. Next are excerpts from their comments following the deliberations.

What were some of the juror comments following the deliberations?

1. The mock trials were a great way to think practically about the lessons learned over the course of the semester. Reading case studies

and coming up with critical discussion questions and answers is very informative, but putting it to use required creativity.

2. The mock trials were a very enjoyable class experience and I thought they showed the class first hand what can happen within the process of law. The juries reached a variety of verdicts and I thought this happened for a few reasons. First, time was limited. Second, much of the evidence presented in the trial was subjective and presented from Brett's and his sister's perspectives so that many of the jurors were confused as to what exactly happened between Brett and his mother and what conditions existed leading up to the killing. The case picked for the trial was a very good one in the sense that there were two different trials to decide and nothing seemed to be cut and dried in terms of culpability rulings. Everyone came fairly well prepared and seemed to understand the case so that stances could be adapted as the trial went on. Overall, a success and recommended for future classes.

3. The mock trials were really enjoyable. The most intriguing part was the different verdict that the juries came up with. For Brett especially, I thought everybody would commit him to some type of rehabilitative program because from the trial, it appeared rather obvious that he had been severely abused by his mother and although he had thought about murdering her, in fact he killed her in a blind rage. I was surprised to learn that one of the groups rendered a verdict of guilty of murder. More discussion of their reasoning and of the dispositions of Mom's and Brett's cases would have been of use.

4. The trials were instructive and informative. I think we got a good idea of the influence of the testimony by expert witnesses in criminal trials. The evidence and arguments presented in this portion of each trial greatly influenced the jury deliberations I was a part of. I also realized the effect jury deliberation can have on influencing the opinions of jurors as in both trials I witnessed other jurors changing their opinions on the cases. Finally, though I had already somewhat considered the complexity of the cases obviously, especially in the case of Brett, I came to see just how complex a decision making process the jury can be asked to go through. With the Brett trial, there was so much grey area that we were asked to deal with. Mom

and Brett cases are especially good cases. I really enjoyed the mock trail and it seemed like everyone else did as well!

5. The mock trials provided a great opportunity to test our knowledge of the legal applications of the insanity defense and civil commitment statute. The divided juries were clearly able to deliberate in a near-objective way, providing a realistic outcome to the trial. For the next mock trial, I would set a simple list of evidence from which attorneys can base their claims. Some material which would have been useful in my decision making included whether or not Brett's Mom administered her beatings in public as for example our jury did not decide whether the road in which she did beat him was heavily occupied or completely empty. To some that would have made a difference.

6. The cases discussed were great for learning about the interaction between psychology and law and how the insanity defense might come into play. I also think it was very interesting that the juries decided on different verdicts.

7. The most interesting part about the mock trials was seeing how three different juries can arrive at very different results despite having heard the same evidence. It just goes to show how important jury selection is because no matter how objective people try to be they cannot help carrying their own personal beliefs and principles into the jury room.

8. The mock trials were a great experience. I really enjoyed applying the principles about which we had been learning, and hearing the various opinions held by my classmates, particularly in jury deliberations. Preparing for the trial put the cases we had read about into new perspective, and for me, acting as a lawyer, first for the prosecution and then for the defense, coordinating with the other lawyers and experts revealed the difficulties of attempting to work with others toward a common goal. Working out the right questions to ask experts from both sides to highlight only the position held by my side was quite a challenge, but introduced me effectively to a new form of thinking. Having the opportunity to participate in the mock trial process was fascinating and opened new possibilities to consider.

9. The mock trials were a great success. Much of the semester was spent on the theoretical legal and psychological aspects of the insanity defense, but it helped to see how it is all put to use in the courtroom. Being forced to decide peoples' fate also added a new dimension to my understanding of the administration of the defense. Additionally, I began to imagine how typical non-Harvard juries who had not spent time understanding the insanity defense would have trouble dealing with such complex issues in deliberation. In all, the simulation was a great addition to more ordinary class material.

10. The mock trials were particularly interesting on account of everyone stepping into their roles with such zeal and creativity. I found it most interesting that my opinion rarely aligned with the law. For example, I felt as though Mom deserved to be sent to prison and have her children taken away from her, not that she had a mental disorder. However, the requirements for civil commitment clearly stated that if a person were posing a substantial danger to themselves or others due to a mental disorder there were grounds for civil commitment. I simply did not think the evidence proved Mom had a mental disorder of any kind, other than being heartless and mean, but I found the overall experience of the trial and the combination of actual and fictional evidence to be rather intriguing.

11. I was most interested by the variance in outcomes for both trials. It seemed interesting that three groups of people, having watched the same video diary and having taken the same seminar and read and discussed the same materials, could come to different unanimously agreed on conclusions when divided into juries. Particularly in the second trial, I would have thought that every jury would have been more lenient toward Brett since his sister's documentary, which we had all watched, had been sympathetic to his situation. Yet one group replicated the exact sentence given to Brett, while the other two delivered much lesser sentences. It is interesting and a bit disconcerting that juries can reach such unanimously different verdicts so easily, which alters the outcome of a person's life. And we were a group of Harvard students in a seminar with presumably more similar experience than a trial jury.

12. The mock trial was a really great time and a chance to get a further glimpse of the personalities of everyone in the class. I also

thought it allowed us to really interact with the material and learn it in an integrated and participatory way. Regardless of where you came in to the trial, working on your portion of it over the week forced you to have a strong opinion which made deliberating the verdict quite a challenge, further proof at the, dare I say, craziness that is our current legal system. I think we may have benefited from having two separate trials and primarily participating in them in different capacities. One of the difficulties others and I faced was that the documentary and materials were primarily from family members who were sympathetic to Brett. A more objective presentation would have been good, but one of the issues often raised is that there really is no objective presentation in an adversary system of justice where each side is strongly arguing its position. Perhaps I was naively asking too much.

13. Most interesting was the struggle that ensued for the trial of Brett. Our jury group had a very difficult time deciding on the verdict, feeling that he did not really exactly fit first degree murder, manslaughter, or not guilty by reason of insanity. Furthermore, even when we tabled that decision and tried to decide based on his crime what sort of punishment he should receive, we still could not decide. We mostly felt that he had to do some prison time just because he killed someone even though we did not think he qualified for murder. Brett's trial was one of those cases where the easy way out of guilty but mentally ill would have been a nice option which would make the jury feel like they were still saying that Brett had done something wrong, and that it was somewhat the result of mental illness. And therefore that he should not receive a severe punishment due to all of his signs of mental illness.

14. It was fun to work together to come up with a strategy for our side. It was also a nice way to have all the components of a trial come together. Those who were more psychologically invested were great at helping everyone with Mom's disorders, and those more legally invested were able to argue their and their experts' views.

15. I thought that the mock trials were a good lesson in the ways in which the insanity defense would actual play out in a court of law. I thought it was effective that everyone committed to their roles and

made their best effort to argue for their side regardless of their actual feelings about the trial.

16. During the mock trails, I was most surprised at the varied verdicts of the juries. There was such variety, two juries civilly committing Mom and one jury even wanting to criminally charge her, and each jury delivering a different verdict for Brett. The differences seemed to be an interesting reflection on the American legal system itself. Each of the jurors heard the exact same evidence, yet, depending on which individuals were grouped together and the particular dynamics of personal opinion and group interaction, varying verdicts were rendered. What was so disturbing about this microcosmic realization was that juries, who essentially hold the lives of the defendant in their hands, are unpredictable and unique. Evidence presented to a group of people is absorbed and processed differently by each individual and the result of this can mean the difference between a defendant simply being placed on parole and being sent to prison for life.

17. The mock trials experience made me realize how important it is in making an argument to argue logically, have a plan for what you are saying, predict what any responses to what you are saying will be, and know how react to those responses such that you stick to your argument. The experience made me realize how much who wins and loses in a court situation depends on so many arbitrary factors not related to the case itself, most notably the ability and preparedness of the lawyers.

Chapter 9.   The Insanity Defense Standard

Among the Harvard contributors to this volume there was a wide array of answers to the questions about the insanity defense standard. Those answers are here grouped by overall question and then by similarity of response. While there seemed to be greater unanimity concerning some of the questions, there was also significant variety with others despite the fact that all contributors studied the same materials, experienced the same issues concerning the insanity defense, participated in research and in a mock trial, and generated, answered, discussed, and shared large numbers of questions. The four questions concerned what the insanity defense standard should be, whether there should be guilty but insane or guilty but mentally ill verdicts, what the role of religion should be in assessing criminal responsibility, and what the relation of the insanity defense to those charged with terrorism should be.

What should the insanity defense standard be?

American Law Institute, Model Penal Code test

1. It would not be just to have no insanity defense, because that would require fully punishing a defendant for an act he did not know was wrong or could not control himself from committing. The M'Naghten

test and M'Naghten test narrowed are unjust because the degree to which a defendant must misunderstand the difference between right and wrong is so severe that the test is almost impossible to pass. The M'Naghten test and M'Naghten test narrowed also make no allowance for mental disease or defect or reference to the ability of the defendant to control his actions. The ALI test recognizes that certain defendants may lack substantial capacity to control their actions or appreciate the criminality of their conduct, and it notes that this lack of substantial capacity may result from mental disease or defect. The ALI test is the only test that sufficiently allows for the very real inability of certain people to fully understand and control their actions.

2. This test states that a person is not responsible for his behavior if he lacks sufficient capacity due to mental illness either to understand the criminality of his conduct or to conform his conduct to the law. This test thus acknowledges that someone can recognize what is right from what is wrong, as does the M'Naghten test, and still be so mentally deficient that he should not be held responsible for his criminal actions. For example, in the Ralph Tortortici case, the jury ruled that Tortortici was guilty because he had an awareness that holding students hostage was wrong. They ignored, however, the fact that he was having severe paranoid delusions about a vast governmental conspiracy and felt his actions were the only way to reveal that conspiracy. In that case, even though Tortortici could differentiate between right and wrong and understand the criminality of his conduct, he did not have the sufficient mental capacity to conform his conduct to the law and should not have been held responsible for his actions but rather treated for his schizophrenia.

3. This test was much broader than the M'Naghten Test and came under more scrutiny after the Hinckley trial. The biggest difference between the two standards was the ALI's wording that a defendant qualifies for the insanity defense if he lacked substantial capacity to understand the criminal nature of the act. The M'Naghten Test was much stricter, requiring that the defendant was completely unaware of what they were doing or was completely unaware of the difference between right and wrong in regards to the act. The M'Naghten Test was difficult in such cases as Andrea Yates, where the defendant was

aware of the nature of she was doing and that what she was doing was wrong. The ALI's wording allowed a defendant to qualify for the insanity defense even if his mental illness did not completely eliminate his awareness or reasoning ability.

4. This test makes the most sense because it would only punish those morally responsible for crimes. An alternate standard which lacks the mental defect prong would be unfair because a person has no control over the composition of their brain. Any statute which punishes people for something over which they have no control and did not choose would thus be unfair. The Model Penal Code test eliminates prosecutions for crimes over which we can exert no control and thus relieves it of moral infirmity.

5. This standard allows more individuals to use the insanity defense successfully. This standard is more complete than the M'Naghten test standard. The M'Naghten test required an individual not know what he was doing, or not understand the action was wrong. This meant that individuals like Andrea Yates, who drowned her children to save them from Satan, would not be legally insane. According to the law, she knew what she was doing, which was killing her children, and she knew it was wrong, as determined by the fact she called the police and reported her crime. However, her mental illness caused her to hear voices and believe her children would be better off dead than living on this planet. There should be an exception for individuals like Andrea Yates, who was clearly mentally disturbed when she killed her children, but would not qualify as legally insane because of the strict standards of the M'Naghten test as she did not in her first trial. But she did on the retrial for the reasons explored elsewhere in this volume. The insanity defense standard should be more liberal because individuals who are mentally ill need actual treatment, not simply to be punished in prison. There must, therefore, be a policy with broader standards to allow for these individuals to receive both the help and consequences they deserve.

M'Naghten test

1. This test combined broad language that did not limit insanity to certain mental disorders with specific language that protected against

abuses of the defense. The success of this combination stemmed from the two prongs of the test. A defendant needed to not understand the nature and quality of the act or that the act was wrong. If the defendant did understand the nature and quality of the act in a physical and natural sense, then he would not qualify for the defense. Likewise, the defense required a person to understand the wrongness of the act committed. By requiring this in the defense, the M'Naghten test created a system that would allow for mental disorders to account for crimes if and only if the person did not understand that the crime they committed was wrong. A person, for example, could have killed a person under the delusion that it was a martian, but still not qualify for the defense if he understood that the act was wrong in a legal sense. This qualifier demanded more than just a mental disorder, and protected from abuses of the defense while protecting the mentally ill from wrongful prosecution.

2. The M'Naghten test is the best way of classifying sane and insane criminals. By forcing the defendant to prove that he did not know the nature and quality of his act or that it was wrong, the line is clearer between the sane and the insane defendant. *Clark v. Arizona* attempted to narrow the insanity defense by excluding this first prong of the M'Naghten test. But this rendered the defense inadequate. If the defendant could not comprehend the action he committed, a guilty verdict would be meaningless and punishment would be nonsensical and ineffective. If the defendant truly did not believe the act was wrong, or it to be wrong in the context of societal rules and obligations, punishment is again purposeless. The American Law Institute's Model Penal Code test is overbroad, and therefore inadequate. That standard is too inclusive. An inability to appreciate the full extent of the criminality of an act should not negate the culpability of a defendant who knew that his action was wrong and was able to comprehend its nature. Committing an act that one knows is wrong begs for criminal responsibility.

3. The American legal system is built on the assumption that individuals have free will and that their decisions are a result of that free will. An insanity defense allows for the possibility that this might not always be the situation, and the two prongs of this test are both necessary and sufficient to challenge this assumption in appropriate

cases. The ALI, on the other hand, is broader in its wording, requiring only substantial impairment rather than absolute impairment as in M'Naghten, and therefore leaves more room for malingering.

4. It is important that the M'Naughten test includes the inability to understand the nature of acts and not just a right or wrong test, because mental illness can cause inability to appreciate actions even when the defendant was fully conscious of whether society would consider the act morally right. In other cases it is also important to separate society's consideration of moral rightness from a defendant's view that a higher power or god was instructing them thus making the act one of moral rightness. In that instance, the line indicating what is right becomes blurred and an action, no matter how malevolent, might be protectable by insanity since the actor could not separate what society considered right and what he perceive as religious rightful guidance.

5. The insanity defense was introduced to help protect people from the law, specifically those who, due to a serious mental illness, could not be held accountable for their actions, regardless of how horrific they were. It seems the most glaring error in applying the insanity defense has become its overextension. It has received unfavorable attention, perceived as a way for criminals to escape their punishment. Yet, especially in the case of gruesome acts, society has become confused about it. Many people assume that no sane person could ever have committed horrific acts and thus assume that the perpetrator must be insane by default. But the question is not whether he is normal, but what his state was when the act was committed, more specifically whether he knew the act was wrong at that moment. Thus, the M'Naghten test is the best for establishing legal insanity. Even, or especially, psychopaths who commit crimes for years without getting caught would recognize that society considered the acts criminal though he did not. That realization was different from the view of another individual who simply could not process that his acts were wrong at the time committed.

6. Most states have chosen to follow the M'Naghten rules. Compared to the more narrowed version of that test, the M'Naghten test seems to be the most just means of dealing with individuals who arguably lack the criminal intent needed for one to receive

criminal punishment. In the one-pronged formulation of this rule applied in the case of *Clark v. Arizona*, which ignored the relevance of the defendant's not knowing the nature of his act, the defense was prohibited from introducing evidence demonstrating that Clark believed he was shooting Martians and not police officers. As a result, Clark, a diagnosed paranoid schizophrenic, was sentenced to life in prison, demonstrating that, as critics of the decision pointed out, if a person believes he is squeezing a lemon, but it turns out to be his sister, then that fact should be allowed as evidence to indicate the defendant's mental illness. In the less narrowed version of these rules, the state has irrationally and unjustly excluded this type of evidence, making the broader M'Naghten test the ideal baseline for the insanity defense.

7. The insanity defense standard should be based on the M'Naghten test. It is important that the insanity defense not be abolished. The M'Naghten test, already widely used, is the best of the tests. The traditional two-pronged approach to determining insanity is important in allowing consideration of mental state without being overly lax in standards for the definition of insanity. The test is best when the defendant bears the burden of proof as an affirmative. Although M'Naghten has been criticized for being overly restrictive, its purpose is to effectively exclude those who would otherwise use the defense as a loophole in the legal system through which to avoid criminal responsibility for their conduct. The other tests under consideration for determining legal insanity may each be ruled out in something approaching a Goldilocks test, leaving the M'Naghten as just right. The American Law Institute Test is too broad and may allow criminals to escape punishment. Narrowing the M'Naghten test may result in sentencing that is too harsh for those who legitimately did not understand the nature of the acts they committed even if they did know right from wrong at the time of the acts.

8. The insanity defense should only be used in extreme cases, or it will lose its validity. The stringent qualities of the M'Naghten test make this an appropriate measure of insanity. While it is not easy for a lawyer to successfully argue this defense for a client, it is still possible in extreme cases, which are the cases the insanity defense should be reserved for in the first place. If not the M'Naghten test,

then the American Law Institute test is the next most appropriate test of insanity. While this test is a more lenient than the M'Naghten test, it is still effective in assuring that in most cases only those that are truly deserving can successfully argue the insanity defense. A test any more lenient would only serve to discredit the insanity defense. Further, the insanity defense should absolutely not be abolished. While there have been highly controversial cases in which it was successfully argued, the defense is only successfully argued, for the most part, in cases in which the defense exhaustively proves that a defendant was mentally incapacitated to the point of insanity. Most criminals deserve to be punished for their crimes, but the insanity defense plays a role in those extreme cases in which perpetrators should not be held responsible for their actions.

M'Naghten test narrowed, as in Clark v. Arizona

1. The emphasis of the narrowed M'Naghten test on whether the defendant knew what he was doing was wrong makes the test fit best with the American legal system. The original two-pronged M'Naghten test is too broad, as it allows a criminal who committed a crime he knew was wrong to escape punishment if he can prove he did not know the nature and quality of the act he was doing. It is hard to believe that someone who knows what they are doing is wrong does not know the nature and quality of the act they are committing. An example of this is the Yates case. She knew that killing her children was wrong as against the law and showed evidence of guilty mind, but she was found not guilty by reason of insanity in her second trial because her defense argued that her mental illness combined with her religious ideation meant that she did not know her drowning her children was wrong. The narrowed M'Naghten test would prevent Yates from being found not guilty by reason of insanity, because she knew when she was killing her children that it was against the law and that there would be consequences for her actions.

2. First of all, the insanity defense should exist because it would not be fair to convict a person of a crime when they were not aware that the action they were committing was wrong. The purpose of convicting someone and of sending him to jail for a wrongdoing

is to punish and to reform. If a person committed a crime yet was not aware that what he did was wrong, then punishing him seems completely counterintuitive. The purpose of punishment should be to make sure that that person and others realize that certain actions have consequences. But if someone is not aware that what they did was wrong, then punishing him seems pointless. Also, the reform purpose of a jail sentence would be better served in a mental institution because a person found insane needs help from doctors, not solitude behind bars. The one-pronged *Clark vs. Arizona* makes more sense than the two-pronged M'Naghten test because the only important factor for distinguishing insanity from criminality should be whether the defendant knew what he were doing was wrong. The first part of the M'Naghten test seems unnecessary because right or wrong is the essential element of criminal responsibility.

Insanity defense should be abolished

1. The fact that there is so much discussion about the appropriate insanity defense standard raises the question of whether the insanity defense should be abolished. Every proponent of one of the possible standards can find fault with the reasoning behind each of the other standards, highlighting their flaws. A few states have abolished the insanity defense and the United States Supreme Court has upheld that action. Since no one wants a murderer on the streets, the legal system should continue its main focus on protecting and preserving society. The most important thing is to keep people that are dangerous confined. Many wrongly believe that abolishing the insanity defense would hurt the mentally ill, throwing them into harsh living conditions in prison where they would not receive the treatment they needed. However, with or without the insanity defense, mentally ill criminals can receive treatment when sentenced, as Yates did. When Yates was found guilty and sentenced to life in prison at her first trial, she was not sent to a regular prison, but to the state secure psychiatric facility where she received treatment. Many people are concerned that others would not receive such care without the insanity defense, but at least those harmful individuals would be off the street, preventing a further threat to society. If this is a large concern, then perhaps if

policies are changed to abolish the insanity defense, another revision could be that juries could mandate that a defendant receive mental treatment immediately following the trial. Furthermore, guilty but mentally ill or insane could easily replace not guilty by reason of insanity. This would satisfy those who are concerned that defendants will slip through without having their mental status evaluated. So if the same end is met with or without the insanity defense, why should it be abolished? There is much confusion surrounding the insanity defense. Juries do not quite know how to use it and in some states, such as Texas, they are not allowed to be adequately educated about it before the trial. Expert psychologists may have opposing views on whether the defendant is mentally sane, so it is unfair for the system to expect the jury to deliver the verdict whether an individual in legally insane. The jury should decide whether the criminal act was committed, and then the court can use the defendant's mental background when considering sentencing.

Uncertain

Should Guilty but mentally ill or Guilty but insane replace the other tests or be added to one of the other tests?

Guilty but mentally ill should neither replace nor be added to other tests

1. Guilty but mentally ill created several problematic legal issues that should not exist when dealing with crime and the mentally ill. Foremost, the test created an easy answer for juries who felt uncomfortable with the conclusion of not guilty by reason of insanity. The issue arose from the fact that people felt the need to ascribe guilt when a criminal-type act was committed, even if the actor did not know the nature and quality of the act or that the act was wrong. Thus, under GBMI, a jury could convict a mentally ill person who had no idea that he did something physically harmful to a human being or that he did something wrong. But many argued that with

this proposed test, the legal definition of guilt stretched beyond acceptable measures. They concluded that a person could not be considered guilty if they do not understand the wrongness or nature and quality of the act, which is just what the GBMI test proposed to do. While some argued that the GBMI verdict could co-exist with the NGRI verdict that would pose several moral and legal issues because redefining guilt to include those who do not understand their actions remains highly problematic. Also, under GBMI, many said that juries which felt the need to ascribe guilt in trials of serious or violent crimes would do so much more readily, even if a person were truly insane and therefore not guilty under NGRI. So, many concluded, when considering the GBMI verdict, one had to also abandon the legal definition of guilt and the practical implications of ignoring the NGRI verdict.

2. The GBMI verdict should not replace the other tests. The GBMI verdict is fundamentally flawed because its effect is to mix the defendant's state of mind at the time of the trial with the defendant's state at the time of the act. What matters in determining guilt is whether the defendant did not understand the criminality of his actions or could not control his actions at the time of the crime. If a defendant did not understand or could not control his actions at the time of a crime but is rehabilitated by the time of a trial, he could receive full punishment under a GBMI verdict even though he did not have mens rea at the time of the crime. The GBMI verdict is appealing to juries because they feel they can have it both ways. Yes, they can conclude the defendant committed the crime, and yes, he was mentally ill. But this verdict ignores evidence that the defendant's mental illness may have prevented him from having mens rea and therefore actually being guilty. Juries may also feel they are ensuring that a defendant gets help for his mental disorder by finding the defendant GBMI. Yet the defendant would also spend time in a psychiatric facility if found NGRI, and might in fact be more likely to spend more time until rehabilitated.

3. The GBMI verdict seems appealing because it allows a jury to show consideration for extenuating mental circumstances while also holding the defendant accountable for his actions. Justice seems to be accomplished with this verdict and not accomplished with a verdict

of NGRI. Nonetheless, the courts should not allow for a verdict of GBMI because this verdict would add further jury confusion through the potential of jurors to reach this verdict for reasons of compromise rather than legal interpretation. The differences in NGRI and GBMI tests can be too subtle for an untrained jury to differentiate. For example, Alaska has implemented a GBMI ruling, but the wording of this and of NGRI are so similar that jury differentiations between the two appear arbitrary. Furthermore, juries might be tempted to use the GBMI as a shortcut verdict, avoiding a tougher or more appropriate verdict because of the ease of reaching a middle ground.

Guilty but mentally ill should be added to other tests

1. While the insanity defense serves as an adequate defense for offenders who did not know their act was wrong or the nature or quality of the act, the legal system leaves the guilty but mentally ill offenders defenseless. Offenders who understand that their act was wrong and grasp the nature of the act may have been influenced in their actions by a mental illness. The presence of a mental illness that alters the state of being of the offender, but does not inhibit him from understanding his culpability or the wrongness of the act, begs for recognition. An offender who knowingly commits a wrongful act should be punished in a different way from an offender who knowingly commits a wrongful act due to a mental illness. The mental illness should be addressed, not just the criminality. It is for this reason that a GBMI defense should be added to the legal standards.

2. Yates provided a great case example of the need for a GBMI verdict. She, ultimately found NGRI in her second trial after a verdict of guilty in her first trial, committed the crime she was convicted of partially as a result of her mental illness. Following Andrea Yates' first childbirth, signs of mental illness and instability began to surface. Upon her meeting Michael Woroniecki, his religious preaching struck a chord in her deepest insecurities as an inadequate mother. Plagued by overwhelming household responsibilities, violent hallucinations and postpartum depression, Yates was unquestionably vulnerable. These initial signs of mental illness would couple with her newfound

religious fanaticism to produce a deadly result. Yates explained to the juries that she had caused her children to stumble and that both she and the children were now doomed. The only possibility for salvation, she believed, existed in killing her children, who then might be spared eternal damnation by God because of their young age and innocence. She knew that killing her children was wrong according to the norms of society and she understood the criminality of her act. She discounted this knowledge, however, partially as a result of her mental illness. Therefore, while Yates was guilty of the crime, a prison sentence alone would have been destructive and counterintuitive with regards to protecting society. To ensure a safe reentry into society, Yates' mental illness had to be treated. For this reason, she should have been found GBMI, and treated as such.

3. GBMI should be added to available verdicts because there are many cases in which an individual is, in fact, mentally ill, but that mental illness does not remove his culpability for a certain crime. When this is the situation, there should be a way for these individuals to get the help that they need before entering jail. With mandated ordinary health care for inmates, this verdict could extend that to mental health care as well to strengthen the argument. Moreover, mental illness can be a mitigating factor in a case, even if it does not absolve an individual of responsibility. As such, there should be a way to note this factor in the verdict so that it plays a part in sentencing.

4. The GBMI verdict should be permitted. The verdict is especially important in states that do not have an insanity defense or states that have a very narrow version of the insanity defense, such as Arizona. In these states, it is very possible for someone who suffers from mental illness to be found guilty of committing a crime and it is important that these people are treated for their mental illness and are differentiated from criminals who do not suffer from mental illness. The GBMI verdict also fits nicely will the narrowed M'Naghten test from *Clark v. Arizona*, because proving that one suffers from mental illness is not enough to prove that he was not guilty and a GBMI verdict could only become an NGRI verdict if the defendant were found to not have known the act he was committing was wrong.

5. Guilty but mentally ill should be added to existing insanity defense standards. Many members of the general public have

expressed concern at the idea of a criminal escaping punishment for a crime because of a mental defect. As an example, a person found NGRI could serve several years in a mental hospital and be released, when he would have served a life sentence in prison. This probably influenced juries into finding mentally ill individuals guilty of their crimes because they were afraid of the offenders receiving lighter sentences. This would eliminate the problem of unequal sentences because individuals found GBMI would still receive the same sentence length, but would be treated properly for their mental disorders in a mental hospital before being transported to a prison.

Guilty but mentally ill but not guilty but insane should be added to other tests

1. The verdict GBI is an oxymoron because insanity is a legal term that by definition removes responsibility or guilt. GBMI, on the other hand, does not have this problem and should become an additional verdict that could be used instead of NGRI. Some defendants are clearly mentally disturbed but not insane. They do not fit any insanity test which requires not being able to differentiate right from wrong or not being able to conform their behavior to the law. A verdict of GBMI would ensure that these people would get the required proper mental health treatment before starting a prison term. That seems important because prisons are so over filled that prisoners with mental illness often do not receive the necessary treatment. Furthermore, a GBMI verdict of would allow juries to take in consideration a defendant's mental instabilities without having to take away all sense of culpability.

    2. GBI should not exist as a verdict because if a person were insane at the time of the crime than he should be considered not guilty under the insanity defense. Insanity should be directly linked to not guilty. GBMI, however, is a sensible verdict and should be considered in a court along with NGRI. GBMI is appealing because a person who fails an insanity defense test, but who was not in a normal mental state or who had a history of mental illness that seemed to have a causal effect on his actions, should start serving a sentence in a mental institution, not in a prison. A person who fails

the insanity defense standard should be found guilty though it would seem illogical to place that person directly into a prison where his mental condition would probably worsen. Even with slight mental illnesses, spending time in a mental institution before prison would give a person a chance to heal mentally before time in prison. Also, time in a mental hospital may give an individual a chance to learn more from their prison sentence because prison reform seems much more likely with a non-mentally ill mind. There seems to be minimal downside to allowing a person mental treatment before they spend the rest of the sentence in jail.

Guilty but mentally ill should be available only if the insanity defense is abolished

1. If the insanity defense were abolished altogether, it would become necessary to have a GBMI verdict to ensure that defendants would receive proper mental care first before going to prison. As long as the insanity defense exists, it is nonsensical to have a GBMI or GBI verdict as well. In most cases, a mental illness should not inhibit someone's ability to know right from wrong or ability to understand the nature of his actions. If mental illness does not do that, then persons should be considered guilty and treated as such.

Guilty but insane should not be permitted

1. GBI should never be allowed because it is a paradox. One cannot be guilty of premeditated murder if he were out of his mind during the time of the act. And while the GBMI verdict may seem slightly more attractive, it would be toothless. After all, such a verdict effectively already exists. In the sentencing phase of trial, the federal rules, and all states, allow for more leniency in the case of a mentally ill defendant. The guilt phase of a trial is meant to determine either guilt or innocence. The sentencing phase of trials ought to determine the mental state of a guilty defendant, and only then ought it to be relevant to any legal proceeding.

Guilty but mentally ill should replace current insanity defense standards

1. GBMI should replace the existing insanity defense standard. The reason many people take issue with the insanity defense is that it seems to excuse criminals because of a preexisting condition. Although certain individuals may not be fully in control of their mental faculties, this should not entirely excuse them from having to pay for their crime. Instead, the legal system should acknowledge that their act differed from others, and thus the punishment should as well. GBMI allows the system to punish mentally ill criminals, but in a different manner than they would the sane ones. It also helps to ensure that the mentally ill who go through the criminal justice system will not simply be released to return to their crazed ways, but that an effort at rehabilitating and regulating their behavior will be made. This would also curb the number of malingerers who simply feign mental illness in order to escape a prison sentence.

2. The insanity defense should be abolished and GBMI should replace NGRI. Adding GBI to the current list of possible verdicts, however, would only confuse juries and the public even more. In both instances the criminal will receive treatment, so those concerned with the mental health of the defendant should be satisfied with either. GBMI is a more appropriate verdict because generally there is no doubt that the defendant committed the crime in these cases and calling them not guilty is misleading. Also, GBMI may satisfy the public more than NGRI does because the convicted criminal will have a set amount of treatment and jail time. Some critics of the insanity defense dislike the possibility that a criminal could receive treatment and then return to society without serving any time in jail. With GBMI, the criminal would receive appropriate treatment and then would be transferred to prison to fulfill the remainder of his sentence.

Guilty but mentally ill should be available in addition to the M'Naghten test

1. GBMI should be available in addition to the M'Naghten test for insanity. GBMI makes available a verdict recognizing a defendant's culpability for an act, while also acknowledging mental illness that requires treatment either before incarceration or concomitant with it. Mental illness and legal insanity are not always synonymous. It is a difficult distinction, but there are those who could not be deemed legally insane while nevertheless clearly in need of treatment for mental illness. For this reason, both are needed. As two distinct considerations, certainly one should not replace the other. Indeed, having both standards available would add greatly to the rehabilitative abilities of the legal system. Even if the legal system focused more on punitive than rehabilitative concerns, it would be important that the system have the capable of treating those who are mentally ill.

Neither guilty but mentally ill nor guilty but insane should be added to the tests of insanity

1. Neither GBMI nor GBI should be added onto the current tests of insanity. Either of these verdicts would only serve to undermine the insanity defense. Someone who found insane is by definition not guilty of a crime. This is simply what the legal term insanity means. However, some take issue with the fact that a person who clearly committed what seems to be a crime is not found guilty of doing so. Either of these other two verdicts get around this by allowing the perpetrator to still be called guilty, but clearly this is contradictory to the defense itself. As it stands, if a person is found guilty and he show signs of mental problems, he can receive mental health care as part of his sentence, so there is no need to create a special verdict for being GBMI. Many people who commit crimes are likely mentally ill. Furthermore, these two verdicts should not replace the insanity defense either. The insanity defense is not an easy thing to achieve, and it should be reserved for only extreme cases of mental illness. If a person meets the qualifications the state has put in place for the insanity defense, then he should not be considered guilty. If there were

many problems with the insanity defense being used successfully too often, there would potentially be arguments for its abolition, but the system appears to be capable of serving justice as it stands.

2. It would be useless to add GBMI or GBI to other tests of legal insanity. In the case that the individual lacked *mens rea* due to his diminished mental capacity, he should not be deemed guilty, but rather innocent by virtue of legal insanity. If, on the other hand, the defendant was perfectly aware of the quality and nature of his act, and understood the wrongfulness of his deed, then he is guilty. In this case, the defendant's mental health should not be an issue in the trial, but rather included in a requisite mental health evaluation upon entrance into the prison system. Ideally, all prisoners should be granted the right to mental counseling and health care. So, unless a defendant's mental health qualifies him for an acquittal, any mental care or rehabilitation of an existing disorder should be dealt with post-trial.

What should the role of standard, extremist, or individualistic religion be in determining criminal responsibility or guilt?

The role should be one of social influence

1. Religion's role in determining criminal responsibility is problematic because it points to the role of a larger group in a crime for which an individual is being punished. The complications surrounding crimes committed in the name of religion or in the presence of other people of the same religion illustrate why, in addition to the ALI insanity defense, society should institute a social influence defense. The ALI insanity defense is concerned with the effect of mental disease or defect on an individual's ability to control or understand the criminality of his actions. The social influence defense should be concerned with the effect of group pressures on an individual's ability to control or understand the criminality of his actions. As numerous social psychology studies have shown, groups can have huge effects on the behavior of individuals, making them commit atrocious acts that they would never have committed in the absence of

social influence. Religion should play a role in determining criminal responsibility if it is either evidence of mental disease or defect or evidence of social influence which might have substantially limited the capacity of the defendant to control or understand the criminality of his actions.

Religion should be taken into consideration

1. Religion should be taken into consideration when trying to determine criminal responsibility. This is because religion can often be a component of a person's mental illness. Brainwashing, for instance, often has a religious element, and hallucinations and delusions can take on a religious tone. Each defendant's particular religious beliefs and behaviors, however, should be examined on a case by case basis. It is dangerous to make generalizations about what specific religious beliefs could mean in terms of mental deficiencies. Extreme fundamentalist beliefs, for example, are not necessarily indicative of a mental disorder and should be careful examined in the context of the defendant's entire psychological profile.

2. If it can be demonstrated that a religion impedes an individual's ability to form *mens rea* or otherwise prevents him from understanding the difference between right and wrong or the nature of his actions, then religion should be taken into account. Belief systems may predispose individuals to think in certain ways, but with the exception of true cases of brainwashing, they do not force people to commit heinous acts.

Religion should play some role

1. Religion should only play a role in determining criminal responsibility if the defendant can be found to have not known what he was doing was wrong due to extreme religious beliefs and brainwashing. However, this would only succeed if the individual was unaware that the religious teachings conflicted with the law. Even if an individual thinks an act is religiously permissible, the individual is still guilty if he knows that what he is doing is wrong according to the law. There should be no distinction made between

standard, extremist, and individualistic religions because it is not the responsibility of the court to determine whether or not a certain religion is extreme or not.

2. Regardless of the extent to which one person's religion is followed by others, it can play a part in determining his criminal responsibility. If due to a person's religious beliefs he meets the criteria for the insanity defense in his state, he should have the ability to defend himself with this defense. While it would be difficult to use widely followed religious beliefs as a basis for the insanity defense, there have been cases in which extremist versions of popular religions have been used successfully for the insanity defense. Yates, for example, held extremist Christian beliefs, leading her to believe that God was telling her to kill her children for their own good. If a person was convinced that based on their religious beliefs the action they were committing was the right thing to do, use of this should be allowed when determining his guilt. Simply because a person may have delusional religious beliefs does not mean, however, that he automatically deserves the insanity defense, but this information should absolutely play some role in determining his criminal responsibility.

Religion should play a minimal role

1. The role of religion in determining criminal responsibility should be extremely minimal, and reduced to the size and relevance of the role of any other type of social influence. As an example, many argued in the Yates case, the woman who drowned her five children in their bathtub because she thought Satan had directed her to do so that it was her religious extremism that was responsible for her acts. They contended that it was her religious belief that caused her to hear the Satanic voices. However, as evidenced by her numerous psychiatric institutionalizations and diagnoses of postpartum psychosis, it was instead a mental abnormality that produced these voices, and not simply her religious beliefs. Too often, it has been assumed that religion diminishes mental capacity for acting criminally. But the possibility should be taken into account that individuals who suffer from depression or psychosis who are also religious may just attribute

their psychotic behavior to religion, when chances are, they would have engaged in these types of criminal behavior under any form of social influence simply because of their mental predisposition.

Religion should have no role

1. Religion, standard, extremist, or individualistic, should play no role in determining criminal responsibility. Offenders who have adhered to a particular religious doctrine must obey the law, even if the religion requires one to break the law. The law must trump all religious demands to ensure public safety and to guarantee a certain quality of life for all. If the law obstructs one's ability to practice his religion, that individual can challenge the law within the legal system. Breaking the law, however, should not be mitigated or permitted by one's religious beliefs.

2. From a general legal standpoint, no religious belief should impact a guilty verdict because the belief does not impair a person's understanding of the act or his understanding of the legal wrongness of the act. Even if his religion states that an act was morally right, the defendant would acknowledge the fact that he understood the legal wrongness of the act, which qualifies him for a verdict of guilty. Although this holds as a general rule, interesting cases could arise in which one attempts to argue insanity for a religious crime. For example, if a religious extremist murders someone under the delusion that the murder was in fact a releasing of the soul, and that the murder did not kill the individual but did release his soul, then he may have not understood the nature and quality of his action. Also, if his religious law did not deride this as a wrongful act, then the individual could possibly not understand the legal sense of wrongness as far as legality applies in his religion. Through this lens, attorneys could possibly argue for the insanity defense in cases of religious extremism, although in most cases, religion could not serve as a reasonable qualifier for absolving guilt.

3. The basis or content of a religion should not come into play with regards to legal rulings of insanity. The courts should not have a role in establishing which religions are legitimate and which are not, so there should be no differentiation between standard religions,

extremist religions, and individualistic religions. Even from a cultural standpoint, the categorization of religions into these groups can be difficult, so trying to legally classify religions into these groups seems futile. Instead, courts should focus on the nature of religious delusions apart from the religions in which they are based. A defendant's delusions of God or Allah speaking to him should not be treated differently than a defendant's delusions of the Holy Spaghetti Monster speaking and commanding him.

4. Religion and the law should be separate. For anyone to blame an action on their religious practice, or a belief in or instruction from a religious figure, should be no different legally from saying that a parent or friend instructed one to do so. An individual cannot freely commit a crime because his faith dictated him to do so because faith must be applied within legal boundaries. Crimes committed with religious motivation are still crimes where the legal consequences should apply. If one's religion dictates he must kill someone to be fully accepted into the religion, then while no legal guideline can prevent one from this holding this belief or performing this action, any individual who does so is punishable because of his crime regardless of what prompted the crime.

5. The role of one's religion should play no role in determining one's criminal responsibility or guilt. A religion is a set of ideals that many, if not all, people possess, and it impacts many people's daily lives. However, a person's religion should not make him more or less responsible for a crime he committed. Religious extremists, such as those who flew planes into the World Trade Center, should not be held more or less guilty because they were motivated by extremist religious beliefs. Society does not operate normatively with extremist religious beliefs, but that does not imply those who believe these are crazy or legally insane and therefore less responsible for their own actions. The only exception to this is individuals who have been coerced or brainwashed into joining extremist religions or cults. These individuals should not be held legally responsible for their actions because they occurred under duress. Any individual who freely engaged in any form of religious activities that motivated criminal activity, regardless of whether it was standard, extremist,

or individualistic, should not be held to a different standard of punishment based on that religion.

6. The *United States Constitution* clearly delineates a separation between church and state. If allowances are not made for religion in the legislative branch, they certainly should not be in the judiciary. Any religion that advocates criminal behavior is not one society should be condoning but rather one society should be regulating and prosecuting. To plead religion, as one might plead the insanity defense, is to completely abandon agency of one's actions. Although some argue that a dogmatic religion can have a brainwashing effect, this phenomenon has not been statistically proven. Allowing it as a defense sets a precedent that opens the door to a wide range of defenses that strip the perpetrator of agency for his actions. The primary purpose of the judicial system is to make people culpable for their criminal deeds, regardless of their religion affiliation.

7. No form of religion should be a legitimate defense in determining criminal culpability. If the defendant knew that his action was illegal at the time of the act, then he should be held fully accountable. Allowing a defendant to claim his religion as the driver of his crime should not excuse the crime. Furthermore, allowing these claims would create a slippery slope and open the door for various other excuses. It may be unfortunate that a fervent believer of a faith is torn between abiding by his faith and abiding by the law, but the law can only be effective and efficient when it is consistent.

8. Since the *Constitution* is said to mandate a separation of church and state, religion should not have any role in determining criminal responsibility. Guilt should be determined without taking religion into account. For anyone charged with a crime the dictates of any individual religion should not be relevant. Religious beliefs cannot act to either mitigate or exacerbate criminal responsibility for illegal conduct. Unless the religion followed was a cult where the individual was brainwashed such that under the M'Naghten test he no longer understood the nature of the act in which he engaged or knew right from wrong, religion should not be a consideration in legal assignation of guilt.

Some extremist religion should be considered a form of insanity

1. Religion should be considered a form of insanity because it seems to be another type of brainwashing and it hinders a person's ability to understand that an act may be criminal. According to the *Clark v. Arizona* test for insanity the only important prong for finding someone NGRI is that he did not know what he was doing was wrong. That test might exculpate a religious person from blame or guilt in some cases where he was sufficiently brainwashed to believe that his religion wanted him to kill someone, making the act in his eyes not wrong. Following a religion to the point where he believes everything regardless of the law is undoubtedly an unhealthy way of living. Through this a person could actually commit crimes like murder and find justification in his actions, which some conclude would be a clear form of insanity. They would argue that if a person is religious to a point where he seems unable to determine what is right and wrong outside of his religion, then jurors should find him not guilty because all he knows to be right and wrong is the law as their religion sets it forth.

Should the insanity defense test or standard be different for those, termed terrorists, who aim to instill fear in and/or destroy large civilian populations as opposed to those, termed ordinary criminals, who aim to attack only the specific individuals against whom their acts are directed?

All the responses to this question assume regular criminal justice system court trials for terrorists and non-terrorists. The military court that may try Major Hasan or others under the *Uniform Code of Military Justice* has its own version of the insanity defense, so the responses include him and his case. What are not included in the materials here are those, labeled terrorists, who are tried under laws of war by military tribunals as opposed to those tried in ordinary courts of criminal law.

The test or standard should be the same

1. The insanity defense standard must be uniform for terrorists and non-terrorists alike. A society must create a legal standard for insanity that can apply to each individual, regardless of the crime committed. Discrepancies in standards would imply a discrepancy in the definition of insanity. A person could not be considered sane under one standard and insane under another. Either an individual was legally sane or insane. Either he understood that the action was wrong or he did not. Either he knew the nature and quality of the act or he did not. This standard must be uniform across type of crime and across offenders. To prevent contradiction and to ultimately support a coherent definition and understanding of insanity, only one standard of insanity can exist.

2. The insanity defense test for understanding the nature of an action and for being unable to tell right from wrong are still applicable for terrorists who aim to terrorize a large demographic or population. Only if they did not know that their action was wrong in the face of the law or could not comprehend the nature of what they had done could the insanity defense apply. A criminal act of terrorism is less likely to qualify for an NGRI verdict because usually terrorists believe that they are doing what is right to further their goals but not what is right or acceptable behavior in society according the dictates of the law. Furthermore, most terrorist acts involve planning and premeditation which indicates that terrorists appreciated the nature of their crime since they knew how many people would be harmed or what property would be destroyed.

3. The insanity defense needs to be the same for terrorists and non-terrorists, but it needs to be broad enough to take into consideration the cases of terrorists. The difficulty with cases of terrorism is the social stigma associated with such criminal acts. Members of society want to hold those engaged in criminal activity to a different standard than other criminals because of the societal violence and fear that these crimes induce. Along the same lines, there might be a desire to apply a different insanity defense standard to terrorists. The law, however, should apply to all cases in the same way, and therefore,

the application of a different insanity defense would not be prudent in terrorist cases.

4. There should not be a specific insanity test for terrorists because the same standards for culpability apply. Whether a person is insane or not should not be determined based on the kind of act they commit but rather the state of mind in which they commit it. Terrorists, therefore, should be subjected to the same insanity test whether it is M'Naghten, M'Naghten narrowed, or American Law Institute, as regular criminals.

5. No, there should not be a difference. The tests and standards employed are meant to take into account a large spectrum of mental disorders, regardless of potential substantial differences between diagnoses. As such, it should be the role of the psychological and psychiatric community to come to an understanding as to whether or not terrorists can be considered mentally ill and if so, what diagnosis and treatment might be appropriate for them. If the scientific and medical communities are able to come to some sort of conclusion about this, then it will be played out in the legal system. Beyond courts' determining the psychology of certain actions, it is up to the community that sets the standard for these psychological questions to do so. For instance, had post traumatic stress disorder not been recognized as a disorder, it might have been more difficult to consistently argue in court that major trauma can predispose people to violent reaction to fear stimuli. Once an understanding of the psychology of terror can be produced, courts will have a scientific standard by which to evaluate terrorists for the insanity defense.

6. The standard should be no different for individuals who target large demographics as opposed to individuals. The standard for insanity, which requires an understanding of the nature and quality of the act along with an understanding of the wrongness of the act, should not change based on the target population of the act. However, if the size of the population or the attempt at a group stemmed from a lack of understanding of the nature and quality of the act, then the insanity defense might be employed.

7. The insanity defense test should not be different for terrorists. While the terrorist nature of the acts committed should certainly be taken into account when determining whether or not the criminal

knew the nature of his act and whether what he was doing was wrong at the time of the crime, the test used should not be different from the test used for a normal crime. Keeping the insanity defense test standard for all types of crime prevents having to make difficult distinctions like determining what constitutes a terrorist act. Even with the same standard for all criminals, it is not very likely that terrorists will be found NGRI. It is not very plausible that a terrorist would be found to not know what he was doing was wrong, because terrorists act with the goal of terrorizing others, something that is not permissible by law. Also, because many terrorist acts are planned in detail, this makes it more difficult to find terrorists to be NGRI because they had lots of time to consider the nature and permissibility of their act.

8. The insanity defense test should not be different for terrorists, for multiple reasons. First, the definition of terrorist is something arbitrarily defined. Is a terrorist someone who aims to terrorize twenty or more people? Ten or more? Two or more? What does terrorize mean? Does it mean to kill? Hurt? Annoy? Threaten? The law would have to make arbitrary distinctions. Furthermore, the law must be blind. And a law which applies a different standard of sanity to terrorists would be unfair to terrorists. Indeed, it would undermine the credibility of the insanity defense itself. If someone is insane, they cannot be held accountable. If they are sane, they must be held accountable. Applying different standards to people based on the crimes they commit disregards that fundamental tenet of the insanity standard.

9. The standard for the insanity defense should not be different for individuals who terrorized large civilian populations than it is for those who terrorized specific individuals. If an individual knew what he was doing, and knew those actions were wrong but chose to do them regardless, he should be held criminally responsible. Conversely, if an individual did not know what he was doing or did not know the actions were wrong, typically because of mental illness or defect, he should not be held criminally responsible and should instead be able to use the insanity defense successfully. The targeted population size should not impact the standards of insanity that are used to evaluate the individual. Some may argue a crime

is more depraved or evil if it was targeted against a large group of people. However, a depraved, evil crime does not imply the criminal was insane. It is the person's state of mind, not the population size or depravity of the crime, that determines whether or not a person is insane. The standard for the insanity defense, therefore, should not be different for individuals who terrorized large populations than it is for those who terrorized specific individuals.

10. The scope of an act does not necessarily affect a verdict, but rather the sentencing after the verdict. Thus the plea should not differ based on how many were affected by the act. Murder is murder. The number of people affected simply allows the prosecutors more chances to try the defendant and the judge a greater opportunity to impose a longer or more severe sentence.

11. The insanity defense should be the same for terrorists and ordinary criminals. The legal system can best function when it is consistent. Furthermore, if the criminal knew that the act he committed was illegal, he is culpable. As far as verdicts go, there should be no difference when deciding guilt in a case, although different sentencing would be appropriate for those termed terrorists who aim to terrorize large groups at a time. The act of killing one person cannot be considered less immoral than the act of killing thousands of people. In each instance the person should take responsibility for his action. However, the harm done to society is more in the latter case and a more severe punishment should follow.

12. The insanity defense test should not be different for terrorists and ordinary criminals. In the case of Yates and other criminals convicted of multiple murders, a life sentence was imposed because of the number of victims and severity of their crimes, and, besides capital punishment, that deprivation of liberty is the most extreme punishment the legal system could give even to an individual who commits heinous mass murder. In all cases of intentional murder, defendants should simply be charged with the number of deaths resulting from their crime, regardless of the scale.

13. The insanity defense must use the same standard for all defendants charged with a crime. The entire basis of the American legal system is that it treats all defendants equally, with a fair trial by a jury of peers and the presumption of innocence until guilt is proven

beyond a reasonable doubt. To treat terrorists differently from other defendants would violate the concept of equal treatment under law.

14. The insanity defense test should not differ based on the number of people targeted by a terrorist or criminal act. In either case, if the defendant was truly mentally ill, they should have the chance to be considered for the insanity defense. As it stands, many major terrorists either perish in suicide bombings they conduct or remain elusive despite attempts made by countries to apprehend them. So there has not really been a chance for the insanity defense to be put to the test in this situation, but it should still remain as a possibility. If a terrorist was found to be mentally deranged enough to qualify for the insanity defense, he should be allowed to claim this defense in court just like any other criminal. The requirements for the insanity should not be made any more or less stringent in that situation.

15. Already very stigmatized, the insanity defense would likely only become more stigmatized if it began to be used by terrorists. This does not mean however that it does not logically make sense that a terrorist should be just as able to use this defense if appropriate as any other criminal. The insanity defense is not an easy thing to successfully argue, and juries would likely be even more skeptical in the case of terrorists, so it is not as if there would be a rush of terrorists declared not guilty by reason of insanity. If the insanity defense stands as it is, it should be available to any person, especially someone who is guided by delusional beliefs, which could be reformed through various forms of therapy.

16. The insanity defense test should not be different for those who aim to terrorize large demographics and those who terrorize only specific individuals. If a defendant can be found legally insane, he should not be held criminally responsible for his acts, regardless of how many victims he has harmed or tried to harm. However, as the number of people targeted increases and the plans to target them grow more complex, it would become increasingly difficult to prove that a defendant was not able to control his actions or did not understand the criminality of his actions. As a result, those who aim to terrorize large demographics will likely find it harder to NGRI.

The standard should be different for terrorists

1. The insanity defense standard should be different for those who aim to terrorize large demographics. If a person terrorized a large demographic, but did not realize that what they were doing was wrong than according to the standard set forth by *Clark v. Arizona* they could be found not guilty by reason of insanity. However, the law should be somewhat different for people who terrorize large demographics. Although in theory all people should be treated with equal rights, sometimes society needs to look at things from a utilitarian perspective. If a terrorist who killed hundreds was ever found not guilty by reason of insanity, society would be in an uproar and the legal system could have serious difficulty. Society would not be able to accept a person who killed a large group of people back as a normal citizen and courts need to recognize this. Although it may be unfair according to the *Clark v. Arizona* standard, those who commit large terrorist acts should be treated by different standards. Time incarcerated could be split between a mental hospital and a prison, but anything less than a life of some sort of imprisonment would be unjust to the people in any society wronged by a large-scale terrorist attack.

Bibliography

Abadie, A. (2006). Poverty, political freedom, and the roots of terrorism. *The American Economic Review, 96, 2,* 50-56

ACLU (2002). How the USA PATRIOT Act redefines "domestic terrorism." *http://www.aclu.org*

Al-Marayati, S. (2009, December 8). Major Hasan and the Quran: Repentance is the only option for the Fort Hood killer. *Wall Street Journal*

Ali, A. (2010, April 27). 'South Park' and the informal fatwa. *Wall Street Journal*

Amador, X. and Paul-Odouard, R. (2000). Defending the unabomber: Anosognosia in schizophrenia. *Psychiatric Quarterly*

American jihadists. (2010, March 10). *Christian Science Monitor*

American Psychiatric Association (1994). *Diagnostic and Statistical Manual of Mental Disorders (Fourth Ed.).* Washington, D.C.: American Psychiatric Association

American Psychiatric Association (2010). *DSM-5*: The future of psychiatric diagnosis. *www.dsm5.org*

Anthony, D., and Robbins, T. (1992). "Brainwashing" exception to the First Amendment. *Behavioral Sciences and the Law, 10, 1*

Anthony, D. and Robbins, T. (1990). *In Gods We Trust: New Patterns of Religious Pluralism in America.* New Brunswick, NJ: Transaction Publishers

Anthony, D., and Robbins, T. (1992). Law, social science and the 'brainwashing' exception to the First Amendment. *Behavioral Sciences & the Law, 10, 1*

Anthony, D. and Robbins, T. (1995). Negligence, coercion, and the protection of religious belief. *Journal of Church & State, 37, 3*

Appelbaum, P., Jick, R., Grisso, T., Givelber, D., Silver, E., and Steadman, H. (1993). Use of posttraumatic stress disorder to support an insanity defense. *American Journal of Psychiatry, 150*

Arehart-Treichel, J. (2007). What can neuroscience teach the legal system? *Psychiatric News, 42, 21*

Argo, N. (2006). The role of social context in terrorist attacks. *Chronicle of Higher Education, 52, 22*

Aronson, E., Wilson, T., and Akert, R. (2007). *Social Psychology.* Upper Saddle River, NJ: Pearson Education

1970s radical Olson due for release. (2009, March 15). *Associated Press*

Atkins v. Virginia. (2002). 536 U.S. 304

Atran, S. (2003). Genesis of suicide terrorism. *Science, 299*

Atshan, S., Gaber, N., and Kacem, R. (2009, November 24). Guilty by association. *Harvard Crimson*

Bainbridge, W. (1984). Religious insanity in America: The official nineteenth-century theory. *Sociological Analysis, 45, 3*

Baker, P. (2010, February 8). Obama challenges terrorism critics. *New York Times*

Barry, E. (2010, April 1). Chechen rebel says he planned attacks. *New York Times*

Barter, J. and Reite, M. (1969). Crime and LSD: The insanity plea. *American Journal of Psychiatry*

Baumeister, R. (2008). Free will in scientific psychology. *Perspectives on Psychological Science, 3, 1*

Beebee, H., and Mele, A. (2002). Humean compatibilism. *Mind, 111, 442*

Beier, M. (2006). On the psychology of violent Christian fundamentalism: Fighting to matter ultimately. *Psychoanalytic Review. 93, 2*

Belzen, J. (2000). Religion, culture and psychopathology: Cultural-psychological reflections on religion in a case of manslaughter in the Netherlands. *Pastoral Psychology, 4, 6*

Bender, B. (2010, February 22). Ft. Hood suspect was Army dilemma: His extreme views possibly overlooked in favor of diversity. *Boston Globe*

Bender, E. (2004). Forensic experts probe mind of mother who killed kids. *Psychiatric News, 39, 24*

Bloechl, A., Vitacco, M., Neumann, C., and Erickson, S. (2007). An empirical investigation of insanity defense attitudes: Exploring factors related to bias. *International Journal of Law and Psychiatry, 30, 2*

Booth, W. (1997, December 26). Kaczynski resists the insanity defense. *Washington Post*

Bortnick, B. and Venezia, T. (2010, March 14). U.S. terror mom brainwashed six-year-old son. *New York Post*

Bowser, B. (2002). Judge declared federal death penalty unconstitutional as questions of innocence, fairness persist. http://www.deathpenaltyinfo.org/PR-DPICRakoff.pdf

Boyle, H. (2006). Memorization and learning in Islamic schools. *Comparative and International Education Society.* Chicago: University of Chicago Press

Braden-Maguire, J., Sigal, J., and Perrino, C. (2005). Battered women who kill: Variables affecting simulated jurors' verdicts. *Journal of Family Violence. 20, 6*

Bravin, J. (2009, November 27). Mental state cited in 9/11 case. *Wall Street Journal*

Brett Killed Mom: A sister's diary. (1996). *HBO Family Video Diary*

Brett Reider is alive and doing well. <http://www.livedtotell. com/2007/10/27/brett-reider-is-alive-and-doing-well>

Brown, A. (2009, December 2). Fort Hood suspect charged with attempted murder. *Associated Press*

Brown, R. (2003). *Social Psychology: The Second Edition.* New York: Free Press

Brown, R. (2007). Alfred McCoy, Hebb, the CIA, and torture. *Journal of the History of the Behavioral Sciences, 43, 2*

Bumiller, E. and Shane, S. (2010, January 16). Pentagon report on Fort Hood shooting details failures. *New York Times*

Burfeind, J. and Bartusch, D. (2005). *Juvenile Delinquency: An Integrated Approach.* Sudbury, MA: Jones & Bartlett Publishers

Burns, J., and Swerdlow, R. (2003). Right orbitofrontal tumor with pedophilia symptom and constructional apraxia sign. *Archives of Neurology. 60, 3*

Burstein, D. and De Keijzer, A. (2007). *Secrets of 24: The Unauthorized Guide to the Political and Moral Issues Behind TV's Most Riveting Drama.* New York: Sterling Publishing Company

Candiotti, S. (2004, June 10). Nichols' sentence still being deliberated. *CNN*

Casselman, B. (2010, January 8). Mental state of Fort Hood suspect takes central role in case. *Wall Street Journal*

Chalk, P. (2009). Chronology of suicide bomb attacks by LTTE Tamil Tiger Terrorists in Sri Lanka. *http://www.spur.asn.au*

Chambers, J. (2010, March 28). Seven arrested in FBI raids linked to Christian militia group. *Detroit News*

Chase, A. (2003). *Harvard and the Unabomber: The Education of an American Terrorist.* New York: W. W. Norton

Chronology of the Unabomber Trial. http://www.courttv.com/trials/unabomber/chronology

Clark v. Arizona. (2006.) 548 U.S. 735

Clay, R. (March 2007). Functional magnetic resonance imaging: A new research tool. *APA Science Directorate*

Closing argument for the prosecution in the Patty Hearst trial by U. S. Attorney James Browning. University of Missouri-Kansas City School of Law. Accessed March 2, 2009. <http://www. law.umkc.edu/faculty/projects/ftrials/hearst/browningclose. html>*CNN.com*

Cole, M., Ross, B., and Atta, N. (2010, April 26). Underwear bomber: New video of training, martyrdom statements: Prior to suicide mission, Abdulmutallab says 'Jews and the Christians' are the enemy. *abcnews.com*

Cornwall, M., Albrecht, S., Cunningham, P., and Pitcher, B. (1986). The dimensions of religiosity: A conceptual model with an empirical test. *Review of Religious Research, 27*

Crazy for jihad: One man's insanity is another man's holy war. (2009, December 17). *Washington Times*

Crimaldi, L. (2010, May 1). It's the max for John Odgren: Teen killer given life without parole. *Boston Herald*

Cultural defense in the criminal law. (1986). *Harvard Law Review, 99, 6*

Curtis, J. and Curtis, M. (1993). Factors related to susceptibility and recruitment by cults. *Psychological Reports, 73, 2*

Daubert v. Merrell Dow Pharmaceuticals. (1993). 509 U.S. 579

Davey, M. (2010, January 29). Doctor's killer puts abortion on the stand. *New York Times*

Davey, M. (2010, January 30). Jury reaches guilty verdict in murder of abortion doctor. *New York Times*

DeAngelis, T. (2009, November). Understanding terrorism. *Monitor on Psychology*

Defense of lack of mental responsibility. *Uniform Code of Military Justice.* 10 United States Code, Chapter 47. Section 850a. Article 50a

Delgado, R. (1984). When religious exercise is not free: Deprogramming and the constitutional status of coercively induced belief. *Vanderbilt Law Review. 37, 5*

Dennett, D. (2003). *Freedom Evolves.* New York: Penguin

Denno, D. (2003). Who is Andrea Yates? A short story about insanity. *Duke Journal of Gender Law and Policy*

Devinsky O, and Lai G. (2008). Spirituality and religion in epilepsy. *Epilepsy behavior, 12, 4*

Downfall (Der Untergang). (2005). DVD. Director: Hirschbiegel, O.

Dijksterhuis, A., Bos, M., Nordgren, L., and van Baaren, R. (2006). On making the right choice: The deliberation-without-attention effect. *Science, 311*

Drinnan, A., and Lavender, T (2006). A qualitative study examining the relationship between religious beliefs and religious delusions. *Religion & Culture, 9, 4*

Dunn, K., Cowan, G., and Downs, D. (2006, September 15). Effects of sex and race of perpetrator and method of killing on outcome judgments in a mock filicide case. *Journal of Applied Social Psychology, 36, 10*

Elliott, A. (2010, January 31). The jihadist next door. *New York Times Magazine*

Emily, J. (2006, October 8). Schlosser and Yates find solace in friendship. *Dallas News*

Erickson, P. and Erickson, S. (2008). *Crime, Punishment, and Mental Illness.* New Brunswick, NJ: Rutgers University Press

Fabian, J. (2007). Methamphetamine motivated murder: Forensic psychological/ psychiatric & legal applications in criminal contexts. *Journal of Psychology and Law*

Federal Justice Service (2008). O'Connor, Sandra Day. *http://www. fjc.gov*

Feinberg, A. (2002). Forcible medication of mentally ill criminal defendants: The case of Russell Eugene Weston, Jr. *Stanford Law Review*

Fersch, E. (1979). *Law, Psychology, and the Courts: Rethinking Treatment of the Young and the Disturbed.* Springfield, IL: Thomas

Fersch, E. (1980). Ethical issues for psychologists in court settings. In Monahan, J. (ed). *Who is the Client? The Ethics of Psychological Intervention in the Criminal Justice System.* Washington, D.C.: American Psychological Association

Fersch, E. (1980). *Psychology and Psychiatry in Courts and Corrections: Controversy and Change.* New York: Wiley

Fersch, E. (ed.) (2005). *Thinking About the Insanity Defense: Answers to Frequently Asked Questions with Case Examples.* Bloomington, IN: iUniverse

Fersch, E. (ed.) (2006). *Thinking About the Sexually Dangerous: Answers to Frequently Asked Questions with Case Examples.* Bloomington, IN: iUniverse

Fersch, E. (ed.) (2006). *Thinking About Psychopaths and Psychopathy: Answers to Frequently Asked Questions with Case Examples.* Bloomington, IN: iUniverse

Fersch, E. (ed.) (2007). *Thinking About Law and Ethics: Answers to Frequently Asked Questions with Case Examples.* Bloomington, IN: iUniverse

Fest, J. (2005). *Inside Hitler's Bunker: The Last Days of the Third Reich.* New York: Picador

Fisher, D. (2001, May 11). A cult leader's 'visions' result in murder trial. *http://www.wwrn.org*

Fort Hood shooter asked about killing Americans in 2008: report. (2009, December 23). *Agence France-Presse*

Friedman, T. (2009, November 24). America vs the narrative. *New York Times*

Frost, L. and Shepherd, R. (1996). Mental health issues in juvenile delinquency proceedings. *Criminal Justice Magazine, 35, 11*

Frye v. U.S. (1923). D.C. Circuit Court of Appeals

Gazzaniga, M. (2006). *http://www.psych.ucsb.edu*

Gerecht, R. (2009, November 22). Major Hasan and holy war. *Wall Street Journal*

Giardino, A., Harris, T. and Giardino, E. (2006, July 17). Child abuse and neglect: Posttraumatic stress disorder. *http://emedicine. medscape.com/article/916007*

Glaberson, W. (1997, November 22). Unabom jury might hear psychiatric evidence. *New York Times*

Glaberson, W. (2008, April 26). Guantanamo drives prisoners insane, lawyers say. *International Herald Tribune*

Glazov, J. (2009, December 22). Fort Hood denial: Why the hard Left can't accept the Islamic roots of Nidal Hasan's shooting spree. *City-Journal*

Graham, F. (2008, March 15). Murder prosecutions costly to county. *North Platte Bulletin*, NE

Greenhouse, L. (2006, April 20). Arizona's strict approach to insanity defense gets a hearing before the Supreme Court. *New York Times*

Greenhouse, L. (2006, June 30). Court upholds Arizona limits imposed on insanity defense. *New York Times*

Hagen, M. (1997). *Whores of the Court: The Fraud of Psychiatric Testimony and the Rape of American Justice.* New York: ReganBooks

Han, S., Mao, L., Gu, X., Zhu, Y., Ge, J., and Ma, Y. (2008). Neural consequences of religious belief on self-referential processing. *Social Neuroscience, 3*

Harlow, J. (2000). Passage of an iron rod through the head. *Journal of Neuropsychiatry and Clinical Neuroscience, 11*

Harnden, T. (2009, December 30). Barack Obama gets an 'F' for protecting Americans. *Daily Telegraph, UK*

Hartog, K. and Gow, K. (2005). Religious attributions pertaining to the causes and cures of mental illness. *Mental Health, Religion & Culture. 8, 4*

Harvard Kennedy School of Government (2003). Frederick Schauer full biography. *http://ksghome.harvard.edu*

Harvard Office of the Provost (2008). Steven E. Hyman, Provost. *http://www.provost.harvard.edu/people*

Heffernan, V. (2010, April 26). Authors unbound online. *New York Times*

Hegeman, R. (2010, April 1). Abortion doc's killer lashes out at court. *Associated Press*

Heyman, G. (2010). *Addiction: A Disorder of Choice.* Cambridge, MA: Harvard University Press

Hixson, W. (2005). Guerilla: The taking of Patty Hearst. *Journal of American History, 92, 3*

Hoberman, J. (2006, October). Unquiet Americans. *Sight and Sound. 16, 10*

Hoffer, E. (1951) The *True Believer: Thoughts on the nature of mass movements.* Harper Perennial

Hotz, R. (2008, June 27). Science journal: get out of your own way: studies show the value of not overthinking a decision. *Wall Street Journal*

Hotz, R. (2009, January 15). The brain, your honor, will take the witness stand. *Wall Street Journal*

Hyman, S. (2007). A question of free will? Coverage of the Provostial Lecture by Steven E. Hyman, M.D. *On the Brain: The Harvard Mahoney Neuroscience Institute Letter, 13, 3*

Ikemoto, K. and Nakamura, M. (2004). Forced deprogramming from a religion and mental health: A case report of PTSD. *International Journal of Law and Psychiatry, 27, 2*

International Sikh Youth Federation (2001). *http://www.satp.org/satporgtp/countries/india/states/punjab/terrorist_outfits/ISYF.htm.*

Jacques, K. and Taylor, P. (2008). Male and female suicide bombers: Different sexes, different reasons? *Studies in Conflict and Terrorism, 31, 4*

Jacquin, K. (2007). The influence of media messages on mock juror decisions in the Andrea Yates trial. *American Journal of Forensic Psychology, 25, 4*

Jacquin, K. and Hodges, E. (2008). The influence of media messages on mock juror decisions in the Andrea Yates trial. *American Journal of Forensic Psychology, 25, 4*

James, D., Mullen, P., Meloy, J., Path, M., Farnham, F., Preston, L., and Darnley, B. (2007). The role of mental disorder in attacks on European politicians 1990–2004. *Acta Psychiatrica Scandinavica. 116, 5*

Jihad as American as apple pie, says US-born cleric. (2010, March 19). *Agence France-Presse*

Johnson, A. and Dugan, E. (2009, December 27). Wealthy, quiet, unassuming: The Christmas Day bomb suspect. *The Sunday Independent UK*

Johnson, R. (2002, March 22). 'Law & Order' saved Yates. *New York Post*

Joshi, K., Frierson, R., and Gunter T. (2006). Shared psychotic disorder and criminal responsibility: A review and case report of Folie à Trois. *Journal of the American Academy of Psychiatry and the Law, 34, 4*

Junge, T. (2005). *Until the Final Hour: Hitler's Last Secretary.* New York: Arcade

Juvenile Justice (2001). *Frontline.* pbs.org

Keim, B. (2008, August 13). Uncle Sam wants your brain. *Wired Science.*

Keiper, A. (2008, July 8). The synapse and the soul. *Wall Street Journal*

Kellogg, A., Etter, L., Johnson, K., and Martin, T. (2010, March 31). Militia's chief mistrust festered, friends say. *Wall Street Journal*

Kent, S., and Szimhart, J. (2002). Exit counseling and the decline of deprogramming. *Cultic Studies Review,* 1, 3

Kershaw, S. (2010, January 10). The terrorist mind: An update. *New York Times*

Kiehl, S. and Gibson, G. (2003, December 19). Insanity defense was risky strategy. *Baltimore Sun*

Knaupp, C. (2008, July 8). Woman who stoned children to death will remain in mental facility. *Tyler Morning Telegraph*

Koenig, H., McCullough, M., and Larson, D. (2001). *Handbook of Religion and Health.* New York: Oxford University Press

Kopacz, K. (2004). Yates was one of Woroniecki's followers. *The Daily Collegian Online,* Penn State University

Kopelson, A. (Producer), & Fincher, D. (Director). (1995). *Se7en* [Motion Picture]. New York: New Line Cinema

Kotlowitz, A. (2005, March 20). The politics of Ibrahim Parlak. *New York Times Magazine*

Krakauer, J. (2003). *Under the Banner of Heaven: A Story of Violent Faith*. New York: Doubleday

Kramer, P. (1993). *Listening to Prozac*. New York: Penguin Books

Kravitz, H. and Kelly, J. (1999). An outpatient psychiatry program for offenders with mental disorders found not guilty by reason of insanity. *Psychiatric Services, 50, 12*

Lapham, R. and Norling, B. (1996). *Lapham's Raiders: Guerrillas in the Philippines, 1942-1945*. Lexington, KY: University Press of Kentucky

Law and Neuroscience Project (2008). *http://www. lawandneuroscienceproject.org*

Layton, J. (2006). How brainwashing works. http://health. howstuffworks.com/brainwashing.htm

Lee, C. (2008). The gay panic defense. *UC Davis Law Review*

Lenman, J. (2006). Compatibilism and contractualism: The possibility of moral responsibility. *Ethics, 117, 1*

Levy, C. and Barry, E. (2010, April 2). Russia says suicide bomber was militant's widow. *New York Times*

Lieberman, J. and Collins, S. How could the Fort Hood massacre happen? (2010, April 26, 2010). *Wall Street Journal*

Liem, M. (2008). Filicide: A comparative study of maternal versus paternal child homicide. *Criminal Behaviour and Mental Health, 18, 3*

Lundegaard, E. (2005, September 5). Saddam Hussein is bombing us! How Hollywood portrayed terrorism before 9/11. *MSNBC*

Major Hasan's smooth ascension. (2010, January 16). *New York Times*

Mallinckrodt Institute of Radiology (2001). Marcus E. Raichle, M.D. http://www.nil.wustl.edu/labs/raichle

Marks, L. (2006). Mental health, religious belief, and the 'terrifying question'. *Journal of Child and Family Studies, 15*

Martin, G. and Contreras, G. (2010, January 16). Ft. Hood inquiry warns of wider security issues. *Boston Globe*

Matza, D. (1990). *Delinquency & Drift*. Piscataway, NJ: Transaction Publishers

McDermott, B., Scott, C., Busse, D., Andrade, F., Zozaya, M., and Quanbeck, C. (2008). The conditional release of insanity acquittees: Three decades of decision-making. *Journal of the American Academy of Psychiatry and Law, 36, 3*

McLellan, F. (2006). Mental health and justice: the case of Andrea Yates. *Lancet, 368*

McNally, R. (2003). *Remembering Trauma*. Cambridge, MA: Harvard University Press

McNulty, S. and Morris, H. (2009, November 6). Call for calm after US military base killings. *Financial Times*

Melton, G., Petrila, J., Poythress, N., and Slobogin, C. (2007). *Psychological Evaluations for the Courts: A Handbook for Mental Health Professionals and Lawyers*. New York: Guilford Press

Military Commissions Act of 2009. Chapter 47A of Title 10, United States Code

Miller, M., Jehle, A., and Summers, A. (2007). From Kobe Bryant to Saddam Hussein: A descriptive examination and psychological analysis of how religion likely affected twenty-five recent high-profile trials. *Florida Coastal Law Review, 9, 1*

Mohr, S., Brandt, P., Borras, L., Gilliéron, C., and Huguelet, P. (2006). Toward an integration of spirituality and religiousness into the psychosocial dimension of schizophrenia. *American Journal of Psychiatry. 163, 11*

Montaldo, C. (2006). Defense rests in Andrea Yates trial. *http:// crime.about.com/b/2006/07/11/defense-rests-in-andrea-yates-trial.htm*

Moran, M. (2006, August 18). Insanity plea successful in Andrea Yates retrial. *Psychiatric News, 41, 16*

Moriarty, J. (2008). Flickering admissibility: Neuroimaging evidence in the US courts. *Behavioral Sciences and the Law, 26, 1*

Morse, S. (2008). Psychopathy and criminal responsibility. *Neuroethics, 1*

Morse, S. and Hoffman, M. (2008). The uneasy entente between legal insanity and mens rea: Beyond *Clark v. Arizona. The Journal of Criminal Law and Criminology, 97, 4*

Murphy, C. (2008, August 20). About 3,200 former militants have completed the ambitious program aimed at persuading them to disavow violent Islamist ideologies. *Christian Science Monitor*

Murrie, D., Boccaccini, M., Zapf, P., Warren, J., and Henderson, C. (2008). Clinical variation in findings of competence to stand trial. *Psychology, Public Policy, and Law. 14, 3*

Neuroscience sparks criminal responsibility dilemma. (2007, November 1). *ABC News* (Australian Broadcasting Corporation).

Newman, M. (2005). Appeals court upholds ruling in Andrea Yates case. *New York Times*

Newman, S., Buckley, M., Newman, S., and Bloom, J. (2007). Oregon's Juvenile Psychiatric Security Review Board. *Journal of American Academy of Psychiatry Law, 35*

Ng, F. (2007). The interface between religion and psychosis. *Australasian Psychiatry, 15, 1*

Nolan, T. (2004). The indoctrination defense: From the Korean War to Lee Boyd Malvo. *Virginia Journal of Social Policy and the Law. 11, 3*

North, S. (2001, May 3). A killing in God's name. *http://www.sullivan-county.com/news/mine/gods_name.htm*

Nussbaum, H. (2005). *Surviving Intimate Terrorism.* Frederick, MD: PublishAmerica

Ostrov, B. (2008, April 14). Free will? Not as much as you think. *Boston Globe*

Overbye, D. (2007, January 2). Free will: now you have it, now you don't. *New York Times*

Pape, R. (2005). *Dying to Win: The Strategic Logic of Suicide Terrorism.* New York: Random House

Parker, L. (2006, June 20). The power of an expert witness. *USA Today*

Pat-Horenczyk, R., Peled, O., Miron, T., Brom, D., Villa, Y., and Chemtob, C. M. (2007). Risk-taking behaviors among Israeli adolescents exposed to recurrent terrorism: Provoking danger under continuous threat? *American Journal of Psychiatry, 164, 1*

People v. Kimura. (1985). Los Angeles Superior Court A-091133

Persinger, M., and Pierre, L. (2006). Experimental facilitation of the sensed presence is predicted by the specific patterns of the applied magnetic fields, not by suggestibility: re-analyses of 19 experiments. *International Journal of Neuroscience. 116, 9*

Pipes, D. (2009, November 20). Major Hasan's Islamist life. *Front Page Magazine*

Pluchinsky, D. (2008). Global jihadist recidivism: A red flag. *Studies in Conflict and Terrorism, 31, 3*

Poll: Do you agree with the guilty verdict and life sentence for John Odgren? (2010, May 2*). Boston Herald*

Post, J. (2005). When hatred is bred in the bone: Psycho-cultural foundations of contemporary terrorism. *Political Psychology. 26, 4*

Pratt, M. and Linder, D. (2006). The trial of Patty Hearst. *http://www.law.umkc.edu/faculty/projects/FTRIALS/hearst/hearsthome.html*

Press Office, University of Oxford News. (2006). One in 20 violent crimes committed by people with severe mental illness. *University of Oxford, UK*

Pronina, L. and Ustinova, A. (2010, April 1). Medvedev calls for brutal anti-terror measures after bombings. *Bloomberg News*

Prothero, S. (2010). *God is Not One: The Eight Rival Religions That Run the World and Why Their Differences Matter.* New York: HarperOne

Prothero, S. (2010, April 25). Separate truths. *Boston Globe*

Psychology of brainwashing. (1957, June 3). *Time*

Pullela, P. (2010, April 1). Vatican attacks New York Times over abuse coverage. *Reuters*

Quinn, P. (2010, March 7). Al-Qaida calls on US Muslims to attack America. *Associated Press*

Rabinowitz, D. (2009, November 9). Dr. Phil and the Fort Hood killer. *Wall Street Journal*

Rabinowitz, D. (2010, April 8). What's not happening to American Muslims. *Wall Street Journal*

Raghavan, S. (2009, November 16). Cleric says he was confidant to Hasan. *Washington Post*

Raine, A. (1999). Murderous minds: Can we see the mark of Cain? *Cerebrum: The Dana Forum on Brain Science, 1, 1*

Raine, A., and Yang, Y. (2006). Neural foundations to moral reasoning and antisocial behavior. *Social Cognitive and Affective Neuroscience. 1, 3*

Raine, A. (2008). From genes to brain to antisocial behavior. *Current Directions in Psychological Science, 17, 5*

Redding, R. (2006). The brain-disordered defendant: Neuroscience and legal insanity in the twenty-first century. *American University Law Review, 56, 1*

Richardson, J. (1991). Cult/brainwashing cases and freedom of religion. *Journal of Church and State. 33*

Riggins v. Nevada. (1992). 504 U.S. 127

Robbins, T. and Anthony, D. (1982). Deprogramming, brainwashing, and the medicalization of deviant religious groups. *Social Problems, 29, 3*

Rodgers, W. (2009, December 21). Terror trials will pose tough questions about Islam. *Christian Science Monitor*

Root, J. (2010, February 20). Plane attack prompts debate over terrorism label. *Associated Press*

Roper v. Simmons. (2005). 543 U.S. 551

Rosen, J. (2007, March 11). Neurolaw: The brain on the stand. *New York Times Magazine*

Roskies, A. (2006). Neuroscientific challenges to free will and responsibility. *Trends in Cognitive Sciences. 10*

Ross, B. and Schwartz, R. (2009, November 19). American official says accused shooter asked radical cleric when is jihad appropriate? *ABC News*

Rubenzer, S. (2004). Malingering of psychiatric disorders and cognitive impairment in criminal court settings. *The Prosecutor, 38, 5*

Salekin, R. (2002). Psychopathy and therapeutic pessimism: Clinical lore or clinical reality? *Clinical Psychology Review. 22, 1*

Satel, S. (2010, March 15). Book review: Review of *Addiction. The New Republic*

Schmitt, E. and Lipton, L. (2010, January 1). Focus on internet imams as recruiters for Al Qaeda. *New York Times*

Schwartz, J. and McKinley, J. (2009, November 16). Experts outline hurdles in trying to defend Hasan. *New York Times*

Scott, C. (2005). *Roper v. Simmons*: Can juvenile offenders be executed? *Journal of the American Academy of Psychiatry and the Law, 33*

Seabrook, J. (2008, November 10). Suffering souls: The search for the roots of psychopathy. *New Yorker*

Shane, S. (2009, December 12). New incidents test immunity to terrorism on U.S. soil. *New York Times*

Shane, S. and Dao, J. (2009, November 15). Investigators study tangle of clues on Fort Hood suspect. *New York Times*

Shane, S. and Mazzetti, M. (2010, May 6). Times Sq. bomb suspect is linked to militant cleric. *New York Times*

Silver, E., Cirincione, C. and Steadman, H. (1994). Demythologizing inaccurate perceptions of the insanity defense. *Law and Human Behavior, 18*

Slovenko, R. (2004). Brian Mitchell - Religious insanity and the law. *International Journal of Offender Therapy and Comparative Criminology, 48*

Springer, J. (2001, April 1). Before and after treatment, stoning mother displayed contrasting emotions. *CourtTV.com*

Springer, J. (2002). Kids drowned, mother faces execution. *Court TV News. http://www.courttv.com/trials/yates/background.html*

Stanford v. Kentucky. (1989). 492 U.S. 361

Stephens, B. (2010, February 15). Major Hasan: The counterlife. *Wall Street Journal*

Stern, J. (2003). *Terror in the Name of God: Why Religious Militants Kill.* New York: Ecco

Strawbridge, P. (1999, July 17). Reider's story of abuse, clean prison record sway parole board. *Omaha World-Herald*, NE

Stryker, J. (2004, August 1). How brainwashing came to life and thrived. *San Francisco Chronicle*

Sullivan, R. (1988, October 27). Judge dismisses murder charge for Nussbaum. *New York Times*

Sweet, L. and Crimaldi, L. (2010, April 22). Doctor: John Odgren was psychotic. *Boston Herald*

The jihad made me do it insanity defense. (2009, December 17). *Washington Times*

The Killer at Thurston High: Kip Kinkel. Frontline. pbs.org

The terror this time. (2009, December 28). *Wall Street Journal*

Thompson v. Oklahoma. (1988). 487 U.S. 815

Thompson, M. (2010, January 20). The Fort Hood report: Why no mention of Islam? *Time*

Trop v. Dulles. (1958). 356 U.S. 86

Tucker, W. (2009, November 17). Major Hasan a true believer. *American Spectator*

Turley, J. (2006). The insanity defense and the future of faith-based killings. *USA Today*

Uniform Code of Military Justice. 10 United States Code, Chapter 47. Section 850a. Article 50a. Defense of lack of mental responsibility

Valencia, M. (2010, April 23). Judge in Odgren case asked to explain insanity verdict details. *Boston Globe*

Valencia, M. (2010, April 28). Jury gets murder case against ex-Lincoln-Sudbury student. *Boston Globe*

Valencia, M. and Wen, P. (2010, April 29). Odgren convicted of first-degree murder, faces life imprisonment. *Boston Globe*

Vertuno, J. (2010, February 18). Man angry at IRS crashes plane into building. *Associated Press*

Vitacco, M., Van Rybroek, G., Erickson, S., Rogstad, J., Tripp, A., Harris, L., and Miller, R. (2008). An empirical investigation of insanity defense attitudes: Exploring factor related to bias. *International Journal of Law and Psychiatry, 30, 2*

Wall, B. (2000). Criminal responsibility, diminished capacity, and the gay panic defense. *Journal of the American Academy of Psychiatry and the Law, 28*

Walsh, M. (2010, January 15). Now they tell us: Ft Hood was terrorism. *bigjournalism.com*

Warburton, I. (2003). The commandeering of free will: Brainwashing as a legitimate defense. *Washington and Lee University School of Law Capital Defense Journal, 16*

Washington v. Harper. (1990). 494 U.S. 210

Weinstein, H. and Blankstein, A. (2008, March 22). Kathleen Soliah re-arrested. *Los Angeles Times*

Wen, P. (2010, May 1). Odgren sentenced to life in prison: No parole option for teen killer. *Boston Globe*

Whitlock, C. (2010, April 27). Obama administration defies congressional subpoena on Fort Hood documents. *Washington Post*

Williams, R. (2010, February 11). What managers need to know about decision-making. *Psychology Today*

Wyatt, E. (2005, January 8). Even for an expert, blurred TV images became a false reality. *New York Times*

Yan, J. (2010, March 5). APA makes *DSM-5* proposals available for comment. *Psychiatric News*

Yates found not guilty in second murder trial. (2006, July 26). *KPRC Houston*